Goths, Gamers, and Grrrls

Deviance and Youth Subcultures

Second Edition

ROSS HAENFLER
University of Mississippi

New York　Oxford
OXFORD UNIVERSITY PRESS

Oxford University Press is a department of the University of Oxford. It furthers the University's objective of excellence in research, scholarship, and education by publishing worldwide.

Oxford   New York
Auckland   Cape Town   Dar es Salaam   Hong Kong   Karachi
Kuala Lumpur   Madrid   Melbourne   Mexico City   Nairobi
New Delhi   Shanghai   Taipei   Toronto

With offices in
Argentina   Austria   Brazil   Chile   Czech Republic   France   Greece
Guatemala   Hungary   Italy   Japan   Poland   Portugal   Singapore
South Korea   Switzerland   Thailand   Turkey   Ukraine   Vietnam

For titles covered by Section 112 of the US Higher Education Opportunity Act, please visit www.oup.com/us/he for the latest information about pricing and alternate formats.

Published by Oxford University Press.
198 Madison Avenue, New York, NY 10016
www.oup.com

Oxford is a registered trademark of Oxford University Press.

Library of Congress Cataloging-in-Publication Data
Haenfler, Ross.
   Goths, gamers, and grrrls: deviance and youth subcultures / Ross Haenfler.—2nd ed.
      p. cm.
   Includes bibliographical references and index.
   ISBN 978-0-19-992483-7
   1. Subculture.   2. Youth.   I. Title.
   HM646.H34   2013
   305.23509'045—dc23   2011052898

Printing number: 9 8 7 6 5 4 3 2 1

Printed in the United States of America
on acid-free paper

To my astonishing daughter,
River.

May you have the strength
to swim
against the current.

CONTENTS

↵⊃

〜⌢

The mid-1980s marked the beginning of my ongoing love affair with youth sub-cultures. As I recall, I was a fairly typical kid, if such a kid exists, playing sports, doing my homework, and listening to Cyndi Lauper, Duran Duran, Bon Jovi, Van Halen, and whatever else was on the radio at the time. That began to change in junior high school, when a metalhead friend passed me a dubbed tape of Metallica's *Ride the Lightning* record and I *knew* I was destined to be a headbanger. I began grow-ing out my hair, listening to Slayer, and wearing a frayed denim jacket on which my mom dutifully sewed an Iron Maiden back patch. It wasn't just the heavy music and socially critical lyrics that attracted me to metal—I enjoyed the outsider status, feel-ing part of a marginalized group foreign to most kids, let alone the adults. It felt more *real*, more authentic somehow than the pop sensibilities played out on the radio and MTV. Little did I know that my subcultural journey had only just begun.

By high school, some friends had turned me on to punk rock, and I was going to shows, reading punk 'zines, and moshing around the circle pit with tattooed, pierced kids, many of whom wanted to change the world. I loved the "question everything" and "do it yourself" ethos of punk, not to mention the raw energy of the live shows. Soon after, bands like Minor Threat and Youth of Today launched my passion for hardcore, and I adopted the clean-living straight edge and vegetar-ian lifestyles. Yet as I finished up high school, Nirvana erupted onto the music scene, bringing grunge and exposing the masses to "alternative" music; I'll admit to having donned a flannel shirt or two. Each of these scenes inspired me and, I can say now, shaped the adult I went on to become. While sometimes dismissed as frivolous stopovers for immature youth on their way to more important (adult) ventures, subcultures occupy a meaningful space in many young lives, as well as teaching us something about the larger society we all live in.

This book emerged from the course "Deviance and Youth Subcultures," which I have taught at the University of Denver, University of Colorado, and University of Mississippi. While there are many great books about individual subcultures, none quite captured the breadth of topics I wanted to cover or the sociological insights I hoped to impart. So, in true DIY fashion I decided that I had to write one. Any book about youth subcultures leaves out more than it can include—this one offers neither a comprehensive survey of every youth scene nor the last word on the sociology of deviance. However, I hope this book gives you a glimpse inside some of the scenes where so many youth have found their subcultural homes. Just as important, I hope you leave the book with sociological tools useful to making better sense of your own life. Studying the "fringe," the "deviants" among us, forces us to reflect on values, beliefs, and ways of life we might otherwise take for granted. This book is more than an academic exercise for me; it's a chance to explore, sociologically, subjects that are *personal* to me and to so many other youth who found acceptance amongst kids for whom being different was a virtue, not a vice.

I am grateful to many people for their help and support. I thank my wonderful editor, Sherith Pankratz, for her patience and encouragement. The following reviewers of the proposal and manuscript in various stages were extraordinarily helpful:

Raymond A. Calluori, Montclair State University

Charles Corley, Michigan State University

Mitch Miller, The University of Texas at San Antonio

Steve Nava, California State University–Santa Cruz

John Siqueiros, University of Texas at El Paso

Steve Vandegriff, Liberty University

Bob Yoder, Goshen College

I couldn't ask for better colleagues than those in the Department of Sociology and Anthropology at the University of Mississippi. I also thank Patti and Peter Adler, my sociological "parents" for their continued guidance. The Huzzah crew—Collin, Ellis, Jimmy, J. P., and Warren—will always be part of my deviant "family." I thank Nate Miller for a lifetime of friendship and for being there as we discovered the "scene." I love my parents and brother for allowing me to be who I need to be, even when it's weird. Finally, I'm grateful for the support of my wonderful partner, Jennifer Snook—I look forward to a lifetime of deviance with you.

CHANGES TO THE SECOND EDITION

- Each substantive chapter now includes discussion questions meant to spark further thinking and debate about the chapter topic.
- New and updated resources appear at the end of each chapter, for students to pursue further learning opportunities.
- New research on youth subcultures, including transitions to adulthood, is now incorporated.
- Additional details on the histories of skinhead, punk, hip hop, and other music scenes, as well as new discussion of the impact of virginity pledgers, have been added.
- The chapter on gamers and hackers has been updated to reflect new developments in technology.
- Explanations in the introduction and conclusion for the social significance of youth cultures and the importance of subcultural studies have been expanded.

~~

CHAPTER 1

Introduction

A few summers ago I went to my first tattoo and body modification convention. Most of my friends had tattoos and piercings, and I had recently been tattooed for the first time. Several of my friends were tattoo artists, and one of my fellow graduate students was writing her dissertation on tattooing, so I was eager to learn more about the scene. The convention took place in a large hotel ball room, each artist or shop with their own booth displaying photos of their work. I'd never seen so many tattoos at once. Beautiful Chinese dragons crawled up arms, and koi fish with multicolored scales swam around thighs. A portrait of Jimi Hendrix grinned at me from a torso, and a collage of birds and flowers splayed across shoulder blades. As I walked around I saw men and women, working and middle class folks, bikers and punks, goths and metalheads, all smiling, talking enthusiastically, and showing one another their "tats," molded into a strange community by their love of tattoos. Some discussed plans for future tattoos with artists; others were tattooed or pierced then and there in front of a curious audience. Old friends caught up with one another, and new friends made plans for the evening. For the most part, the convention met my expectations—a friendly gathering of people with common interests, only with participants covered, sometimes from head to toe, in colorful ink.

One afternoon, however, revealed something I didn't expect, as an artist used a surgical scalpel to cut a large, swirling "tribal" design into a client's back. The procedure, called "cutting" or "ritual scarification," would leave scars roughly in the shape of the design. As blood ran down the man's back, I wasn't sure whether I should be fascinated or disgusted. I knew that many cultures have practiced scarification for centuries. Peoples across Africa used stylized scars as beauty markers as well as indicators of lineage, group membership, or status. Other forms of body modification have been prevalent as well, such as foot binding in China, neck stretching in Burma, and Incan skull binding that elongated the skull into an alien-like shape. Closer to home, plastic surgery is increasingly popular in the United States, with millions of people seeking breast implants, nose jobs, and liposuction every year, not to mention reality television shows such as *Extreme Makeover* and *The Swan*, and the drama *Nip/Tuck*, which make cosmetic procedures seem increasingly normal and desirable. Yet as I watched the scarring at the convention

I couldn't help but think, "This is so *weird*." As the artist finished, some in the crowd applauded while others shook their heads in bewilderment. It seems that, even in a subculture known for tolerance and diversity, not everyone could agree whether scarification is an art form or a travesty. The client stood up, smiled, and took a bow, his back a canvas painted with thin cuts and glistening blood.

Whatever your opinion about scarification, there are surely people and practices that *you* find strange. Even stranger, though, is how we often have different ideas regarding what is strange. One person's beauty mark is another's blemish, and what disgusts one excites another. But *why* do we find some things disturbing that others find completely acceptable, even enjoyable? *How* do people become involved in subcultures like tattooing and body modification? What leads some of us to pursue lifestyles outside the norm? Digging deeper, who gets to decide what's normal anyway? It's questions like these that led me to a passion for sociology, for studying youth subcultures, and for writing this book.

Most public high schools are home to groups such as goths, theater kids, athletes, skaters, computer and band "geeks," hip hoppers, emo and metal kids, among others. Whether they coexist peacefully, in open hostility, or simply avoid each other entirely, these groups form a stew of different identities available for youth. Each subculture has its own interests and usually its own style, though interests and styles certainly overlap. Each knows its approximate place in the pecking order and can identify its allies and antagonists. My goal with this book is to describe a variety of contemporary youth subcultures while explaining the ways scholars have tried to make sense of subcultural experiences. Whether you have identified with a subculture or not, I hope that the book will give you the tools to examine subcultures in new and more interesting ways. I also discuss the sociological study of *deviance*, or how society defines what is strange or normal, acceptable or unacceptable. Not only will you learn about some interesting groups, you'll pick up some theoretical tools that can help you examine virtually any group you encounter in the future.

While subcultures are interesting objects of study in their own right, I believe their significance transcends a fascination with "spectacular" styles and unfamiliar activities. They serve as windows into how youth learn about and struggle with issues of identity—for example, racial, gender, class, or sexual identities—and the hardships that marginalized groups often endure. Subculturists' questioning and challenging of widely accepted beliefs and practices highlight the hypocrisies, shortcomings, and even failings of more conventional "adult" society, providing in some ways as a mirror in which we might discover social problems reflected back at us. Thus in learning *about* subcultures we also learn *from* them something about the larger social world beyond any particular "scene." Studying individuals and groups deemed "deviant" encourages us to question the social rules that we so often take for granted, rules that often upon reflection make little sense. Before we get to the subculture chapters, it's important to understand how scholars have used and defined some of our basic concepts, especially subculture, resistance, and deviance.

OVERVIEW OF SUBCULTURAL THEORY

Many of us find subcultures incredibly fascinating. Circus freaks, sexual swingers, and extreme skateboarders can seem exciting or unsettling, and body modifiers who tattoo their entire bodies or implant horns on their heads are interesting and exotic. Reading descriptions of any of these groups might be intriguing and fun; however, our goal as scholars is not just to describe different youth subcultures but to discover the patterns across subcultures and answer questions about subcultures in general. For example, maybe the process of entering and exiting a subculture follows a similar pattern regardless of whether we're looking at graffiti artists or Christian athletes. Perhaps hip hoppers and metalheads have similar gender relations. While we may not come up with grand overarching theories that explain *everything*, we can attempt to put our observations about subcultures in some kind of theoretical context.

Scholars have studied youth for a long time and have created many theories attempting to explain how and why subcultures exist. They have struggled even to define just what a subculture is. The word is often used as a way to describe "any aspect of social life in which young people, style and music intersect" (A. Bennett 1999, 599). Subculture is a muddy concept, and scholars have, as you shall read, thoroughly critiqued it and offered alternatives. For our purposes, a **subculture** is a social subgroup distinguishable from mainstream culture by its non-normative values, beliefs, symbols, activities, and often, in the case of youth, styles and music (see A. Bennett 2001; Baron 1989). Subcultures are rarely clearly delineated, closed groups; rather, they are fluid networks constantly interacting and overlapping with other scenes and elements of popular culture. Throughout the book I occasionally refer to people involved in subcultures as "subculturists," rather than being members of a subculture, because being a "member" of a group implies some sort of organization and set of boundaries, which many subcultures do not have. Participants engage in non-normative (or deviant) activities that in some significant way differ from more conventional cultural, political, religious, gender, sexual, or other meaningful social categories. Thus, in my usage, members of cooking clubs, marathon runners, people who read comic books, and most sports fans are not automatically subculturists, even if they share norms and values that may seem particular to their own passions. Likewise, fraternities and sororities are not subcultures; they may be social subgroups with particular ideologies, symbols, even secrets, but in most significant ways they reproduce the values and practices cherished in contemporary society. Clearly, this loose definition potentially includes a variety of beliefs and practices, making it difficult to definitively say one "group" is a subculture while another is not. In fact, I want to avoid placing strict, artificial boundaries around the term. However, if *any* cultural grouping counts as a subculture, then the concept becomes nearly meaningless. Rather than using subculture as a static conceptual category, it may be useful to consider the "subcultural" aspects of social objects, viewing social subgroups as an ongoing series of interactions and negotiated meanings.

There are many different schools of thought that seek to explain subcultural participation, significance, and so on. Before we take a look at specific subcultures and these theories in more depth, let's take a brief tour of the history of subcultural studies and explore the concepts of resistance and deviance. I expand upon each of these ideas later in the book.

The Chicago School, Social Ecology, and Strain Theory

As one of the first established sociology departments, the University of Chicago's Department of Sociology and Anthropology had a long-lasting impact on how sociologists study subcultures. Theorists associated with the "Chicago school" often studied elements of urban life, including immigrants, "taxi-dancers" (women who danced with men for money), jazz musicians, and life on street corners, among many other subjects (Park 1925; W. Thomas and Znaniecki 1918; Cressey 1932; Whyte 1943; A. Cohen 1955; Becker 1963). Among this era's vital sociological contributions was an insistence that talking with people and observing their interactions was the best way to discover the social patterns of their lives. In other words, theory should be grounded in empirical observation. Early social reformers strove to explain urban problems such as poverty and crime in the rapidly growing cities of the time, and a variety of theories emerged. Common medical and psychological theories put the responsibility squarely on criminals, the poor, and delinquents, claiming they were somehow mentally or psychologically deficient. Religious reformers claimed that delinquents and criminals were less moral and proposed spiritual renewal as the cure. Early sociologists took a different approach, proposing that delinquency is a more or less "normal" reaction to one's social surroundings. In other words, to understand why a group of kids turns to crime it is necessary to understand the external social settings in which they live, including their opportunities—or lack thereof. Members of the Chicago School hung out with the people they studied in the settings in which they lived. They talked with people and attempted to understand their subjects' lives rather than applying a theory with little empirical basis.

For the Chicago School, subcultures emerged in response to the struggles of urban life (A. Cohen 1955). As an example, faced with few legitimate opportunities (and often with discrimination), marginalized individuals sometimes turn to gangs for a sense of belonging and opportunity. Therefore, in seeking to explain delinquent youth and youth subcultures, one *must* understand the cultural surroundings and opportunity structures in which youth live. The focus on the urban surroundings in which subcultures (and gangs) emerge is sometimes called **social ecology**. Some in the Chicago School studied, mapped, and contrasted the different "zones" or territories in Chicago, noting in particular how poverty, slums, and different ethnicities were distributed throughout the city (Jenks 2005). Like any ecological system, the city generally exists in a state of equilibrium. However, during periods of rapid social change, economic struggle, fast growth, or political unrest, the system may become dysfunctional, giving rise to delinquent subcultures, especially in "zones of transition" characterized by "social disorganization"

(Shaw and McKay 1942). Again, to properly understand deviance we must understand the social context in which it occurs.

Alongside the Chicago School, strain theory arose as another brand of American theory relevant to the study of subcultures. This theory grew from a branch of sociological theory called structural functionalism, which proposes that pieces of society—the different structures such as family, education, and economy—more or less fit together into a functional whole, making social order possible. For a society to properly "function," people must be able to achieve the goals society sets forth (Merton 1938, 1957). If they cannot, they experience psychological strain and may question the legitimacy of society's rules. For example, if a culture values hard work and individual success there must be adequate jobs that provide the means to achieve that success. People who cannot legitimately achieve the society's cultural goals—basics such as food, clothing, and shelter, but also status, wealth, and power—collectively create alternative values and means of achievement, often as part of a subculture. If one cannot gain respect and status through conventional means, then unconventional, even illegal, means might become appealing. Subcultural participants adopt an alternative set of values, legitimating or even glorifying deviant behavior. They also may find in subcultures a deviant path to society's goals, such as making money through criminal activities.

These early subcultural theories had several weaknesses (Williams 2007). First, they placed too much emphasis on subcultures being reactions to larger cultural forces, especially economic forces. Subcultures emerge for reasons other than the difficulties of achieving the American Dream. Second, these theorists' studies focused primarily on the urban poor, giving the impression that only working-class youth, often ethnic minorities, take part in subcultures and deviant behavior. Finally, strain theory leaves the impression that involvement in subcultures is abnormal (even if it serves some sort of societal function) or undesirable, something to be fixed to bring society back into balance. Adopting a subcultural identity is hardly abnormal given the vast numbers of contemporary youth, from a variety of backgrounds, who participate.

Centre for Contemporary Cultural Studies

Much like the Chicago School, the Centre for Contemporary Cultural Studies (CCCS) saw subcultures as a way for disadvantaged or marginalized kids to "solve" their status problems (S. Cohen [1972] 1993; Hall and Jefferson 1976; Mungham and Pearson 1976; Hebdige 1979). However, while the Chicago School focused more on the micro level, studying youth and their neighborhoods, the CCCS gave more attention to the macro analysis of social class and the economic conditions of society as a whole. Examining British subcultures such as mods, skinheads, rockers, punks, and football hooligans, these theorists held that subcultural youth form an active, but largely symbolic, resistance to the larger society in which they find themselves trapped. They saw working class kids with little opportunity resisting an oppressive system and glamorizing working class identity (Willis 1977).

Subcultures were collective responses to larger structural changes in British society, especially the growing postwar economy that boosted consumerism while reinforcing divisions between the working and upper classes (A. Bennett and Kahn-Harris 2004). However, many in the CCCS saw this resistance as "magical," or illusory (Hebdige 1979). In adopting outrageous styles (like the punks) and anti-social behaviors (like the skinheads) youth did not do much to change their lot in life. While meant to challenge "adult" society, such "rituals" and "signs" accomplished little—wearing a safety pin through your ear might be provocative or repulsive, but it doesn't change the society's class hierarchy. In fact, by refusing to strive for upward mobility, subculturists actually *reinforced,* rather than resisted, their class position, ensuring that "subcultural empowerment is empowerment without a future" (Gelder and Thornton 1997, 87). As you'll see later, however, the CCCS still tended to take a sympathetic view towards subculturists. You'll learn more about the CCCS in Chapter 2 about skinheads.

"Post-subcultural" and "Clubculture" Theories—Scenes and Tribes

The CCCS theories have prompted a slew of critiques falling under the umbrella of "post-subculture studies" (Widdicombe and Wooffitt 1995; Muggleton and Weinzierl 2003; A. Bennett and Kahn-Harris 2004). First, the CCCS (with some exceptions) lost sight of the empirical rigor of the Chicago School studies, instead formulating theories that did not always accurately capture subculturists' experiences. For example, theorists explained the meanings behind punk style without always talking to punks. Second, post-subculture theorists call into question the very notion of distinct, stable, coherent subcultures, recognizing that subcultures are fluid, often overlapping with one another and sharing styles. You may have noticed this with the blending of punk and goth, or hip hop and heavy metal. Subcultures also vary by region and country; rave culture in Detroit may be different from rave culture in New York, let alone in the United Kingdom. Third, the CCCS didn't pay enough attention to girls' experiences, often viewing girls as little more than accessories to boys (McRobbie and Garber 1976; McRobbie 2000). Fourth, rather than being tied to the working class, subcultures appeal to middle and upper class youth as well (Muggleton 2000). This may be even truer today as middle class youth "buy into" all sorts of subcultural groups. Fifth, as you'll see later, post-subculturists also question the CCCS picture of "heroic" youth somehow resisting an oppressive, hegemonic mainstream society. Perhaps such youth are interested primarily in having a good time rather than making some sort of critical statement about the larger culture.

Post-subculture theories take several forms. "Clubculture" theories focus more on the consumer tastes of youth and the ways in which the media constructs subcultures (Thornton 1995). In reporting on youth scenes, the media actually helps construct somewhat coherent subcultures—rave wasn't really rave until it was reported on by the media. Studies of the 1990s rave culture highlighted the diversity and smorgasbord of styles present in one scene (Redhead 1993; Redhead, Wynne, and O'Connor 1998). Youth of all different races, classes, and genders congregated in clubs, raising questions about the CCCS focus on class and race divisions among youth. Rather than being class-based, subcultures offer youth the means to distinguish themselves as cool and "in the know." Similarly, another way of viewing contemporary "subcultures" is as a form of "neo-tribe" (Maffesoli 1996; A. Bennett 1999), or a fluid, ever-changing hybrid of many styles and scenes. Emphasizing the pleasure orientation and impermanence found in dance-music culture, neo-tribes periodically come together to have fun rather than to express a political message or form a more permanent group. Rather than coherent, stable *subcultures*, youth congregate in diffuse, heterogeneous scenes. The important insight to remember from these theories is their focus on subcultures' complexity, fluidity, and often impermanence.

One of the tricky problems in describing any subculture is avoiding stereotypes and overgeneralizations. Can we realistically discuss trends and patterns within subcultures when micro-level studies reveal extensive variety of meaning and experience? There are many kinds of metal and goth. One virginity pledger may have completely different motivations from another. There certainly is no single type of hip hop head, punk, hacker, fic writer, or athlete. Another post-subculture contribution is accounting for the diversity and complexity of different *scenes*, perhaps a more useful way to characterize youth groupings. While subculture implies deviance from a coherent dominant culture, **scenes** are porous and diffuse, with members coming and going and few living completely subcultural lives (A. Bennett and Peterson 2004). Scenes form around musical genres or local areas but imply more fluidity than subculture. This reflects an *anti-essentialist* view—there is no all-encompassing way to describe any particular subculture. As we will see with goth in Chapter 7 and virtual communities in Chapter 8, scenes are not necessarily tied to one geographical locale. Similarly, other scholars see the emergence of **neo-tribes**, very fluid, pleasure-oriented, and mostly apolitical groups united by shared symbols and rituals (Maffesoli 1996); Juggalos—fans of the hardcore rappers Insane Clown Posse—might be a good example. In increasingly mobile, consumerist societies emphasizing the individual, many people long for some kind of community but are unwilling to fully commit to one single group. We're all shopping in the **supermarket of style**, trying on various fashions and even identities as the mood strikes us, mixing and matching at our leisure until we find some sense of belonging (Polhemus 1998). Shopping for a subcultural identity isn't so different from trying on different outfits:

> As in pop music, the predominant tendency in appearance style today relies upon sampling & mixing diverse, eclectic, often contradictory elements into a unique, personal statement. Celebrating the confusion and diversity of our age, we surf through both history and geography to find our own reality—in the mix.[1]

Another ongoing struggle in subculture studies is how to define "mainstream" society, if such a society even exists. Part of the post-subculture critique includes questioning the CCCS image of relatively distinct and stable subcultures engaged in pseudo-class struggle against hegemonic mainstream society. Subculturists, of course, nearly always define themselves against some other group or against some vague notion of "society," but this implies that there is some coherent, all-powerful, oppressive society "out there" that responds en masse to quash subcultural individuality. Clearly, this is too simplistic—societies are extremely complex. Countercultures strive to make space for people to flex their individuality in defiance of "the system." Yet some argue that there is *no* tension between "mainstream" and "alternative" as both exist in a capitalist world with a consumerist ideology (Heath and Potter 2004). Nevertheless, subculturists construct (and critique) a symbolic mainstream that serves as a foil for their attempts at individuality (Williams 2003). One's authenticity and subcultural capital, and therefore one's status, depends upon distinguishing oneself from the mainstream; therefore, subculturists will always invent new ways to differentiate the mainstream from the "underground" (Thornton 1995). Indie rock kids might claim that wearing Converse Chuck Taylor shoes, vintage t-shirts, and skinny jeans sets them apart from their mainstream peers, but the separation is largely symbolic—the indie kids are still buying into the fashion industry and often paying top dollar to look like an "individual."

From Class 1/28

Despite the diversity within scenes and the lack of a single mainstream society, there are still recognizably distinct subcultures, characterized by *relative* distinctiveness, a common identity, commitment, and community (Hodkinson 2002). For all the overlap between subcultures and subcultural identities, for all the blending, sharing and mixing, many youth still tend to distinguish their identity from that of others, congregating in relatively coherent groupings. The concept of subculture is not yet dead—it's just been going through a serious overhaul.

The Concept of Resistance

Subcultural youth are typically known for rebelling in some way against adult society, resisting the demands and pressures of their parents' generation. The hippies of the 1960s, for example, dressed, spoke, and acted differently from their often more conservative parents. They set themselves apart by using drugs, listening to folk music and acid rock, and postponing families and careers to enjoy and extend their youth. The hippies *resisted* mainstream lifestyles for a way of life they believed was more fulfilling and free. The notion of cultural rebels taking a stand against a conformist society is one of the things about youth subcultures many of us find intriguing.

Fact!

Resistance has been one of the most central concepts of subcultural studies and perhaps one of the most controversial (Muggleton and Weinzierl 2003). The CCCS tended to paint a "heroic" portrait of subculturists resisting a domineering and often unjust society that pushed conformity while offering little opportunity, particularly for working class youth. Such scholars claimed that working class youth joined subcultures to resist the capitalist/consumerist society. Rather than being misguided deviants or simple delinquents, subculturists highlighted the contradictions in society, even if their resistance was largely symbolic. Thus, while politicians and most of the mainstream press saw subculturists as a "problem," CCCS scholars viewed them in more political terms.

The CCCS notion of resistance has faced a lot of criticism. One of the main problems of examining youth subcultures as a form of resistance to parent culture is the assumption that there are coherent and readily identifiable youth and adult cultures. Perhaps there is no single, monolithic mainstream culture to resist in the first place? Many societies are increasingly complex and multicultural; rather than a perfectly blended melting pot, we've become a stew of many different ingredients. Furthermore, while subculturists may not be the devils society sometimes makes them out to be, they are also not always the heroes portrayed by the CCCS (Muggleton and Weinzierl 2003).

While the CCCS did not expect much from subcultures in the way of political change, they saw the potential in subcultures for *cultural* resistance. If the CCCS takes a mixed view of subcultures' potential for resistance, post-subculture and club culture theorists are often more pessimistic. Geared more toward consuming a particular style than creating structural change, subcultures may carve out symbolic cultural spaces for youth but are often little more than hedonistic, apolitical, consumerist escapes (e.g., Polhemus 1998). In fact, contemporary subcultures may be more about identity shopping and personal fulfillment than social resistance (ibid.).

These criticisms have led some researchers to pay more attention to the subjective understandings of resistance held by youth (Leblanc 1999). It is important to understand resistance from subculturists' point of view because they may have different understandings of its meaning. While "symbolic" resistance may not produce radical change at a societal level, it may empower individuals to live more fulfilling lives on their own terms by resisting peer pressure, parental abuse, and societal expectations (Haenfler 2006). Even contemporary scholars associated with post-subculture studies acknowledge the political/cultural significance of youth (Muggleton and Weinzierl 2003).

Finally, the focus on youth resisting adult culture misses the fact that many youth are also busy resisting other youth (Haenfler 2004c). For example, skinheads and punks despised and defined themselves against the hippies. Virginity pledgers resist what they see as the promiscuity of other young people. Virtually all youth cultures define themselves apart from other youth, and their resistance manifests in actions and behavior.

THEORIES OF DEVIANCE AND DELINQUENCY

You may have noticed that our lives can be fairly predictable—the majority of people act in pretty conventional ways. We generally follow the current fashions of the day, and more or less conform to the path many others have trod before us. But there are always those people who stand out from the crowd. **Deviance** is a broad concept encompassing all sorts of beliefs and behaviors that violate established social norms. You might think of deviance as "breaking the rules," including anything from talking loudly during a movie to stealing a car. The term "deviance" comes from the statistical idea of *deviation* (Best 2004); when an event occurs relatively rarely it deviates from the general pattern. Pierced ears may be statistically common in the United States, but facial piercings such as lip and eyebrow rings are uncommon and judged strange or ugly by many. As such piercings become more common, one could foresee, possibly, a time in the future when they would not be considered deviant.

"True Story."

Distinguishing Between Deviance, Delinquency, and Crime

What is the difference between deviance and a *crime*? It is tempting to think that crime is just one kind of deviance and that all crime therefore is deviant. But is driving over the speed limit deviant? Clearly it is a crime, but is exceeding the speed limit really deviant? Not if many people do it and it doesn't provoke a reaction. In fact, on urban freeways it is likely deviant *not* to speed! So you see, just because society labels something a crime by enacting laws does not make a particular action deviant, and simply because something is legal does not mean it is not deviant. Having a tattoo on your neck is legal, but it certainly falls outside the norms of society.

From a legal perspective, a **crime** is an act that defies a legal definition of right and wrong—societies establish laws to protect citizens, maintain order, and promote the interests of the state. A more critical perspective would suggest that criminal definitions and the courts that enforce them are also used to stigmatize and control certain groups of people, such as prostitutes or the homeless. **Juvenile delinquency** is legally defined criminal behavior by perpetrators who fit the socially defined category of children or youth—in the United States these are individuals under age eighteen. Deviance, the focus of this book, is a much broader category of violating cultural norms, encompassing crime, delinquency, and more benign breaches of social convention. It is useful to distinguish between these categories because, as I've said, not all crimes are broadly considered deviant—a twenty-year-old who drinks alcohol responsibly at a family gathering may be breaking the law, but she is not necessarily violating a norm in that context.

The field of deviance studies is closely tied to subcultural studies, as both often examine marginalized groups. Social scientists have come up with a variety of theories in an effort to better understand how we define deviance, whom we label deviant, and why people engage in deviant behavior.

Differential Association

One explanation for why people engage in deviance is that they learn it from the deviant people around them. If you associate with criminals, you are more likely to become a criminal yourself, and if you live amongst law-abiding people you are likely to be law abiding. Criminologist Edwin Sutherland (1939) called this explanation of deviant behavior **differential association**. Perhaps your parents warned you to stay away from the "bad apples" in your school, believing that you might pick up smoking, drinking, vandalism, or other behaviors they wanted to shelter you from. Differential association acknowledges that a person's social environment impacts the likelihood that they will break the rules (Sutherland and

Cressey 1978). Deviant or criminal behavior is not inherited (through genetics) but is learned. People learn both the *techniques* of deviance, such as how to forge a check, and the *rationalizations* for deviant behavior. The notion that criminals, in particular, *learn* criminal behavior rather than being somehow biologically or psychologically abnormal or deficient was a fairly radical idea in the early twentieth century.

Consider the decision to get a tattoo. Though more and more common, tattoos are still considered deviant in many contexts. Differential association theory would predict that if you hang out with people who have tattoos and who believe tattoos are cool (whether rock stars, soldiers, bikers, or athletes), you will be more likely to get a tattoo. Plus, you will have access to tattoo artists and knowledge about how to go about getting a tattoo. Likewise, if you associate primarily with people who shun tattoos and believe they are gross, dirty, or even evil, you will be less likely to be tattooed yourself. We tend to adopt the beliefs of the people we value, are closest to, and most associate with, including beliefs about what is deviant and what is "normal." If you grow up in a family where smoking pot is acceptable and normal you (a) probably also would find it acceptable, (b) would have an avenue to learn how to smoke, and (c) would have easier access to pot than most kids.

Labeling

Differential association theory explains that we learn deviant and criminal behavior, but it takes for granted that some behaviors and lifestyles are deviant while others are not. Who decides what counts as deviant and what passes as normal? **Labeling theory** proposes that actions or people are deviant only when society *labels* them deviant. Is there something *inherently* weird about Ozzy Osbourne or the members of Green Day wearing eye makeup? Or professional athletes covered in tattoos? Not really. Labeling theorists hold that something or someone only becomes deviant when we label it as such (Becker 1963). Which groups have the power to define and label deviants is an important question for labeling theory (and conflict theory, as you'll see later). Once upon a time, schools and universities required women to wear dresses or skirts; wearing pants was deviant, but only because certain groups in power established social norms and rules that labeled pants-wearing women as less feminine. According to Becker, after being labeled deviant, youth commit further deviant acts, which in turn reinforce the deviant label.

Comparing different cultures' beliefs about tattoos offers a nice illustration of labeling theory. Tattoos have been part of human cultures for millennia, from ancient Japan and China, the Celts of the British Isles, and the tribes of Africa and Polynesia. Some societies even encouraged facial tattoos, which as you know would be particularly deviant in modern Western nations. However, people in these other cultures found tattoos beautiful and honorable—totally normal— rather than subversive or deviant. Tattoos marked rites of passage, provided spiritual protection, and served to distinguish different classes and castes of people.

Again, there is nothing inherently deviant in tattoos or people who have them—we only think of tattoos as deviant after social groups label them deviant. We'll look at labeling theory again in Chapter 5 as we discuss heavy metal.

Conflict Theory

Advocates of **conflict theory** take an even more critical approach to defining deviance. Labeling theory assumes that there is some consensus in society about what is "normal" and what is "deviant" and that people generally follow the rules. Conflict theorists claim instead that society is made up of continually struggling groups and that more powerful groups use their resources to control and exploit those with less power (e.g., Collins 1975). Conflict theorists tend to be critical of those with power in society, such as the police, lawmakers, and the wealthy. Using arrest and prosecution data, such theorists show that law enforcement, for example, serves the interests of the wealthy class by fervently prosecuting and harshly punishing street crime with greater effort than white-collar crime perpetrated by privileged, high-status individuals (Shrover and Wright 2000). Laws, made by those with power, function to control those with less power, and certain groups may be singled out. Juvenile courts, for example, may be less about "reforming" kids than about controlling lower-class youth (e.g., Platt 1969). A conflict perspective would be especially attentive to who is in charge, who makes the rules, and how they enforce those rules in their interests. Sentencing for drug-related crimes shows disparity along racial and class lines: even after reforms passed in 2010, penalties for distributing and using powder cocaine carry, on average, a much lighter sentence than for the cheaper crack cocaine, more commonly used by the poor and in communities of color.[2] The dominant group creates laws/rules in its favor. In Chapter 7 I further discuss the conflict perspective as we explore goths and stigma.

Regarding tattoos, a conflict theorist might ask how powerful institutions have used tattoos and who benefits from the social stigmas surrounding tattoos? In the past, governments tattooed people who committed crimes, and during the Holocaust the Nazis tattooed Jews and other groups in the course of imprisonment and genocide. In promoting fairly narrow standards of beauty, the fashion and beauty product industries can more easily control demand for their products. The fact that the law prohibits artists from tattooing minors also reinforces the control and domination of minors by adults. For young people, especially, tattoos may become marks of *retaliation* against what they perceive as forced conformity.[3] More broadly, tattoos may symbolize the symbolic and "real" conflicts between outsider groups and society.

Control Theory

As you read about deviance and delinquency, you may be thinking your life is fairly mundane in comparison. But let's face it, most people follow most social norms most of the time. Instead of asking what draws people toward deviance, we could ask what keeps people from it. Studying juvenile delinquency, Travis Hirschi

(1969) developed the **social control theory** of deviance, focusing on the social networks that keep us *out* of trouble. Like differential association theory, control theory emphasizes relationships between people; whom you associate with and whom you have ties to influences whether or not you engage in deviant behavior. A person who has a strong bond to society and has little reason to break the rules will be dissuaded from deviance. For example, someone with a job, family, and religious community has a variety of social networks. Someone disconnected or alienated from society has less reinforcement to follow the rules.

Thinking about tattoos, if you have strong ties to a variety of social networks, such as student clubs or a religious group, you will be less likely to get a tattoo. These networks might not only disapprove of tattoos, but they reinforce their own definition of normalcy, rewarding those who follow their rules. If you have a certain career path mapped out you might worry that having a tattoo will jeopardize your employment possibilities. Or you may get a tattoo but place it in an inconspicuous place rather than on your neck or forearm. If you lack stable communities or have few job prospects, you may have fewer ties to mainstream life and thus may be more inclined to become tattooed. I explore the social control theory of deviance more in Chapter 6.

Constructionist/Interactionist Theories

Constructionist theories emphasize that what we label deviant depends on context and how we interpret the meanings of deviance. You may have noticed that what society considers deviant changes over time. Miniskirts, once considered scandalous by most of the population, are now commonplace. Actions have different meanings depending on their context. Belching might be OK on a hunting trip but considered deviant in church. Similar to labeling theory, **social constructionist theories** treat deviance as subjective rather than objective (Rubington and Weinberg 2005). In other words, deviance is not automatically understood as an objective fact but as constructed and interpreted meanings that are subject to change. Constuctionists are interested in how behaviors and traits come to be labeled deviant, how persons labeled deviant manage others' impressions of their deviant identity, and how the cultural context influences definitions of deviance.

Returning to tattoos one last time, constructionist theories might address the various meanings people construct around tattoos and how they interpret people with tattoos. They would pay attention to the context in which tattoos are perceived and judged. For example, when are tattoos considered "art" and when are they symbolic of gang membership or other identities? Constuctionist theory would also prompt us to wonder how the meanings of tattoos change over time. Will TV shows like *Miami Ink*, *New York Ink*, and *LA Ink* normalize tattoos or make them even more "outlaw"? Will heavily tattooed hip hop artist Lil Wayne's popularity change the meanings of facial tattoos or reinforce their deviant meanings? Following the Chicago School, we would also want to study how tattooed people understand their tattoos. Middle-class people often avoid "antisocial" tattoos and frame their tattoos according to conventional norms such as commemorating a special life event (K. Irwin 2001). Talking with tattooed people demonstrates how they attempt to legitimate their tattoos and avoid social stigma. I investigate constructionist theories of deviance more deeply in Chapter 2.

OVERVIEW

From here on out, this book will help you tackle some of the most pressing questions about youth subcultures:

- How and why do subcultures emerge?
- Do subcultures mount a meaningful resistance to mainstream/adult society?
- How do subculturists determine who is a "true" member and who is a "poseur"?
- How do men and women enact gender in their scenes?
- How do subcultures relate to one another?
- What is the impact of commodification on subcultures?
- How do subcultures influence racial and sexual identities?
- What does it mean to be "deviant"? Who decides what is deviant and what is "normal"?

In each chapter, I use a subculture to help me illustrate sociological concepts and theories. While I would have liked to include even more subcultures—skaters, bike messengers, street artists and graffiti writers, lowrider and Kustom Kulture car enthusiasts to name but a few—writing about so many groups in such a small space proved impossible. Thus I chose relatively familiar and well-researched subcultures that helped me discuss the theoretical ideas central to deviance and subcultural studies and that represented a wide range of identities and experiences. Even if you don't find the group most interesting to you, you will be able to ask meaningful questions about *any* subculture using the theoretical tools in this book.

Chapter 2 covers the meanings of social class in skinhead culture while exploring how the larger structural context influences the emergence of subcultures. We'll look at both the racist and nonracist skinhead factions as I outline the basic premises of symbolic interactionist theory. In Chapter 3 we take a look at punk and its offshoots, including hardcore, emo, and straight edge. Punk reveals the status hierarchy present in any subculture as well as the role of style and politics in music scenes. I examine race and gender in Chapter 4 as we discuss hip hop, one of the most popular and influential contemporary subcultures. Hip hop articulates minority groups' frustration with racism and poverty while demonstrating how we "perform" race and gender in our interactions with others. Chapter 5 turns us to heavy metal where we revisit the themes of race, gender, and class before discussing moral panics and satanic scares. We'll see how "moral entrepreneurs" create subcultural "folk devils" as scapegoats and diversions from larger social problems. In Chapter 6, virginity pledgers help us explore the meanings of sex and sexual identity. Though seemingly out of place in this book, pledgers illustrate "positive deviance" and the social control theory of deviance, showing that religion establishes norms that set these youth apart from their peers. Chapter 7 looks at the goth subculture while discussing the concept of social stigma. We will see how dominant groups stigmatize people who are different as well as how people manage or cope with stigma. Chapter 8 looks at virtual subcultures and online communities, especially computer hackers and gamers. Massively Multiplayer Online Role-Playing Games and virtual profile sites such as Facebook show the elements of a virtual scene such as economy, communication, gender, and identity. Chapter 9 uses two girl-centered youth subcultures to discuss the relationship between young women and media. Riot Grrrl, a feminist-inspired subculture connected with punk and indie music scenes in the 1990s, shows how girls resist sexist media portrayals by creating their own media, and fan fiction subcultures offer women a space to explore sexuality as they (re)write stories featuring their favorite fictional characters. In Chapter 10 I conclude with several discussions relevant to virtually all subcultures: resistance, commodification, and what happens as subcultural youth grow up.

Each chapter begins with a brief description and history of the scene before diving into the more theoretical material. One of the challenges of a book examining youth subcultures is that participants in subcultures are often a very diverse bunch. Trying to describe a "typical" punk, hip hopper, or virginity pledger is very tricky and runs the risk of reinforcing stereotypes or giving a scene more coherence than it may actually have. I've done my best to outline each group's basic beliefs and practices and describe the variety of subgroups in each subculture, but remember that my descriptions are brief snapshots of very complex scenes. Subcultures change constantly, and with a little research you can discover the latest trends in any of these groups.

~~~

CHAPTER 2

Skinheads—The Symbolism of Style and Ritual

For many of us, the word "skinhead" brings to mind very frightening images of violent racists perpetrating hate crimes or offering the Nazi "Seig Heil" salute in a white power parade. Media reports of skinhead violence were prevalent in the 1980s and 1990s, fueling fears of a growing, organized white supremacist youth movement (Wooden and Blazak 2001). Talk show hosts Geraldo Rivera, Oprah, and Jerry Springer devoted episodes to skinheads—Geraldo's popularity skyrocketed after he received a broken nose during a brawl involving skinheads and anti-racist activists. Racist organizations in the United States and right-wing political movements in Europe and Russia have used the skinhead movement and its music as a powerful recruiting tool (Pilkington, Garifzianova, and Omel'chenko 2010). Despite the impression these horrific incidents leave, there is more to the skinhead culture than you might think. Our culture teaches us many things about subcultures, some relatively true and others blatantly false. Often our image of subculturists rests upon **stereotypes**, oversimplified generalizations applied to all members of a group. Stereotypes are often based upon distorted facts, half-truths, and even outright lies. They deny individual differences and often carry a negative connotation. Systematically studying subcultures, rather than relying on popular beliefs, can produce some surprising results. Did you know that many skinheads are actually *anti*-racist? Or that some skinheads are *black*? That there are *female* skinheads? Certainly some skinheads are violent white supremacists, but many others are not. Throughout this book you will see that there is more to subcultures than meets the eye. In this chapter, I outline skinhead history, beginning with their roots in rude boy, mod, and working class cultures. Then I focus on the context in which skinheads emerge before distinguishing between racist and non-racist skins. Finally, I use skinheads to demonstrate the theory of symbolic interaction, explaining how members of subcultures create and maintain symbolic meaning around their actions and their styles.

ORIGINS OF SKINHEAD

Roots of Skinhead Culture—Rude Boys and Mods

Subcultures often evolve into new forms, adopting fresh styles and changing to fit different times and places. Early studies of subcultures emphasized both the "spectacular" styles and the many interconnections between various youth groups. The skinhead lineage begins, perhaps, with the Teddy Boys, fashionable British youth who sported "Edwardian coats, tight pants, and very short hair styles" often fixed into a pompadour (Zellner 1994, 2). They enjoyed drinking and dancing to the newly popular rock and roll, and their style, including drape jackets and waist coats, appropriated a wealthy facade that contradicted their working class roots. From the teds came the mods and the rockers. The mods rode scooters (typically Vespas), wore trendy clothing, frequented dance clubs, and listened to bands such as The Who and The Kinks, embracing the future even as they struggled against the constraints of their mostly working class backgrounds (see Feldman 2009). Rockers, riding motorcycles in their leather jackets, fought their rival mods for territory, symbolizing for mods a clinging to the past.[4] Eventually the "hard mods," who were more working class than their counterparts, became the skinheads (Hebdige 1979). Since then, skinheads have branched into various subgroups. As you can see, the history of any subculture takes many twists and turns.

The roots of skinhead culture, believe it or not, can be traced to people of color, especially black Jamaican immigrants to the United Kingdom. Early skinheads owe much of their music and style to reggae and soul music (Hebdige 1979; Marshall 1994), and many were black/West Indian. British youth fused the ted and mod styles with the Jamaican "rude boy" culture. "Rude boys" were a 1960s Jamaican subculture of youth trying to get by in the poverty and unemployment of the post-independence era.[5] Frustrated by a declining economy and disappointed by the lack of expected improvements after the British departure, many of these youths turned to crime and violence. Eventually, some rude boys migrated to the United Kingdom, subsequently introducing white working class lads to Jamaican music, especially rocksteady and ska artists like Desmond Decker, Prince Buster, and the Skatalites. Ska music still maintains a strong presence amongst some skins, though punk, Oi!, and power metal bands have followings as well. Ska is distinctive for fusing Caribbean music with jazz and rhythm and blues and, eventually, a horn section, and for expressing optimism and hope for a better future. Fans dance, called "skanking," in place to the beat in a sort of skipping, bobbing, motion that resembles running in place. Integrated bands such as the Mighty Mighty Bosstones and others on the Two Tone label, such as The Specials, The Selecter, and Madness, drew racially mixed audiences. Skinhead and punk have shared members at various times in their histories (J. Moore 1993). Racist skins, however, increasingly distinguished themselves from punks and their perceived left-wing ideology (Burghart 1999).[6] (See "Skins Online" at the end of this chapter.)

Working Class English Skins

Like the teds and the mods, skinhead culture grew among the working class. However, while the former groups tended to emulate upper class fashions and lifestyles, temporarily escaping their workaday lives, skins celebrated their working class roots, making no pretensions toward upward mobility. Skinheads often wore a working class "uniform" of denim jeans, work boots (often Doc Martens, and sometimes steel-toed), and a white tank top shirt. Braces (suspenders), flight jackets (usually olive green in color), and Fred Perry polo shirts or Ben Sherman button ups are other markers of skinhead culture. Of course, the most distinguishing feature of skinhead style is the close-cropped hair. Not only is this an intimidating symbolic rejection of mainstream hairstyles, it also serves a practical purpose: in a fight, a skinhead's opponent can't grab a handful of hair, and at work a shaved head is easier to keep clean. British skinheads were also avid football supporters (soccer fans), identifying strongly with their local teams. They drank and fought their way across Europe, following their teams from match to match. Some engaged in football "hooliganism," generally drunken rowdiness and violent clashes with police and opposing clubs' fans (Dunning, Murphy, and Williams 1986; Buford 1992). Female skinheads, often called Chelseas, sport the shaved head but retain bangs or a "fringe" of hair. Their fashions vary, but can include bleached hair, plaid/checkered skirts, or the flight jackets and jeans of their male counterparts.

SOCIAL CLASS

Structural Context and Subcultural Emergence
Every subculture emerges in a larger social context that shapes the form the subculture takes. It is tempting to believe that subcultures emerge as ideas from individuals—some might think, for example, that skinhead culture is the result of deviant (and possibly disturbed) individuals who individually choose to come together into a deviant subculture. Sure, individuals *do* have an impact, but social scientists are always interested in the larger social factors that influence individual choices. In other words, we must study the **structural context** in which subcultures emerge if we are to understand their appeal. Structural context includes the historical, social, political, and cultural environments in which we exist. Hippies, for example, reacted against the perceived stifling conformity of the 1950s and the Vietnam War. Further, the increased access to college education prolonged youth (creating adults without adult responsibilities) and fostered a space in which to question the status quo. In short, subcultures do not exist in a vacuum; to understand them, we must also understand something about the society, or structural context, in which they exist.

Remember that for the CCCS, the social class structure and the economy were the most salient structural aspects of subcultural emergence, especially with groups such as mods, skinheads, and punks (Willis 1977; Hebdige 1979). **Social class** designates one's economic standing in a society and therefore many of one's opportunities. We typically divide our class structure into lower, working, middle, and upper classes, each characterized by a certain amount of income and wealth as well as power and opportunity. Class also has cultural elements; the working and upper classes have different tastes in (and ability to afford) music, food, and clothing. For example, wealthy people might avoid Bud Light, Velveeta cheese, and clothing from Target, preferring higher status wines, fancy cheeses, and expensive designer clothing. Thus class also implies a pattern of consumption. In a class system, people ideally have opportunities for social mobility, a chance to "move up the ladder" through persistence and hard work. However, our perception of opportunities often exceeds the reality (Esping-Andersen 2007). More than likely, you will remain in the social class in which you were born. Skinheads (and other members of working class subcultures) recognize that their opportunities are limited and, perceiving relatively little recourse, join deviant groups as a **symbolic form of resistance** (Hall and Jefferson 1976). If the world can't live up to its promises of opportunity, then reject the world.

Subculturists and the CCCS theorists who studied them see subcultures as resistance to "hegemonic" culture. **Hegemony** is another word for dominance. Antonio Gramsci (1971) suggested that people in power preserve their dominance not only through politics and force of arms but through *cultural* domination. They manipulate the working classes by enforcing beliefs (through schools, religion, nationalism and so on) that further the interests of the powerful. For example, people in the United States tend to believe if they work hard they can "get ahead" and therefore people who are poor are poor due to some personal failing such as lack of motivation or irresponsibility. In short, people who are rich deserve their wealth; people who are poor are somehow deficient. These beliefs perpetuate a focus on individual success and prevent questioning of the economic system. As the working class (the *proletariat* in Marxist terms) identifies with the upper classes, especially the owners of industry (the *bourgeoisie*), and adopts their beliefs, it is less likely to revolt. Skinheads, in creating a working class culture and identity, could be seen as challenging the cultural hegemony of the upper classes. For Gramsci, a distinct working class culture is a precursor to revolution. Subculturists of all sorts question the hegemony of dominant groups and mass culture.

Skinheads emerged during the deindustrialization of Europe, when the future of the working class seemed especially in doubt. The secure factory jobs that had provided millions with stable, secure middle class lifestyles were slowly eroding and along with them the working class culture. Immigration and the close proximity of working class whites and blacks provided pieces of the puzzle that skinheads would become (Hebdige 1979). Recall that Merton (1957) proposed that youth become deviant in reaction to **blocked structural opportunities**, or inadequate legitimate access to society's rewards. Working class youth turn to groups like the skinheads in a ritualistic effort to "solve" their problems (Hall and Jefferson 1976). Rather than organize a formal political challenge against the state, subcultures tend to offer a symbolic opposition glorifying their outsider status. Ironically, according to the CCCS, by celebrating manual labor and disparaging education and middle class work, kids reinforce their own working class position, *ensuring* a lack of upward mobility (Willis 1977). This sort of resistance is therefore "magical," or illusory, giving skinheads the feeling of resistance while really challenging the system little, if at all (Hebdige 1979).

Core Values

Though skinheads hold diverse ideologies, they tend to accept several core values related in one way or another to social class. First and foremost, skinheads express working class pride. They value common sense, hard work, camaraderie, and worker unity, distinguishing themselves from intellectuals and managers who they consider spoiled, lazy, or effeminate. Some skins exhibit tattoos such as "Working Class Pride," and the shaved heads and work boots symbolize worker solidarity. Even contemporary middle class youth who adopt the skinhead style tend to idealize the working class as somehow more authentic than the backstabbing, shallow middle class work world.

Pride is a general skinhead theme, whether pride in one's self, friends, family, or country (Marshall 1994). Skins are often patriotic, sometimes wearing patches of their country's flag on their jackets. Some are especially nationalistic, tattooing patriotic slogans across their bodies, and for a few, nationalistic pride turns to xenophobia, leading them to join anti-immigrant neo-Nazi groups. In any case, the CCCS theorists would see this patriotism as misplaced and counterproductive; why glorify your country that perpetuates the very system that keeps you poor and struggling? However, for skins, the flag symbolically represents the "real," common people rather than the rich who profit most from the capitalist system.

Many skins also respect "aggro," or hypermasculine, behavior. Toughness, bravado, and being ready to fight are hallmarks of skinhead pride. Groups tend to build a masculine camaraderie, defending each other from threats, both perceived and real; standing up for one's friends is a must. Some are inspired by the hooliganism and random violence of the "droogs" in Stanley Kubrick's controversial film *A Clockwork Orange* (based on the Anthony Burgess novel of the same name), but most simply put on a masculine pose. Homophobia, the irrational mistrust, fear, and hatred of lesbians and gay men, is yet another way for skins to express and "prove" their masculinity. Some skinheads go so far as to perpetuate violence on gays and lesbians (Marshall 1994). These skinhead characteristics clash with the hippie lifestyle, which skinheads despise for its perceived laziness, lack of patriotism, poor hygiene, and pacifism.

RACISM VERSUS ANTIRACISM

The history of skinhead race relations is fairly complicated. Some skinheads, of course, are adamantly racist, sometimes engaging in violent criminal activity (Hamm 1993). Early U.K. skinheads, both white and black, engaged in "Paki-bashing," or harassing and beating immigrants of color (many presumably from Pakistan but also from other Asian countries). Seen as a threat to workers' livelihoods and neighborhoods, immigrants became the scapegoat for a struggling manufacturing economy and a changing working class culture. Yet it wasn't just whites doing the bashing; West Indian skins, who had assimilated into the local culture more than the new wave of Asian immigrants, engaged in their fair share of violence as well. Further, black skinhead gangs fought white skinhead gangs, but typically more for territory than as part of a racist ideology (Marshall 1994). Skins went after (white) greasers as much as people of color. Clearly, race played an important role in skinhead violence, but a full-fledged ideology of racial suprem- acy had not yet developed. Skinheads' anti-immigrant sentiments reflected the feelings of much of white society and mirror the same racist worries that exist in the United States or any society struggling with its borders and/or identity, albeit in a more aggro form.

Eventually, organizations such as the British National Front recognized the potential of an "army" of angry youth. Bands like Skrewdriver provided a sound- track to the new movement, which gained momentum in the United States during the 1980s. White supremacist Tom Metzger and his organization White Aryan Resistance (WAR) aggressively recruited skinheads, playing up fears of invasions of brown-skinned immigrants and white decline (J. Moore 1993). Music has been central to the white power skinhead scene, and Metzger used many genres to attract new recruits, including punk, goth, and especially black, noise, and death metal (Burghart 1999). Some racist skins affiliate with groups or "crews" such as the Hammer Skins, and others join gangs while incarcerated in prisons.

In Europe and parts of the United States, **neo-fascist** movements continue to use skinhead nationalism to enforce anti-immigrant sentiments. Fascism is a totalitarian political ideology based upon the belief that one's nation and/or people is superior to others. Promoting hypernationalism and racism, fascists often seek to isolate or eliminate ethnic groups, as Hitler's Nazis perpetrated genocide against Jews, communists, gypsies, and homosexuals. Thus, in Europe, authorities con- sider skinheads a political threat, while in the United States they are considered primarily a gang. The violence perpetrated by skins is similar on both continents.

Despite the ongoing racism of certain skinhead factions, many skinheads are *not* explicitly racist, and North American skinheads did not emerge as a racist movement, as many believe (Wood 1999). Skinheads fall into several categories including nonracist, separatist, anti-racist, and political skins (Young and Craig 1997; Wooden and Blazak 2001). A lot of skinheads are not necessarily white supremacist but rather nonpolitical, rejecting racist beliefs but not taking an active stance against racism.

Non- and anti-racist skinheads despise racist skins for giving their movement a bad name, calling them "boneheads" to represent racists' lack of intelligence or "Nazis" to frame them as an evil that must be stopped. Anti-racist skinheads, often called SHARPs (Skinheads Against Racial Prejudice), seek to confront rac- ism wherever they find it. Racist and anti-racist skinheads occasionally come into violent conflict, each faction sharing the original skinhead penchant for aggro violence. Some join groups such as Anti-Racist Action (ARA) and distribute con- sciousness-raising materials to right the racism they see in their local communi- ties, families, or scenes (Wooden and Blazak 2001)—a central tenet of the ARA is that members do not rely on the police and/or legal system to fight racism; racists must be actively confronted. Others are former racist skinheads who wish to educate the public about nonracist skins. Just as racist skins wear swastikas and other racist paraphernalia, anti-racist skins often sport buttons, t-shirt slogans, or patches advocating their point of view (e.g., a swastika within a circle with a line through it or two clasped hands, one white and one black). I personally encountered one skin who had tattooed "This machine kills fascists" down his arm. SHARP zines feature smashed swastikas, articles on racism, and pieces advocating violence against racist skins (Wood 1999). Not only are SHARPs against racism, they also tend to oppose sexism and homophobia, reflecting the official stance of ARA. There are even Web sites for queer skinheads. By now your head is probably spinning—anti-racist, anti-sexist, gay-positive *skinheads*? This just goes to show you how difficult making generalizations about subcultures can be.

Traditional skinhead culture went through a minor revival with the resurgence of ska's popularity in the mid- to late 1990s. Inspired by ska/punk groups such as The Mighty Mighty Bosstones, No Doubt, Reel Big Fish, and Rancid, kids brought back ska fashions such as plaid pants, checkered belts, and flight jackets. The so-called third wave of ska had a relatively short life span, but nevertheless nonracist skinheads began showing up in a variety of scenes. Kids continue to adopt the skinhead and rude boy styles. Suits (often with pants cut just above the ankles), ties, dress shoes, pork-pie hats, and dark sunglasses are typical of the "rudie" uniform, while "rude girls" favor a sort of retro 1950s look of dresses or skirts, bright lipstick, and bobbed hairdos. Today's rudies are into the fashion and the connection to the Two Tone era of ska more than any sort of social protest or violence. White power skinheads tend toward various kinds of metal (see Chapter 5) and have developed an online presence on sites such as Stormfront.org.

SYMBOLIC INTERACTION

If you were to see a bunch of skinheads walking down the street wearing steel-toed boots, checkered suspenders, and shaved heads you might be amused, repulsed, or scared, depending upon the meanings you associate with skins. By now you understand that your interpretation of any particular skins may or may not be true. You would need more clues than simply shaved heads and boots to tell if this group was racist, anti-racist, or nonpolitical because the meaning of skinhead varies, even between skins. Recall from Chapter 1 that a constructionist or interactionist analysis of deviance pays attention to how we interpret the world and how we construct the meanings of deviance in interaction.

Much of my understanding of subcultures comes from a broad theoretical paradigm called **symbolic interaction**. Symbolic interactionists recognize that human beings are *meaning makers*. We interpret the world around us and create meaning through interaction. The theory is based on several assumptions (Blumer 1969; Sandstrom, Martin, and Fine 2006):

1. We act toward people, things, and events based upon the meanings we have for them. We do not passively perceive the world "as it is." We actively transform the world into images and concepts, giving it meaning and

order. We see the world through "filters" such as our social class, gender, religion, nationality, race, and sexual identity.

2. Meaning is created through interaction between people. Furthermore, meaning is not inherent—there is no fixed reality. Rather, we *interpret* reality. Reality passes through our various filters, coloring our conclusions. This seems simple enough, but really acknowledging this can be a bit unsettling at first. It means things you have taken for granted all your life are open to questioning.

3. We learn meanings. Parents, teachers, friends, coaches, the media, and so forth teach us our initial interpretations of the world. The process begins at birth, when parents dress baby boys in blue and daughters in pink; we start learning right away what it means to be a girl or a boy.

4. Meanings change through an interpretive process. As we interact in different contexts, we learn new meanings and must somehow reconcile them with our old understandings. Meanings change over time.

What is the implication? *The same "objective reality" can hold vastly different meanings depending upon our filters.* Consider a cow, for instance. For Hindus in India, a cow represents a sacred incarnation of a deity to be revered and not harmed. The same cow—the *exact* same cow—would be lunch in the United States. It's the same cow! Yet our interpretation of that cow depends upon our filters, in this case based upon religion, history, and culture. "Reality" (if there is such a thing) passes through our filters, prompting us to draw certain conclusions.

Something as seemingly simple as a shoelace can hold significant meanings. To some skins, wearing white laces signifies white pride, red laces white power, and yellow laces hatred of police (Wooden and Blazak 2001). Still other skinheads think giving such meaning to laces is a stupid myth concocted by law enforcement and media. Obviously shoelaces have no inherent meaning. Yet skinheads have **socially constructed** meaning around these supposedly meaningless, functional things. To say that reality is socially constructed is another way of saying that we create meaning through interaction rather than meaning being rooted in some objective reality (Berger and Luckman 1966). There is nothing inherently meaningful in shoelaces, but some skinheads construct particular meanings, common understandings that have real consequences. To complicate matters even further, other skins find little meaning in the particular visual styles associated with early skinhead culture, especially as they get older, instead deriving meaning primarily from the performative *activities*—fighting and tattooing, for example—of their crew (Pilkington 2010).

Identifying with the working class carries a host of meanings. In seeking to revive working class culture, skinheads often wear clothes associated with the working class, work traditionally working class jobs, and favor beer over beverages that symbolize the upper class. Wine, especially *expensive* wine, might symbolize upper class pretentiousness, snobbishness, or even femininity. *Real* men drink beer and work at *real* jobs—that is to say, manual labor (see Willis 1977).

So you see, even choice of beverage is layered with meanings rooted in social class, gender, and even race. Through their dress, language, and other lifestyle choices many skinheads reinforce particular meanings for what it means to be working class. This contrasts with the mods, who while also working class wore expensive fashions in imitation of the higher classes. The mods could look good, party in style on the weekend, and then turn back into a "working stiff" during the week.

For mods, the make and type of scooter carried symbolic significance. They favored Vespas or Piaggio (European brands) over Bajaj and SIL branded Lambrettas (made in India). American-branded Vespas—Allstates—are even lower on the totem pole. The scooter itself was a "classier" alternative to the motorcycles ridden by rockers. Mods also customized their scooters with multiple chrome-backed rear-view mirrors, flags or raccoon tails, and two-tone paint; a straight stock scooter indicated a potential poseur. A typical mod bike might have six or seven mirrors *on each side*. Thus an affordable, practical means of transport became a meaningful statement meant to distinguish the group from both the mainstream and other youth subcultures.

Racist skins have a whole variety of symbols that embody their ideology. Swastikas and SS lightning bolts draw upon Nazi imagery. Some use the number 88 as shorthand for "Heil Hitler," eight signifying H, the eighth letter of the alphabet. The Celtic cross worn by some members symbolizes European ancestry, and the Christian cross connects white supremacy to a religious duty or even crusade. Nonracist skins often wear buttons with a crucified skinhead, half black and half white, or a broken or crossed-out swastika. Each of these symbols communicates membership to a group, a connection to a collective identity that other members can recognize.

Drugs offer another good example of how people construct a variety of meanings around the same thing. Drugs carry vastly different meanings for different groups. For hippies, drugs such as marijuana and LSD were casual, relatively harmless indulgences or even catalysts to expanding awareness. Some skinheads use drugs, but many reject them based upon a perceived connection to hippies. Even hippies' meanings for drugs were more complex than most people realize. "Dope," mind-altering substances such as marijuana, hashish, and LSD, were acceptable and good, while "drugs" such as heroin and PCP were bad.

DEFINITION OF THE SITUATION

While it is true that reality is socially constructed, we interpret our surroundings and then act upon our interpretations as if they are real and true, based upon how we define a situation. Sociologist W. I. Thomas (1923) wrote about the **definition of the situation**: What people believe to be real is real in its consequences. When people agree on a definition of the situation they act in predictable ways. For example, college students and professors tend to have similar definitions around how a class proceeds—the professor lectures, provides notes, assigns homework, gives exams, and so on, and students listen, take notes, do homework, and take exams. Conflict often emerges when we define situations differently. Think of the many cultural debates in the United States, each of which boils down to vastly different definitions of the situation: abortion rights, gay marriage, gun control, and the role of religion in society. As I've pointed out, racist and anti-racist skins occasionally come into violent conflict based upon their very different perceptions of race. Each faction's members are *certain* they are right, based upon the filters through which they perceive the world.

Skinhead values sharply contrast the hippie lifestyle, based on the meanings these groups construct. For hippies, opposing war meant (among other things) resisting a larger unjust system. It's not difficult to see how skins might interpret this as a cowardly shirking of duty. However, the meanings run more deeply. War resistance also has class connotations. Skins may conclude that hippies are middle class kids who use their privilege to avoid service, thereby shifting even more of the burden of war onto the working classes. Hippies defied conventional standards of appearance by letting their hair (often including, for men, facial hair) grow and rejecting business attire. Skins might interpret these actions not as a challenge to conformity but as a lack of pride and perhaps, in the case of men, a sign of femininity.

CONCLUSION

This chapter offers three important insights for the study of subcultures. First, at the macro level, it is important to examine a subculture's relationship with the larger culture. The social context in which a subculture exists influences the possibilities for that group. Think of it as looking at the big picture. Second, at the micro level, subculturists produce and maintain meanings about the world. To understand a subculture, we must try to grasp the meanings, the definitions of reality that its members construct. Third, subcultures change and diverge into different factions over time, and members grouped into the same general subculture may have vastly different definitions of the situation, as is the case with racist and anti-racist skins. Thus, while it can be useful to describe distinct subcultures, it is also easy to overgeneralize and paint all members with the same brush. I return to these issues later in the book.

Skinheads come from a long and complicated history interwoven with other subcultures. Today, some of the different factions share little more than the style and the championing of the working class. Some are in scooter clubs, others a part of racist movements, and still others find a place in the punk, ska, or metal music scenes. You might think that the practices of some subcultures are weird, wrong, or even crazy. However, to really understand a group in all of its complexity requires that we try to grasp subculturists' meanings *from their point of view*. That is not to say you have to agree with or support the subcultural lifestyles represented in this book; I certainly hope you reject the beliefs and goals of racist skinheads. However, I am suggesting that before you make assumptions or pass judgment you should recognize that your interpretation of reality is simply one among many, and your definition of the situation is simply one definition. With effort, we can learn to better recognize the set of filters that affect our perception, gradually coming to our own conclusions.

DISCUSSION

- Describe some markers of social class present in your workplace, on your campus, in your town/city, and in your daily life.
- What societal changes in the past forty years have made the skinhead identity susceptible to cooptation by white power organizations and ideologies?
- Which subcultures or groups do you find especially strange? Give some examples of how their definition of the situation might differ from yours.

KEY IDEAS

Blocked structural opportunities: The theory that youth join deviant groups due to inadequate legitimate access to society's rewards, including wealth and prestige, as well as decent jobs, health care, and luxury goods.

Definition of the situation: An interpretation of "reality." We define any given situation largely according to what we have been socialized to believe. People may define the same situation in different ways, producing conflict.

Fascism/neo-fascism: A totalitarian political ideology based upon the belief that one's nation and/or people is superior to others. Promoting national unity, hyper-nationalism, and racism, fascists often seek to isolate or eliminate ethnic groups. Neo-fascism draws inspiration from past fascist leaders but generally fails to win large-scale public support or political victories.

Hegemony: The dominance of one group over another. Typically associated with the powerful wealthy classes and nations exercising political and cultural domin-ion over the rest of society in order to keep their power.

Ritual: A recurring pattern of behavior that has symbolic meaning.

SHARPs: Skinheads Against Racial Prejudice—a skinhead faction formed in the late 1980s to oppose racism. While few formally organized SHARP groups remain, individual skins still claim the identity.

Social class: A system of stratification based upon income and wealth. Social class impacts one's opportunities, tastes, and power in society.

Socially constructed: The idea that we create meaning through interaction rather than meaning being rooted in some objective reality. Assumes that meanings (i.e., beliefs) can change and be challenged.

Stereotype: A simplified overgeneralization, usually negative, about a group of people. Stereotypes are often based upon incomplete or false information and can be used to label groups as deviant.

Structural context: The historical, social, political, cultural, and economic circumstances in a society that influence subcultures' emergence and form. The "big picture" in which subcultures exist.

Symbolic interaction: A major theoretical paradigm based on the work of George Herbert Mead, Herbert Blumer, Erving Goffman, and others. Symbolic interactionists are especially concerned with how humans use and interpret symbols, creating meaning in their interactions with one another.

Symbolic resistance: The theory that, rather than being truly revolutionary and making actual political change, subcultures offer symbolic challenges to society that in reality produce little social change.

RESOURCES

Anti-racist Action

www.antiracistaction.org

Anti-racist Action (ARA) is a network of groups dedicated to fighting racism, sexism, and homophobia across North America. Many anti-racist skins have been associated with ARA. You can also search the site for articles on skinhead history.

Southern Poverty Law Center

www.splcenter.org

The Southern Poverty Law Center advocates for civil rights of all kinds. Their site features many articles about racist skinheads.

Skinheads: A Guide to an American Subculture

By Tiffini A. Travis and Perry Hardy. 2012. Santa Barbara, CA: Greenwood.

A short introduction to skinhead history and various types of skinheads, co-authored by a self-identified skin.

Skinhead

By Nick Knight. 2011(1982). London: Ombibus Press.

A book of photos and commentary about London's skinhead revival in the early 1980s.

We Are the Mods: A Transnational History of a Youth Subculture

By Christine Jacqueline Feldman. 2009. New York: Peter Lang Publishing.

A fascinating study of mod cultures in the U.S., U.K., Germany, and Japan.

The Spirit of '69: A Skinhead Bible

By George Marshall. 1994. Lockerbie, Scotland: S. T. Publishing.

A former insider's take on skinhead history and one of the more respected books among traditional skins.

www.modculture.co.uk/

A U.K. site featuring all things mod, from fashion and music to scootering and art.

This Is England (film, Shane Meadows 2006)

Set in early 1980s United Kingdom, a drama following a boy torn between traditional skinheads and the racist National Front.

American History X (film, Tony Kaye 1998)

A drama following the story of one young man's conversion to and later rejection of racist skinhead ideology.

Quadrophenia (film, Franc Roddam 1979)

A drama based on The Who's 1973 record of the same name, depicting mods and rockers in a coming-of-age story.

Romper Stomper (film, Geoffrey Wright 1992)

A drama of a skinhead gang in Australia that has become a cult classic.

SKINS ONLINE

"Skinheads in 1988"

www.youtube.com/watch?v=PFxhGyfnhuE&feature=related

A newscast showing both SHARP and racist skins.

YouTube: "Oprah vs. Skinheads 1988"

Oprah interviews white power skinheads as traditional skinheads offer a different point of view.

YouTube: "People are Talking—Skinheads After Geraldo Show"

A series of interviews with various types of skinheads, including anti-racist skins, following the infamous episode of *Geraldo* featuring a fight between skinheads and a black activist.

CHAPTER 3

ᐩ

Punk Rock, Hardcore, and Straight Edge—Status and Hierarchy in Subcultures

By the mid-1990s, punk had burst from the underground and into mainstream culture. If you went to high school after 1995, you probably noticed that the punk clique grew from a socially isolated band of outcasts into visible, well-established groups of kids from a variety of backgrounds. Today, punk has a widespread presence on both radio and MTV. Wal-Mart and Target carry punk CDs, and Hot Topic stores in suburban malls across the country sell punk clothing complete with spikes and rips. This was not always so. Punk's full transformation from socially isolated tribe to commercially profitable trend took nearly twenty years. Even today, a new generation of kids in the punk underground puts on shows in basements, produces its own low-budget records, and silk-screens its own shirts. For every band like Blink 182 performing to sellout crowds of thousands of fans, there are twenty underground bands playing in front of fifty to one hundred kids. In this chapter, I first discuss the origins of punk and its various offshoots. Next, I outline punks' core values, including the style, "Do It Yourself" ethic, and the politics of punk. Finally, I use punk to illustrate how subculturists rank themselves according to their own status hierarchy, continually trying to prove their authenticity.

ORIGINS, SOCIAL CONTEXT, AND FRAGMENTATION OF PUNK

Punk emerged in the late 1970s, influenced by U.S. garage bands, new wave music, and the New York art rock scene (A. Bennett 2001), and it has since evolved and fragmented into a variety of genres. New Wave music such as Blondie and other bands like MC5, The Velvet Underground, the Stooges, the Ramones, New York Dolls, and Talking Heads set the stage for the emergence of punk (Heylin 1993), forming a scene around the famous Manhattan venue CBGB. David Bowie's glam rock persona, "Ziggy Stardust," dressed in bright, flamboyant outfits and wearing heavy makeup, influenced punk's early androgynous look. From the start, punk was an in-your-face movement out to shock adult society. The sound was often abrasive, and adherents valued passion and presence at least as much as musicianship and probably more. Since its beginnings, the punk subculture has spread around the world, splitting into a variety of subgroups including hardcore, straight edge, riot grrrl, and emo. Over time, subcultures tend to both blend with other subcultures in a process called **syncretism** and splinter off into other groups, called **fragmentation** (Campbell 1972). The history of punk illustrates both.

British Punk and American Hardcore

Punk's distinctive style really came together with British punk around 1976, taking off with the popularity of the Sex Pistols, the Clash, the Damned, and Siouxsie and the Banshees (Henry 1989). The Sex Pistols' onstage antics and blatant derision for mainstream conventions grabbed newspaper headlines and worried adults. Malcom McClaren made teddy boy, punk, and new wave fashions available in his London clothing shop while also managing the Sex Pistols and New York Dolls, marketing their outrageous behavior and offensive style. Bassist Sid Vicious, who joined the band in 1977, became legendary for his drug abuse, onstage drunkenness, and self-inflicted wounds that left blood running down his body. Their songs "Anarchy in the U.K." and "God Save the Queen" illustrated punk's earliest values: personal freedom, disorder, and disrespect for tradition and authority. As with any subculture, understanding punk depends in part on grasping the social context in which it emerged. Early American punk was partly a reaction to the hippies, the disco culture, and arena rock bands like KISS, Styx, Foreigner, and Journey. These bands played in front of tens of thousands of fans, living a rock-and-roll lifestyle of celebrity. Music was becoming increasingly commercial and professional, leaving many kids feeling that the dream of being in a band was beyond their reach and that established record labels wanted little to do with risky, groundbreaking music. Instead of concerts, punks attended more intimate "shows" in which the crowd often ended up on stage with the performers or vice versa.

In the United States, bands like The Ramones ushered in an Americanized pop punk sound in New York while the Dead Kennedys, Bad Religion, and Black Flag spearheaded a West Coast hardcore scene (Blush 2001). While punk was fairly androgynous, tongue-in-cheek fun, hardcore had a distinctly masculine feel, as the music became faster, the dancing rougher, and the attitude more antagonistic (Leblanc 1999). Punk style was meant to repulse the straight world, especially the yuppie Reaganites of the 1980s. Some sported the skinhead look while others wore their hair in a variety of spiked, shaved, and sculpted styles, the most well known being the Mohawk and liberty spikes (named after the Statue of Liberty's spiky crown). Like the skinheads, early British punks were primarily from the working class (Hebdige 1979), though since then the style has become a suburban middle class phenomenon, especially in the United States.

Early American hardcore evolved into a faster, more aggressive sound complete with its own style. Bands stripped most of the pop sound and melody from their songs, favoring instead very fast guitars driven by repetitive drums and screaming vocals. Guitar solos came to symbolize the perceived pretentiousness of professional rock musicians and were pared down or scrapped entirely. Hardcore kept punk's DIY ethic but gradually shed much of its style; athletic shorts, sweat-shirts, and high tops replaced studded leather jackets, Mohawks, and ripped cloth-ing. The Cro-Mags, SS Decontrol, Minor Threat, Agnostic Front, Bad Brains, and 7 Seconds were among the first hardcore pioneers. CBGB in New York served as a hub for hardcore acts, hosting Sunday "matinee" shows with low door prices. By the early 1990s, the punk and hardcore scenes had grown increasingly distinct— many kids were fans of both hardcore and punk, but increasingly they identified with one scene more than the other. Today's hardcore kids often overlap with the metal scene (see Chapter 5) but retain many of the original hardcore ideals.

Straight Edge

While the heavy drug and alcohol use in the early scene has led to popular por-trayals of punks as drunks and addicts, some punks take a strong stance against substance use. Hardcore and punk produced straight edge, a clean-living youth movement whose adherents make a lifetime commitment to abstain from alcohol, drugs, tobacco, and "promiscuous" sex (Haenfler 2006; D. Irwin 1999). Straight edge emerged from the Washington, D.C., hardcore scene around 1980 with the band Minor Threat but quickly spread across the United States and eventually the world. Straight edge was a reaction to the heavy drug use and nihilism of some segments of the punk scene; straight edgers appreciated punks' questioning of the status quo, aggressive music, and unconventional ideals but didn't like the heavy drinking, drug use, and cynical "no future" attitude.[7] Kids today become straight edge for a variety of reasons, including to resist a family history of substance abuse, personal addiction, or more often as a way to challenge alcohol and drugs' prominence in youth culture (Haenfler 2004c). Early members took the "X" as the movement's symbol. Club owners would mark underage kids' hands with a black X so the bartenders would not serve them alcohol, but straight edgers transformed this symbol into a badge of defiance. Members often wear or tattoo Xs and straight edge slogans (such as "Poison Free") on their bodies (Atkinson 2003).[8] Like many subcultures, straight edge has a large presence on the Internet (Williams 2003, 2006). Many straight edgers also adopt vegetarian or vegan (no animal products whatsoever) lifestyles, inspired by past bands such as Youth of Today, Insted, and Earth Crisis. While most straight edge kids try to spread their drug-free message by example, some adopt a more "hardline" stance, aggressively pushing their beliefs and ostracizing kids who drink or smoke (Wood 2006).

Emo and Indie Rock

By the 2000s, punk has branched into so many subgenres that it is more difficult than ever to say what punk really is. Like straight edge, "emo" has its roots in the Washington, D.C., scene, inspired especially by the bands Rites of Spring and Embrace.[9] Difficult to define, emo is simply short for "emotional"; songs express feelings of "nostalgia," "romantic bitterness," and "general poetic desperation" (Greenwald 2003, 12–13). Musicians usually don't call themselves emo, but the label has stuck among fans. Groups such as Sunny Day Real Estate and Jawbreaker paved the way for later bands such as Dashboard Confessional and Taking Back Sunday. All encourage a deep, almost desperate introspection and catharsis of emotion at their shows (Bailey 2005). It is not uncommon to see kids crying as they sing along at an emo concert. By encouraging kids to express a variety of emotions, emo stretches gender boundaries, especially for young men. Emo kids adopt several styles; both the musical and stylistic boundaries are contested. Many are distinguishable by their tight jeans and vintage t-shirts, thick-rimmed glasses (imagine Buddy Holly), thrift store jackets, brightly colored athletic shoes, and unruly hair, while others adopt "goth" styles or focus on "Do It Yourself" (DIY) practices rather than any specific fashion. "Indie rock" may be the new catchall phrase, replacing "alternative rock" and used to describe any rock music slightly out of the mainstream. Emo and indie rock have firmly established their place in pop culture, and though they emerged from punk they now influence punk. Even hardcore and straight edge kids who sometimes mock emo's sensitivity have adopted much from the indie style.

CORE VALUES

Punk Style and Nonconformity

Punks, like many subculturists, despise conformity, including conformity of thought, fashion, and lifestyle. Early punks adopted the "question everything" mentality of their subculture forebears, writing songs criticizing the government, big business, police, parents, and other authority figures. Unlike the skinheads, punks were decidedly *not* patriotic. Like the hippies, punks emphasized the present, advocating a "live for the moment" attitude—why go to school, get a job, buy a house, and raise a family just to end up as miserable as your parents? However, punks also believed society was in irrevocable decline, the "no future" mantra capturing their attitude about the world (Henry 1989). Punk shows reflect the chaos punks see in the world, with kids diving off the stage into a crowd of stomping, flailing, "moshing" fans. "Pogoing" entails repeatedly jumping up and down in place and "slamming" involves running around in a circle (called the "circle pit") while bouncing off of fellow punks. To outsiders, such dancing seems violent, but most insiders claim it is a harmless way to vent anger and frustration, observing a "slam etiquette" to prevent injury (Baron 1989, 231). Hardcore and straight edge kids take moshing to a new level of intensity, spinning, "windmilling" their arms, kung fu kicking, and punching the air with abandon. Surprisingly, while fights and injuries do occur (in some local scenes more than others), overall they are relatively rare.

When you imagine punk style, you probably think of tall mohawks, ripped clothing, combat boots, metal studs, and safety pins. As I described previously, today's punks are a much more eclectic group sporting a variety of styles. Some wear outrageous clothing and others are virtually indistinguishable from their more mainstream counterparts. Piercings and tattoos have grown even more popular among all versions of punk, and spikes, whether on leather jackets, carrier bags, or belts, are still a common feature. Hardcore and straight edge kids, especially, favor large stainless steel guages in their ears, some even stretching the holes to an inch or more. Riot Grrrls often blend traditionally feminine styles (e.g., makeup, skirts) with brightly colored hair, tattoos, and facial piercings, challenging standards of feminine beauty. In short, while there are recognizable trends in punk style, contemporary punks are a pretty diverse lot, and no one look dominates the scene.

Theorists such as Paul Willis (1978) have claimed that style is symbolic of subcultural values and subcultures' relationship to the mainstream. Punks' spikes, therefore, have meaning beyond fashion, symbolizing untouchability and toughness. Even the apparently thoughtless, chaotic melee of the mosh pit can be read as a symbolic statement expressing the frustrations of youth and yearning for some kind of visceral community. Punk mixes a variety of styles into a bricolage. **Bricolage** entails taking aspects of popular culture and reworking and combining them into new forms. It is evident in punk clothing and zines. Many punks cover leather or denim jackets with patches or scrawled messages (e.g., an "A" in a circle, standing for "anarchy") or piece together pants with different materials. Before the advent of computers, punk zines were cut-and-paste projects including mix-and-match fonts and crooked pictures; some punks still cut and paste, upholding punks' roots. Though there is certainly some kind of meaning behind subcultural forms and fashions, contemporary scholars criticize Hebdige and the CCCS's focus on the symbolic meanings of style for reading too much into style, imposing meaning rather than recording meaning as understood by subculturists themselves.

DIY—Do It Yourself

Perhaps the most enduring ideal from the punk scene is "Do It Yourself," or DIY for short. Reacting against the corporate music industry that was virtually inaccessible to most kids, punks made doing it yourself a virtue (Gosling 2004). Making music does not require fancy instruments, years of training, professional producers, or unattainable talent; *anyone*, according to punks, can make music. If a major record label will not sign your band, form your own label. In fact, forming your own label is *better* because you have more creative control over your music and are not supporting the corporate music industry. If promoters will not book your band, find your own venue and put on your own show. According to the DIY ethic, corporate involvement commodifies art and risks business executives meddling with the creative process. In addition to serving the practical purpose of making music and art production accessible, DIY symbolizes independence and a rejection of mainstream mediocrity. Of course, despite this ideal, many punk bands have signed with major labels, fueling debate about the bands' integrity and authenticity, an issue I address later in this chapter.

One of the most significant symbolic markers distinguishing punk's DIY ethic is the difference between concerts and shows. A concert is a large, professional, for-profit event with an expensive cover charge and a barrier between the fans and the performers. A show is a smaller, more intimate affair with a reasonable door price often booked by the fans themselves. Concerts take place in sports arenas and civic centers, whereas shows happen anywhere from VFW halls and small clubs to youth centers and basements. The lack of a barrier at most shows symbolizes the idea that musicians are fans and fans could be musicians, that punk bands should not be put on a pedestal, and that musicians should avoid an arrogant "rock star" attitude. Indeed, the presence of a barrier is perhaps the easiest way insiders distinguish between a show and a concert, though as punk music has grown in popularity (necessitating larger venues), barriers have become increasingly common.

Punks have established a DIY **underground economy**, both due to being shut out of mainstream opportunities and in outright rejection of the corporate model. Ideally, an underground economy is smaller in scale, run by scene insiders, focused on artistic rather than commercial concerns, and tied to a local scene community. Subcultures often launch their own network of businesses: photography, video production, newspapers/zines, music promotion and management, boutiques, and comics inspired by or affiliated with a subculture are common (see Gaines 1994). Hundreds of independent records labels, including Alternative Tentacles, Dischord, Epitaph, SST, and Revelation release recordings by a range of artists otherwise ignored by larger labels. Eventually, successful, localized independent enterprises may gain national and international prominence, as is the case with the long-running punk zine *MaximumRocknroll* or hardcore label Victory Records. However, members of most scenes establish their own, localized zines and labels, often at little or no profit to themselves, simply to make a creative contribution to the scene (Gosling 2004).

Punk Politics/Personal Is Political

Some sectors of punk quickly evolved from hedonism and self-destructiveness to politics and social change. Punk helped many kids find a progressive political voice, similar to the hippies but without the peace, love, and flower power. The Dead Kennedys certainly were out to shock people—as album title *FrankenChrist* suggests—but singer Jello Biafra also expressed a political point of view; the song "California Uber Alles," for example, criticized California governor Jerry Brown. In Washington, D.C., kids organized Rock Against Reagan campaigns, staging concerts that also served as platforms to criticize what punks saw as the president's anti-poor, anti-gay, and pro-war policies (Andersen and Jenkins 2001). The D.C. organization Positive Force has helped punks and straight edge kids work for social change, including supporting the anti-apartheid movement in the 1980s. On the other side of the Atlantic, the British band Crass promoted anarchism, vegetarianism, and communalism in both their music and their lifestyle. For Riot Grrrls, so often excluded from equal participation in the scene, forming a band or creating a zine were political statements in themselves. Like many subcultures, they claimed that the **personal is political**, a phrase coined by feminists to engage women in the fight against sexism. The notion that the personal is political rests on several assumptions:

- Our personal lives are interwoven with our social, cultural, and political surroundings. Politics in some ways determines our personal lives. For example, being a woman in U.S. society is loaded with expectations. Some women refuse to wear makeup not only as a personal choice but to make a political statement that society places too much emphasis on women's appearance.
- To improve our personal lives, we must address political structures. For example, if we want universal access to health care or we want a livable wage (believing these things will improve our personal lives), we must act together.
- Our personal choices have political implications. For example, what we choose to eat, wear, and drive has implications for other people. Shopping at locally owned businesses rather than chain stores helps mom-and-pop stores stay in business and can maintain the distinctiveness of a community.

Straight edge kids make the personal political by using their *personal* choice of abstinence to make a *political* statement against alcohol and tobacco companies and a youth culture that pressures kids to use. They seek to carry on Ian MacKaye's "revolution by example" (Andersen and Jenkins 2001, 397–398). Their stand against "promiscuous sex" is a rejection of a perceived masculinity encouraging men to pursue sex wherever they can get it, often at the expense of women (Haenfler 2004b). Subcultures differ from many social movements in that they are less likely to challenge government directly (though this does occur). However, many subculturists engage in social change in a more personal way, crafting a lifestyle of resistance to dominant norms and values (Baron 1989; Leblanc 1999; Haenfler 2004a). Riot Grrrls especially combined their love of punk music with their commitment to feminist politics, as you will see in chapter 9. Creating and publishing feminist-punk zines raises consciousness of sexism, racism, and homophobia.

Other factions of punk, known as gutter-punk, crust punk, and anarcho-punk, choose to live communally, reject conventional work, and avoid capitalism whenever possible. Some "squat" (illegally occupy) in abandoned dwellings and panhandle on the streets (Baron 1989). Others organize into anarchist collectives, pooling resources and living in a cheap apartment or rented house. Such punks make a conscious choice to live outside (as much as possible) of the capitalist system that to them represents greed, oppression, and exploitation, occasionally engaging in a variety of causes, including the peace and anti-racism movements (Roberts and Moore 2009). Lyrics of bands such as England's Crass and Canada's Propagandhi condemn imperialism while promoting alternatives to capitalism. Queer punks, also known as the queercore scene, challenge the heterosexism of both mainstream society and music scenes (J. Taylor 2009).

Finally, not all punk politics run in a progressive direction. Punks have been part of racist and anti-Semitic movements, recruited, like skinheads, to groups such as the National Front (Sabin 1999). Others have engaged in gay-bashing and anti-immigrant movements. The majority of more progressive punks disavow any connection to reactionary, right-wing Punks, as demonstrated in the Dead Kennedys' song "Nazi Punks Fuck Off."

SCENESTERS, POSEURS, AND "TRUE" MEMBERS

Punks, and most other subculturists as well, pride themselves on their egalitarianism. They despise the competition and hierarchies of the mainstream business world, claiming to be interested in values, art, and equality rather than status, power, and money. The hippies with their "peace, love, and happiness" ethos promoted an alternative to a society that ranked and rewarded individuals according to their race, gender, sexual identity, and social class (T. Miller 1991; 1999). In their scene, equality would enable each individual to live a creative and more intentional life. As noble as these goals may be, research shows that even subculturists that aspire to unlimited individuality and free expression battle over hierarchy. Ask yourself, "Who is a *real* punk, and who is a *poseur*?" and you see that some punks are supposedly more "true" or "authentic" than others. Who represents *real* hip hop and who are the fakes? Who are true Christians and who are the imposters? Virtually every group has ways of designating authenticity.

For all their acceptance and tolerance, punks spend a great deal of time and energy discussing who is really punk and who is a fake. Can you call yourself a punk and listen to Britney Spears? Are you a punk if you wear a sweater? Do real punks drive expensive cars? Can you be a Riot Grrrl and hold your boyfriend's coat at a show? Are Green Day, who worked their way up from a small Berkeley band to performing at (and winning) the Grammy Awards still punk? The fact that these questions arise indicates that punks informally organize themselves into authentic and inauthentic members.

Most subcultures have their own version of the "poseur." A **poseur** is someone who wears the trappings of a subculture but who others perceive to fail to live out or truly believe in the subculture's ideals. In the minds of subculturists, poseurs are all style and no substance. Each punk offshoot has its own means of designating who is true and who is an imposter. For goths, "tourists" are people who attend a goth event trying hard to dress the part but looking like they bought their goth gear straight off the rack at Hot Topic.

Status and Hierarchy

Punks have many ways of distinguishing between "real" punks and "pretenders" (Fox 1987). Before we tackle that we need to show how status and hierarchy are ubiquitous features of social life. Every society has some form of **social stratification**, a way of rank ordering people based on characteristics deemed important by that society. In India, the caste system demarcates one's position, while South Africa's apartheid system and the United States' segregation formerly stratified people according to race. **Status** is your position or rank in society. Your status defines part of who you are and therefore how people relate to you. You have **ascribed status**, or status you were born with and did not choose. For example, you were born with your sex (male or female), your race and/or ethnicity, and into a certain social class (such as working, middle, or upper class). You also have **achieved** status, or status that you voluntarily adopt or achieve through your own efforts. You might achieve the status of honor student, athlete, boyfriend/girlfriend, or soldier. Ascribed and achieved statuses typically overlap—achieving the status of President is far easier for individuals born into an upper class family with political connections and credentials. A **status hierarchy** is an arrangement of statuses where some are more valued, honored, or rewarded than others. Imagine a ladder or a pyramid where those at the top have more respect and resources than those at the bottom. Where you fall on the ladder impacts how others treat you, your access to society's rewards, and your opportunities in life. The military, with its clear ranks, rigid protocols, and bureaucratic structure, is a clear example of a hierarchy. So are a corporation, a police department, and a church. But even less structured groups have hierarchies. Think of a street gang's "pecking order" or the cliques in a high school; some people wield more power and influence than others.

Levels of Status in Punk

Subculturists typically question, challenge, or even reject society's status hierarchy. Just like the hippies they disdain, punks profess to be anti-hierarchy, even mocking wealthy, powerful people at the top of the status structure. Clearly, however, subcultures produce hierarchies of their own. In her study of punks, Kathy Fox (1987) found four main positions in the scene: the hardcore, softcore, preppie, and spectator punks. Participants held the *hardcore* punks (not to be confused with the hardcore genre/faction of punk) in highest esteem as they most closely lived the scene's ideals. These were the kids with the most commitment who were punk all the time and claimed to be permanently punk. More likely to be gutter/street/anarcho punks, the lifestyle wasn't something they did only on the weekends. Their appearance was the most radical, including Mohawks, flashy makeup, visible tattoos, and swastikas. Some lived on the streets, and many used hard drugs. Though relatively few in number, the hardcores wielded the most power in the scene, determining who and what was cool. The *softcore* punks were less committed but still maintained a visible presence in the scene. They frequently attended shows and dressed similarly to the hardcore punks but were less likely to fully embrace the punk lifestyle and ideology. They used drugs less and held more of a temporary commitment to punk. Both hardcore and softcore punks looked upon the more numerous *preppie punks* with a measure of contempt. Preppie punks are more interested in the fashion and novelty of punk than making a long-term commitment to the scene. Both hardcore and softcore punks criticized and mocked preppies for taking off their punk "costumes" when they went home or to work. *Spectators* included those who were not punks but attended shows and appreciated the music. They didn't bother trying to look the part and attracted little attention from other punks.

The hardcore punks, having the most status, are at the top of the hierarchy while the preppies and spectators occupy the bottom. Though Fox's analysis focuses on punks, other subcultures have similar hierarchies. In the computer-hacker subculture, for example, someone who performs an especially ingenious, daring, and illegal hack gains status amongst her or his peers.

"Proving" Your Roots—Stratification as an Ongoing Interactional Accomplishment

Once you have reached a certain status in a subculture, your work isn't done. Even after achieving the status of a "real" punk, maintaining status is an ongoing project; subculturists must continually "prove" their authenticity or risk being labeled a "sellout." Subculturists define **authenticity** as being involved for the "right" reasons, generally meaning living the *values* of the group rather than simply sporting the costume, having a lasting commitment to the scene rather than a temporary escape from "real" life. Punks *perform* or *do* authenticity in order to maintain their status as true or authentic punks while continually contesting its meaning. Subculturists use status symbols to communicate their membership and authenticity. A **status symbol** is a marker of status, a way of communicating social prestige and membership to a group. For Americans, second (or third) homes, expensive cars (Hummers or Ferraris, perhaps), and designer handbags (Prada, Gucci) might all be status symbols. For punks, wearing an *original* (rather than a recent reprint) t-shirt of a classic punk band such as the Misfits can be a status symbol. It communicates that one knows punk's roots and was around in the early days instead of jumping on a bandwagon. Hardcore and straight edge kids joke about earning "scene points," another way of saying status. Straight edge tattoos can earn someone scene points because they reflect the permanence of straight edge commitment. Having "Str8 Edge" tattooed across one's knuckles, for example, indicates a high degree of commitment and therefore authenticity.

Each of these is an example of what Sarah Thornton calls **subcultural capital** (Thornton 1995). Subcultural capital "confers status on its owner" in the scene, coming in the form of material objects (e.g., owning the right records and clothes) but also embodied in mannerisms, style, and speech (ibid., 11). Displaying knowledge of a subculture's roots and using the appropriate slang are other examples of subcultural capital. A punk who loves Sum 41 or whichever band currently occupies the Top 40 list has less status than one who can explain the history of pioneers Black Flag and TSOL or who has knowledge of less known "underground legends" such as Born Against. A hardcore kid who follows popular bands Hatebreed and Killswitch Engage but has no knowledge of classic Bad Brains or Minor Threat is held in less esteem. A Riot Grrrl who likes Avril Lavigne but has never heard Bikini Kill is suspect, and so on. Owning rare records, longevity in the scene, and knowledge of underground bands are all worth scene points. For straight edgers, the distinction between authentic members and sellouts seems a bit easier to manage. Anyone who takes even a sip or alcohol or a drag off a cigarette is automatically considered a sellout. However, authenticity is still under dispute. Some straight edgers argue that one *must* be part of hardcore to be truly straight edge, while others claim people who are *not* part of the scene are more true because they are not caught up in scene fashion and politics (Williams and Copes 2005). Another way to reinforce your own status is to emphasize what you *are not* (Mullaney 2006). Some hardcore and straight edge kids, for example, partially define their status as *not punk*; to them, punk represents a co-opted, silly, apolitical fashion show. Likewise, punks may distinguish themselves from straight edge kids by claiming to be more open-minded or tolerant. Given that there are no real written "rules" on what it means to be Riot Grrrl, hardcore, or straight edge, managing status can be quite complicated! The point is that members of subcultures continually assess authenticity and therefore also *deliberately create* ways to communicate their authenticity. Trendsetters in the scene define what is "hip," but the media (such as MTV) also play an important role in determining what counts as subcultural capital (Williams and Copes 2005).

When punk bands become commercially successful, they run the risk of being dismissed as sellouts, regardless of their underground origins. Green Day, The Offspring, and Blink 182 serve as good examples. As they rose to prominence, some punks negatively compared them to contemporaries NOFX and Rancid, both of which stuck with independent labels and maintained more of a DIY ethic. Other punks argue that since Green Day and The Offspring became popular without significantly modifying their sound they shouldn't be held in contempt for their success. Still others contend that making videos, playing arenas, and signing multimillion dollar deals disqualify the bands as punk. Popular band Rise Against sells thousands of records, makes music videos, and signed with a major label but remains authentic in the eyes of many hardcore kids and punks by maintaining vegetarian and straight edge lifestyles, singing about contentious social issues, and championing progressive causes such as animal rights. Others subculturists seek to prove their underground roots as well. Successful black rappers such as 50 Cent repeatedly emphasize their street credentials, their roots in the "hood," and their connections to gang culture even as they live in mansions and drive expensive cars. Underground hip hoppers, in contrast, are more likely to find authenticity in originality, simplicity, political voice, and contribution to the community.

CONCLUSIONS

The British punk band Crass famously claimed that punk was dead way back in 1978, yet it seems their pronouncement was a bit premature. Or was it? Self-proclaimed punks exist all over the world, living out various incarnations of punk style and politics. But are they *really* punks or just the flickering shadow of a once cutting-edge movement? Punk's movement to the mainstream calls into question its credentials as an oppositional subculture. Although I won't presume to pass judgment one way or the other, I do hope that this chapter has provided you with some tools to analyze status and hierarchy in punk or any other subculture. Punks proclaim there should be "no rules," that individualism should rule the day. However, maintaining some sort of boundaries or, dare I say, rules is perhaps essential to subcultures. Otherwise, anything goes and it becomes impossible to determine an "us" and a "them." And if anything goes, what is left to strive for? On the other hand, perhaps the "real" punks are those busy upholding the DIY ethic, creating art, pursuing politics, and creating fulfilling lives without worrying about who is punk and who is not. As punks grow older, many realize that the movement's strength is less in its shocking attire and colorful hair and more in its relentless DIY attitude and willingness to step outside conventional boundaries, be they sexual, political, musical, occupational, or otherwise.

DISCUSSION

- Which bands/musicians do *you* consider "authentic"? Why? What characteristics or practices signify authenticity?
- Describe the status hierarchy in an organization you belong to, such as school, work, sorority/fraternity, or religious body. Who has the most status and why?
- Is "true" punk "dead"?
- How do punks create ways for youth to actively challenge or "resist" social hierarchies? How is punk successful, and how does it fail?

KEY IDEAS

Achieved status: Voluntarily adopted status or status achieved through one's own efforts.

Ascribed status: A social status one is born into and does not choose. Ascribed status is difficult to change.

Authenticity: Symbolic ways subculturists designate who is "real" or "true" in the scene and who are poseurs. Authenticity is often connected with status; the more authentic one appears, the higher one can climb in the status hierarchy. Authenticity is also a way to separate insiders from outsiders and is often contested within the scene.

Bricolage: Taking aspects of popular culture and reworking and combining them into new forms, thereby creating new (and subversive) meanings.

DIY: "Do It Yourself"—a philosophy of punk and many other subcultures based upon maintaining independence and wresting control of the creative process from corporations.

Fragmentation: The process by which a subculture splinters into specialized subgroups over time, each its own variation of the original.

Hierarchy: A system of ranking people, whether by status, wealth, race, gender, or other social characteristics.

Personal is political: A feminist philosophy and slogan meaning that our personal lives are interwoven with our social, cultural, and political surroundings and suggesting that our personal choices and identities are political statements.

Performing authenticity: The ongoing process of proving one's authenticity and simultaneously reinforcing a subculture's status hierarchy.

Poseur: A derogatory label signifying one who wears the trappings of a subculture but who others perceive to fail to live out or truly believe in the subculture's ideals.

Social stratification: A way of rank ordering people based on characteristics deemed important by that society.

Subcultural capital: Insider knowledge, experience, and style that confers authenticity and status on members of the scene.

Status: A position or rank in society. Status defines part of who you are and therefore how people relate to you.

Status symbol: A marker of status; a way of communicating social prestige and membership to a group.

Syncretism: The process by which subcultures tend to gradually overlap, sharing elements of both style and belief.

Underground economy: The array of independent, DIY businesspeople who facilitate subcultural production while operating under the mainstream radar. Includes independent record labels, promoters, artists, and so on who are often part of the scene.

RESOURCES

Punkrock.org

www.punkrock.org

Punk77—History of U.K. punk

www.punk77.co.uk

Sells Like Teen Spirit: Music, Youth Culture, and Social Crisis

By Ryan Moore. 2010. New York: New York University Press.

This study examines how the political and economic changes of the last thirty years influenced punk, grunge, alternative, metal, and retro scenes.

Straight Edge: Clean-Living Youth, Hardcore Punk, and Social Change

By Ross Haenfler. 2006. New Brunswick, NJ: Rutgers University Press.

An in-depth study of straight edge youth that covers the history, different factions, and gender dynamics in the scene.

Pretty in Punk: Girls' Gender Resistance in a Boys' Subculture

By Lauraine Leblanc. 1999. New Brunswick, NJ: Rutgers University Press.
An important work in the subcultures field that tells how the women in punk carve out their place in a male-dominated scene.

The Decline of Western Civilization (film, Penelope Spheeris 1981)

Documentary about the early Los Angeles punk scene showcasing early punk style and beliefs and featuring bands such as Black Flag, Circle Jerks, X, and the Germs.

NOFX: Backstage Passport (Fuse TV 2008)

A television series chronicling DIY band NOFX's 2008 world tour. Available on DVD and on YouTube.

Afro-punk (film, James Spooner 2003)

Documentary delving into the experiences of black punks, including interviews or footage of Fishbone, Candiria, and Bad Brains.

Another State of Mind (film, Adam Small and Peter Stuart 1984)

Documentary following a Youth Brigade/Social Distortion tour and showcasing early U.S. DIY punk.

American Hardcore (film, Paul Rachman 2006)

Documentary that traces the emergence of hardcore in the United States, related to the book of the same name.

~⌀

CHAPTER 4

Hip Hop—"Doing" Gender and Race in Subcultures

Rap music has become a billion dollar industry, with artists from Kanye West and Nicki Minaj to 50 Cent and Jay-Z selling millions of records, while hip hop style is ubiquitous in any high school or shopping mall. What began as the soundtrack for inner city black youth in the United States has burgeoned into a worldwide subculture that crosses racial and economic lines. Youth from Sao Paulo to Tokyo, Moscow to Sydney share a passion for hip hop music, culture, and fashion (Condry 2006). Still, hip hop and rap began as African American art forms, meaning they are rooted in traditions and experiences of black people in the United States (Bianco 1998). Rap music has been an outlet for African American and Latino youth to express their struggles within impoverished urban areas, criticisms of law enforcement, and hopes for a better future, even as hip hop culture has grown into a way of life for people of all races, including white kids in the suburbs. Although some rap glorifies violence and degrades women, beyond hip hop's "bling" often lies a deeper message from marginalized youth striving to find a voice. In this chapter, I begin by explaining the origins of hip hop and its relationship to rap music before discussing each element of the hip hop scene. I then consider hip hop as an ongoing dialogue about race and racism. I continue with a discussion of the sexual politics in hip hop, especially how female rappers express their own sexual power. The chapter concludes by examining hip hop's appeal to white youth.

ORIGINS OF HIP HOP

Hip hop traces its beginnings to the streets of the South Bronx in 1970s New York City. The early pioneers were DJs (disc jockeys) who performed live in clubs, at block parties, or even in parks, encouraging enthusiastic crowd participation. They began to manipulate the music using two turntables, which allowed mixing and rearranging of songs rather than simply playing music as it might be heard on the radio. Jamaican-born DJ Kool Herc introduced "break" spinning, repeatedly playing instrumental bits of songs using two copies of the same record, prolonging the parts most popular with dancers. Grandmaster Flash perfected "scratching," the art of using the turntable and record needle to create a high-pitched rhythm and "punch phrasing," playing a quick burst from one record while the other continues playing on the opposite turntable. Influenced by spoken word musicians such as Gil Scott-Heron and Jamaican DJs' "toasting," MCs began talking or chanting over the music, working the crowd as the DJ played records. "Turntablists," led by pioneer Grand Wizzard Theodore, pushed the musical foundations of early hip hop further, scratching a needle over the record to produce one of rap's distinguishing sounds.

Rap music really took off in 1979 with the Sugarhill Gang's "Rapper's Delight," a fifteen-minute opus that became rap's first gold single, demonstrating that rap could be commercially viable. Afrika Bombatta is perhaps the most well known of hip hop's originators. His 1982 song "Planet Rock," with its synthesized voices, keyboards, and drum machines, was hugely influential in electronic music generally. Formerly a gang member, Bombatta founded the Zulu Nation to help other young people avoid a life a crime. Meanwhile, b-boying (popularly called breaking or breakdancing) exploded with crews like Rock Steady Crew and New York City Breakers. In 1984 Run DMC earned rap's first gold record for *Tougher than Leather*, gaining the music increasing attention. Soon after, three white MCs with roots in the punk scene formed the Beastie Boys, fusing rap, metal, and college rock on *Licensed to Ill*. Meanwhile, rap's first supergroup, Public Enemy, and others such as KRS-One began making music with a political message. Reflecting hip hop's growing mainstream attention, MTV took notice of the growing culture, airing the show *Yo! MTV Raps* in 1989.

Hip Hop Classics

Type these titles into YouTube:
"The Revolution Will Not Be Televised"—Poet and musician Gil Scott-Heron's classic from the early 1970s.
"Sugarhill Gang Rapper's Delight"—early rap hit by one of hip hop's seminal groups.
"KRS One Sounds of da Police"—early song critical of the police.
"Queen Latifa Ladies Choice"—classic pro-woman song featuring Monie Love.

In the late 1980s, gangsta rap emerged as the dominant force in rap, with Ice T, NWA, and Dr. Dre leading the charge from the West Coast and Snoop Dogg, Tupac Shakur, Wu-Tang Clan, and Notorious B.I.G. popularizing the style in the 1990s. Songs about gang life, especially crime and violence, worried parents and law enforcement officials. Often criticized for glorifying violence and degrading women, gangsta rappers also described the struggles of living in poor, urban environments. The late 1990s and 2000s brought new hip hop styles, including Crunk, a club-oriented genre that emerged with Three 6 Mafia and other groups in the

Southern United States. As rap has become increasingly mainstream, hip hoppers, like punks, have had to wrestle with the growing popularity of their subculture, and some underground artists take great pains to set themselves apart from the commercially successful mainstream, claiming to be more authentic than the fare offered on MTV. Artists such as Immortal Technique, Medusa, Fugees, and Sage Francis have pursued less commercial paths, often incorporating more explicitly radical or political messages into their songs.

From the outset, hip hop developed its own fashions—Run DMC even sang a song about their Adidas shoes. Baggy pants and shirts, athletic shoes, and baseball caps have been hip hop mainstays, although designers now branch into many different styles. Today, hip hop moguls such as Russell Simmons (Phat Farm), P Diddy (Sean John), OutKast (OutKast Clothing), Eminem (Shady Ltd.), and 50 Cent (G-Unit) have their own clothing lines. The late 1990s saw a shift from gangsta style to "bling," showcasing wealth through expensive jewelry, cars, and clothes. Hip hop has arguably had a greater influence on all youth style than any other subculture, as white, Latino, and Asian, upper, middle, and lower class kids alike adopt hip hop imagery, speech patterns, and fashions.

HIP HOP CULTURE—STATUS AND ROLES IN THE SCENE

Hip hop is a *culture*, not simply a musical form, and an underground subculture has grown steadily alongside hip hop's mainstream popularity. One might claim to listen to hip hop music without really being part of the subculture, which encompasses much more than a musical style and street fashion. Hip hop culture, as outlined by Afrika Bombatta and the Zulu Nation, consists of four basic **elements**, or art forms: DJ-ing, MC-ing, breakdancing, and graffiti. **DJ-ing**, as you might expect, involves playing records for a crowd. However, the hip hop DJ does much more than simply play one song after another. Rather, she or he uses two turntables simultaneously, jumping back and forth between records, mixing in samples, scratching over the music, and pumping up the crowd with chants, cheers, and call and response. As part of a hip hop group, the DJ lays down beats that the MC(s) raps over. An **MC** (Master of Ceremonies or Microphone Controller), popularly called a rapper, writes and performs rhymes over a beat. Rap's most basic definition is a vocal laid down over music (Ridenhour and Jah 1997). Technically, one could rap over country, classical, jazz, or any other type of music. Rap groups, such as the legendary Run DMC, include one or more MCs and a DJ like Jam Master Jay,[10] although solo artists are much more popular today. Their songs include samples, or small pieces of other artists' songs; hence, part of a James Brown song might end up in more contemporary rap music.

Having emerged alongside DJ-ing and MC-ing, **b-boying** (also called breakdancing) is the dance form most associated with hip hop culture. B-boying requires exceptional balance, strength, and skill, as dancers regularly assume difficult poses ("freezes"), such as holding their entire bodies up on one hand, or "power moves" such as spinning on their heads. Breaking is an exhibition or showcase style, where one dancer at a time takes center stage, showing off her or his moves as others watch and wait to take their turns. Some breakers form teams, or "crews," and face off in b-boy competitions.

The final element of hip hop culture is **graffiti** art, sometimes called graffiti writing or bombing. Though typically viewed as deviant vandalism or associated with gangs, the hip hop world considers graffiti a true art form. Writers gain fame and respect for their art and symbolically lay claim to urban space (Macdonald 2001). Each "street artist" coins her or his own "tag," their personal logo or signature that other writers identify, and more experienced artists create "pieces" (short for "masterpiece"), which are larger, more elaborate murals depicting their tag (ibid.). In an interesting (and practical) twist that reflects some mainstream recognition of graffiti art, some cities have erected "safe walls" where graffiti is not only legal but encouraged. Although graffiti culture has often been connected with hip hop, many artists have little or no connection with the scene, considering themselves their own, unique subculture (Pray 2005).

DJs, MCs, b-boys, and graf artists are all examples of statuses in the hip hop scene. As we saw in the last chapter, status is not the same as *prestige*—it is rather a *social position* recognized by the larger culture or community. Different people hold the same status; for example, there are many individuals with the status of MC or b-boy. Each person simultaneously holds many different statuses. You, for example, might be some combination of a student, an employee, a sister or brother, a mother or father, an athlete, and a member of a church, mosque, or synagogue. Each status comes with a set of expected behaviors and/or obligations, called roles. A **role** is the set of behaviors associated with a status. In hip hop, the status of graffiti artist entails performing the artist role by designing and painting tags and murals. Holding the status of MC requires performing the roles of lyricist and live performer. Members of every subculture hold at least one status and perform multiple roles. Someone who is completely involved in hip hop culture is known as a "head" (Ridenhour and Jah 1997). Authentic "headz" know hip hop history and take an active role in shaping its future. Like "hardcore" punks, they are more committed to the scene than the average hip hopper. Each of the four hip hop statuses demand, in their own ways, respect (see Macdonald 2001). While arguably every member of any subculture might be searching for or demanding some kind of respect, hip hoppers more regularly and explicitly articulate this demand. The importance of respect comes from African Americans and other marginalized groups who have faced struggle, discrimination, and a *lack* of respect.

HIP HOP, URBAN LIFE, AND RACISM

In 2005, shortly after Hurricane Katrina wreaked havoc upon the U.S. gulf coast, rapper Kanye West claimed during a telethon that "George Bush doesn't care about black people."[11] His comments, reflecting the widespread frustration with mismanaged federal relief efforts, raised unaskable questions: Did race play a factor in the delay, given that most of the stranded New Orleans residents were black?

Would aid have arrived faster had the victims been white? These were uncomfortable questions for a society that prides itself on fairness and equality for all.

Hip hop is one response to inner city urban life and contributes to an ongoing dialogue regarding racism and race relations in the United States. Rap music and hip hop culture originally flourished in marginalized communities that experienced poverty and racism. Subcultures, according to Brake (1985), point out the inconsistencies in the larger culture, the gaps between a society's values and its reality. People in the United States value the "American Dream" that claims that those who work hard will be rewarded with upward mobility and secure, stable lives for their families. The reality is that many people work hard yet remain in poverty with inadequate access to health care, affordable housing, and good education. Hip hop becomes a tool youth use to point out these inconsistencies, and not just in the West. MCs in Tanzania use hip hop to critique the inequalities exacerbated by globalization (Ntarangwi 2009). Even in Japan, often believed to be a racially homogenous nation, hip hoppers shine a spotlight on ethnic discrimination against "outcaste" groups such as *burakumin*, who face bias finding jobs and marriage partners (Condry 2006).

Race in the United States

The United States has had a troubled history of race relations, to say the least, from slavery and Jim Crow laws to school segregation and debates over affirmative action, immigration, and reparations for slavery. The occasional racist incident aside, many Americans believe that equal opportunity exists for all, regardless of the color of one's skin, and that racism was by and large an unfortunate problem of the past, resolved for the most part during the civil rights era. The election of President Barack Obama surely reinforced such beliefs. Undeniably we have as a nation made some progress toward racial equity, and relationships between whites and nonwhites have significantly improved. We are a diverse country in which many different ethnicities work, live, and socialize together. Yet problems persist, including racist violence. The terrorist attacks of September 11, 2001, renewed stereotypes of people of Middle Eastern decent and raised concerns about racial profiling. African and Native Americans make up a disproportionate number of the poor and the prison population. The country still struggles over immigration policies, with politicians and pundits taking opposing stands on illegal immigration. These struggles reflect a **racial ideology**—the widely held system of beliefs about race—that on the surface champions equal opportunity while covering significant inequality, tension, and racism. Far from being a harmonious, "color blind" society, race significantly impacts our lives and profoundly affects how we experience the world (see Bonilla-Silva 2009).

Like many people, you might believe that individuals of different colors are somehow fundamentally different from one another, that race somehow determines characteristics like intelligence, work ethic, morality, and propensity for criminal behavior. Sociologists, however, recognize that there are no fixed or permanent characteristics of race. **Race** encompasses biological traits such as skin color, facial structure, and hair texture that society considers meaningful. However, the actual meanings of race are socially constructed; what people think about race depends on their social surroundings, varies from place to place, and changes over time. There is no fixed biological meaning associated with race; in fact, race doesn't necessarily depend upon the color of one's skin, as was evident in nineteenth- and early twentieth-century immigration to the United States when waves of Italian, Irish, Polish, and other immigrants were not considered "white" (Margolis 2005). **Racism** is a belief system asserting that one race is inherently inferior to another (Healey 2005). Again, racism is not entirely based upon skin color—racism existed between the Hutus and Tutsis of Rwanda despite the fact that both groups are black, virtually indistinguishable in terms of skin tone. People's perceptions of skin color and race vary from culture to culture. In France, for example, racism is based more upon immigrant status than skin color (Lamont 2003). Racism always, however, involves a more powerful group judging a less powerful group as somehow morally inferior. Racism is embedded in the structures of society—our politics, education, housing, prisons, economy and so on.

Although race is socially constructed, it still has vital consequences for what we believe and the opportunities we have. The cultural meanings connected with race influence our perceptions of people. Young black men, in particular, are often presumed to be "troublemakers or criminals" (Anderson 1991, 167). Chicano youth are viewed as gang members or illegal workers. Even people who think of themselves as "color blind" or opposed to racism often subscribe to negative stereotypes. **Racial scapegoating**, or blaming social problems on a racial or ethnic category, fuels anti-immigrant movements today that blame unemployment and the health care crisis on Mexicans and other Latinos. Likewise, our racial category often influences our perceptions of others. Consider that after the devastating 2005 Hurricane Katrina 12.5 percent of whites believed race played a factor in rescue attempts, whereas 60 percent of African Americans felt that if the victims had been white they would have been evacuated more quickly.[12] Regardless of the reality, a racial divide in perceptions still exists.

Hip hop as a culture has consistently challenged the notion that racism has disappeared by drawing attention to the lives and problems of inner city youth. Remember that subcultures often uncover the hidden contradictions in society (Brake 1985). Hip hop, in a sense, asks how a country that prides itself on its freedoms and opportunities still harbors poverty and racism. It emerged in the midst of "**white flight**," or the migration of whites (and often industry) from urban to suburban areas—the urban middle class stagnated or shrank, leaving in its wake deteriorating schools and a scarcity of jobs. The hip hop response initially followed two veins, "sixties-inspired hip hop nationalism" and "Afrocentric hip hop nationalism" (Decker 1994, 99–100). Black nationalism draws upon black power movements of the 1960s and 1970s, condemning the disenfranchisement of contemporary poor, urban blacks. Afrocentric nationalism glorifies precolonial African empires, promoting a spiritual connection to African heritage and freedom from Western/colonial thought and oppression. Beyond these historic inspirations, today's underground hip hop (for example, dead prez and Immortal Technique) focuses on additional issues such as corporate control of the media, war, and welfare. As an initially urban phenomenon, hip hop culture constitutes a symbolic "taking back" of urban areas (Rose 1994b). Street artists tag their names and paint murals on trains, buildings, and public spaces, staking out territory and remaking their surroundings. Early DJs tapped into streetlight electricity to throw block parties, and b-boys often performed on street corners.

The "other side of racism" is white privilege (Rothenberg 2005, 1). Privilege is another way of saying unearned advantage (McIntosh 1988). For example, a child born into a wealthy family automatically has more opportunities than a child born into poverty (such as better health care, education, and housing). The child born into wealth did nothing to earn those advantages; they are there whether she or he wants them or not. **White privilege** includes the unearned advantages white people have simply by virtue of their skin color. For example, as a white person I never worry about being pulled over by the police because of my skin color. I never question whether people think I have an education or a job because of affirmative action rather than my own merits. I belong to a racial grouping that enjoys overall better health, less poverty, and better access to education than do African Americans and Latinos. Most of the powerful people in the United States, from CEOs to politicians, come from backgrounds of privilege. Political hip hop not only sheds light on these disparities, it seeks to empower the less privileged with a voice. "Conscious" hip hop, especially, uses the four art forms to build positive communities in marginalized areas.

Hip Hop Politics and "Conscious" Rap

In 2001, hip hop mogul Russell Simmons convened a hip hop "summit" in New York City, bringing together musicians, artists, activists, politicians, and religious leaders to harness the cultural and political power of the hip hop generation (Kitwana 2002). As perhaps the most prevalent contemporary cultural movement, "conscious hip hop" has always held sway with its millions of fans, and Simmons believes it could potentially be a meaningful political force. Other hip hop celebrities have exerted their influence in politics, including Sean "Diddy" Combs' "Vote Or Die" registration drive in 2004 and Jay-Z's 2008 "Last Chance for Change" rallies on behalf of President Obama. Conscious hip hop contains a range of socially conscious and politically progressive messages, from feminism and socialism to peace and democracy, and is distinguished from "commercial" hip hop characterized by violence and misogyny and controlled largely by major media conglomerates (Rose 2008). It is generally more underground and DIY (e.g., Immortal Technique, dead prez, Jedi Mind Tricks), although artists such as Common, Nas, and The Roots are commercially successful. Writing about rap, Rose (1994a, 99) claims, "Under social conditions in which sustained frontal attacks on powerful groups are strategically unwise or successfully contained, oppressed people use language, dance, and music to mock those in power, express rage, and produce fantasies of subversion." Rap exposes power and wealth inequalities and serves as an outlet for anger and a conduit for community consciousness about a variety of issues: police brutality, mandatory minimum sentencing, racial profiling, poverty, and political repression. A Tribe Called Quest, Sister Souljah, Disposable Heroes of Hiphopricy, and KRS-One were all part of early conscious hip hop. Public Enemy, one of the most successful groups of the 1980s and 1990s, released *It Takes a Nation of Millions to Hold Us Back* and *Fear of a Black Planet*, both full of political discontent. Songs such as "Fight the Power" and "911 Is a Joke" expressed a deep distrust of the police and other authorities, and the group faced controversy for some members' connection to the Nation of Islam, a black Muslim organization to which Malcolm X once belonged.

Many African Americans view the police with suspicion at best and as a source of oppression rather than protection at worst (see Weitzer and Tuch 2004). As the Black Panther Party for Self Defense, a social movement of the 1960s and 1970s, put it, some residents of poor black communities see the police as an "occupying force" (Seale [1970] 1991). The 1992 beating of Rodney King by police in Los Angeles touched off several days of rioting, and the 1999 killing of Amadou Diallo by New York City police fueled beliefs in some communities that young black men were targets for violence. Rappers have continually brought critical attention to police brutality, such as KRS-One's song "Who Protects Us from You?" and Ice-T's "Copkiller," performed with his heavy metal band Body Count. Early gangsta group NWA's ("Niggas With Attitude") "Fuck the Police" condemned the injustice of police brutality in South Central Los Angeles, and contemporaries such as dead prez carry on the fight.

Less Commercial Artists

Medusa

Onry Ozzborn

dead prez

Sage Francis

Immortal Technique

Jedi Mind Tricks

Other groups, such as Tribe Called Quest, Fugees, and the Disposable Heroes of Hiphopricy, explicitly link racial, economic, and sexual oppression, writing progressive lyrics that call for racial and gender equity (Niesel 1997). The Beastie Boys left behind their sexist frat rock roots for explicitly anti-sexist and anti-homophobic lyrics, as well as organizing benefit concerts to help free Tibet from Chinese rule. Clearly, as a *subculture* hip hop is more than baggy clothes, gold chains, and expensive cars. Yet drawing strict boundaries between conscious and commercial hip hop relegates conscious rap to the underground and promotes a kind of elitism that conscious rappers want to avoid (Rose 2008).

SEXUAL POLITICS OF HIP HOP—GANGSTA RAP
AND WOMEN RAPPERS

Sexism, Gender Inequality, and Misogyny

While conscious hip hop often articulates a socially progressive message, other strands are profoundly misogynistic. One aspect of **male privilege**, or the unearned advantages associated with being male, is the dominance of popular culture by men that often results in music/movies/TV produced by men, for men, from men's point of view. Like heavy metal, some rap lyrics, rap videos, and rap record covers degrade women, treating them as voiceless sexual playthings. Gangsta rappers in particular regularly depict women as devious and domineering, relegating them to little more than potential sexual conquests. White rap artist Eminem drew substantial criticism (despite support from openly gay pop star Elton John) for songs depicting violence against women and gays. NWA criticized the police and debased women in the same songs. Just as punks and skinheads have contradictory elements, rap often simultaneously critiques racism while reinforcing sexism and homophobia.

No subgenre of rap gains more negative attention than gangsta rap. While artists claim they are simply singing about their experiences of ghetto life, critics charge rappers like Snoop Dog and 50 Cent with glorifying violence and sexual domination. The now-defunct Parent Music Resource Center waged a campaign against rap (and metal), targeting 2 Live Crew in particular for its raunchy lyrics. Bragging about one's physical and sexual power is part of the hypermasculine image many rappers cultivate. Influenced by Al Pacino's portrayal of Sicilian mafia boss Michael Corleone in *The Godfather* and his role as a Cuban gangster in *Scarface*, self-described "gangstas" prove and perform their masculinity through two primary roles: the "tough guy" and the "player of women" (see Oliver 1989). Prior to his murder in 1996, rapper Tupac Shakur, with "Thug Life" tattooed across his muscular torso, exemplified the "cool pose" prevalent among young men and ubiquitous in gangsta rap, and 50 Cent carries on the tradition today.

The "**cool pose**" generally entails baggy clothing, a cocky swagger, physical intimidation, and sexual prowess (Majors and Billson 1992). It is a performance, meant to convey specific meanings to whomever happens to be the "audience." **Interactionist theories of gender** focus in part on how we *do*, or create and recreate, the meanings of gender through our everyday actions. Candace West and Don Zimmerman (1987, 140) claim that "a person's gender is not simply an aspect of what one is, but, more fundamentally, it is something that one *does*, and does recurrently, in interaction with others." Rather than a fixed characteristic, gender is an "interactional accomplishment." We produce, reinforce, and sometimes challenge what "masculine" and "feminine" mean in our interactions with others. You've probably seen guys "proving" their masculinity by showing off or women producing "femininity" by carefully managing their makeup and hair. In hip hop, particularly in gangsta rap, young men perform the cool pose and so reinforce a fairly narrow masculine script.

One explanation for the prevalence of the tough, cool, sexually powerful pose is the blocked status opportunities discussed in Chapter 2. Lacking viable legitimate opportunities to attain culturally valued statuses and rewards, some people will turn to illegitimate means to succeed (Merton 1957). In particular, young men who are unable to fulfill the roles that society says "real" men should fulfill (such as having a high-paying, high-status job and providing for a family) may seek to compensate in the only ways available to them: athleticism, violence, and bragging about their sexual conquests (Rose 1994b). This dynamic is hardly restricted to young black men, as our discussions of skinheads and heavy metal fans demonstrate. Indeed, the sexism and racism in youth subcultures may merely reflect, sometimes dramatically, the patriarchal, white supremacist values of the larger society (hooks 1994). Black rappers' misogynist attitudes may conceal the anger, pain, and depression that go along with the struggles many of them face (Morgan 1999). Finally, women's struggle for power and access to formerly male-exclusive domains produced a backlash meant to reduce women's value to their sexual availability. Thus "the codes of male privilege were challenged even as the culture of misogyny doubled in force," which in the case of hip hop included lyrics rife with "bitches" and "hos" as "linguistic bombs exploding on the identities of assaulted women" (Dyson 2001:178). Ironically, as women gained some measure of legal justice and representation in politics, business, and the arts, sexist depictions of women proliferated throughout popular culture and perhaps especially in music.

Women Rappers

Women in hip hop have not sat idly by while men degrade or exclude them. While in many ways mainstream hip hop culture glorifies patriarchal masculinity, some female artists use rap music and culture to encourage and empower women. There have been a number of successful female rappers, such as Salt-N-Pepa, Queen Latifah, MC Lyte, Foxy Brown, Missy Elliott, Lil' Kim, Beyoncé, Nicki Minaj, and MIA. Tricia Rose (1994a) finds that both male and female rappers illuminate and confront a variety of social problems. While male rappers primarily challenge police, government, and other oppressive institutions, female rappers focus much of their social critique on "sexual politics," challenging both male rappers and the culture at large (ibid., 147). Queen Latifah's song "Ladies First" emphasizes that women can be a powerful force in hip hop. Underground artists such as Medusa insist that, rather than objects to be acted upon, women should be respected as capable in their own right with something important to add to the hip hop scene. Like most subcultural resistance, the results are mixed. Many women construct images of sexually powerful, beautiful black women—images often neglected by mainstream media. However, this also sexually objectifies these women.

Cheryl L. Keyes (2002, 189) identifies four categories of female rappers: "Queen Mother," "Fly Girl," "Sista with Attitude," and "The Lesbian." The Queen Mother, exemplified by Queen Latifa early in her career, portrays herself as African royalty, dispensing knowledge and guidance to her people, demanding respect for black women, and often dressing in stylized African clothing. Fly Girls, such as the members of Salt-N-Pepa and TLC, wear the latest fashionable clothing while delivering an image of strong, independent, empowered women in charge of their sexuality. Like the Fly Girl, the Sista with Attitude (such as Lil' Kim) is an independent woman, only with a more aggressive, in-your-face, "bad girl" posture, sometimes even reclaiming the word "bitch" as a positive label. The Lesbian, of which Queen Pen is the exemplar, addresses lesbian identity from a black woman's perspective, a daring challenge in the often homophobic rap world. Although these categories are merely loose archetypes, they give an idea of the diversity of women's performances of gender in the hip hop world.

Although from a certain point of view female rappers are engaging in feminist resistance, according to Rose (1994a) and Morgan (1999), feminism has not resonated with many black women, who associate it with white women and an anti-male attitude. They are wary of a feminist movement that emphasizes gender inequality at the expense of racial inequality and are sometimes reluctant to criticize sexist black men for fear of further marginalizing that group. In addition to balancing calls for sexual and racial equality, women in hip hop are caught between challenging men's sexual exploitation of women and confidently asserting their sexuality (Pough 1999). Various contemporary pop singers, including Lady Gaga, Pink, and Nicki Minaj, simultaneously satirize sexist portrayals of women while suggesting women are culpable in their own objectification. Traditionally, white feminism has focused more on stopping sexist exploitation (by challenging pornography, for example) than on celebrating women's sexuality and sexual power. Yet women in hip hop sometimes wear skimpy outfits and dance "suggestively." Is dancing with little clothes on an example of shameless exploitation or a statement of sexual power? Can feminists demand an end to the objectification of women without denying their sexuality? Hip hop feminist Joan Morgan (1999, 74–78) claims that the responsibility lies on both men and women to challenge the sexism in hip hop, writing, "Any man who doesn't truly love himself is incapable of loving us in the healthy way we need to be loved" and "sistas have to confront the ways we're complicit in our own oppression." She insists that the hip hop community can be "a redemptive, healing space for brothers and sistas" (ibid., 80). Still, the financial rewards of sexist mainstream hip hop will likely confine much of conscious hip hop to the underground.

HIP HOP AND WHITE SUBURBAN YOUTH— THE "PERFORMANCE" OF RACE

Although hip hop sprang from African American communities, it has since spread throughout the world. MCs from Japan to Brazil adapt the medium to their own circumstances, and in the United States Latino, Asian, and Native American youth have all joined the hip hop revolution. However, the largest consumers of hip hop music in the United States are white youth; the subculture has spread from the inner city to suburban America (Kitwana 2005), and various white performers have found mainstream success—Beastie Boys, Vanilla Ice, Marky Mark (now actor Mark Wahlberg), Everlast (and House of Pain), and most recently Eminem. In the early 1990s, Cornell West (2001) foresaw the "Afro-American-ization of white youth" as young black athletes and entertainers gained significant attention and were subsequently admired and emulated by young, white, and (mostly) male fans. Perhaps nothing more clearly illustrates this trend than the mass appeal of hip hop.

The rise of hip hop's appeal to white youth has sparked a politically incorrect moral panic—in short, some white adults, whose conceptions of blackness are mostly negative, worry that their children are trying to "be black" (Kitwana 2005). Exactly what attracts white youth to rap music is difficult to say, especially since rap often contains explicit critiques of dominant (white) society. But perhaps this critique holds the attraction; what could be more subversive to an adolescent than to glorify the very artists who condemn your own (and therefore your parents') group? In the early 1990s, white kids who wore Public Enemy shirts likely unnerved their elders, stoking the "Fear of a Black Planet" the group represented. Interestingly, adolescent white males tend to identify with the violence and sexism of gangsta rap rather than the anti-racist themes of political hip hop. The performance of a narrow, powerful, sexual version of black masculinity may lie at the heart of rap music's attraction. It could be that white kids are also alienated from mainstream American life and its uncertain job opportunities, stagnant wages, and growing inequality (ibid.). Yet apart from popular rap music, hip hop as an underground culture is likely attractive because it offers a community that, ideally, nurtures artistic and political expression and becomes a voice for struggling kids of all races (ibid.).

The phenomenon of white hip hoppers offers a clear example of how we construct race. White kids who adopt (in their minds) "black" manners of speech, dress, and demeanor evoke a variety of responses from their peers (Roediger 1998; Kitwana 2005). Some, white and black, reject whites that "act black" or who "wish they were black" as inauthentic poseurs. Outspokenly racist whites in particular slander other whites that violate their perceived racial norms. Sometimes, however, the label "wigger" is a term of endearment used by blacks to designate whites "seriously embracing African American cultural forms and values, in contrast to 'wanna-be' dabbles in the externalities of rap" (Roediger 1998, 360). The confusion or strangeness that white hip hoppers evoke demonstrates that we act out our race as well as our gender and that a flawed (or unconventional) performance is deviant. Several movies and TV shows illustrate conventional performances of race. In the movie *Can't Hardly Wait* (1998) a white kid "acts black," and *White Chicks* (2004) depicts two black men posing as white women. Both situations are funny to the audience precisely because they break the expectations of how we perform racial identity. Likewise, black kids who act "white," such as the Carlton character on the old TV show *Fresh Prince of Bel Air*, face derision from their peers for failing to follow the unwritten rules of racial performance. Pointing out racial performances is not meant to essentialize or stereotype any racial group—in other words, there is not one way to "act" white, Asian, Latino, black, or any other grouping, because there is no essential whiteness, Asian-ness, or Latino-ness. Nevertheless, we have unspoken norms and expectations regarding how people of different races and ethnicities act, and when people bend or break these rules we notice.

As I pointed out earlier in the chapter, we all hold a variety of statuses. Sometimes those statuses contradict one another in important ways. **Status inconsistency** occurs when a subculturist holds two or more seemingly contradictory statuses. Imagine a gutter punk who comes from a loving middle class family or a gansta rapper from the suburbs. Thus, when he raps about street life, 50 Cent is not simply relating his experience as a drug dealer and victim of gun violence; he is reminding his audience of his authentic roots. White rappers must reconcile their whiteness with a cultural form still associated primarily with African Americans and Latinos. They may face even greater pressure to show their rap credentials, hence Eminem's continual reminders that he struggled to rise above a humble background and his surrounding himself with a largely African American entourage. I am not questioning these artists' credibility, but clearly rappers construct and manage their authenticity as much as any other group, and authenticity depends, in part, on demonstrating one's racial and social class credentials.

You may be wondering if white hip hop fans develop a sort of racial consciousness, an ability to examine their own privilege, question racist beliefs, and grapple with social problems affecting people of color. Does hip hop have these positive outcomes? There is some evidence that hip hop has fostered a multicultural perspective and raised consciousness about race (Kitwana 2005). However, it may be that most whites are simply consuming a "black" art form without having to really engage with black or Latino people. One can purchase hip hop music, watch music videos, and so on without ever actually encountering a black person.[13] Some people fear that white kids have appropriated hip hop, as they appropriated rock and roll, and have removed it from its racial and political context as it assimilates into the mainstream (McLeod 1999). Furthermore, it could be that white kids feel that identifying with a "black" cultural form is in itself revolutionary—in a sense, they might feel they are "doing their part" without really changing anything. After all, white youth have rejected their "whiteness" as an act of rebellion since at least the early 1900s. And finally, white kids may find the more outrageous portrayals of violence, drugs, and sexuality in some gangsta rap simply funny, chanting along to Wu-Tang cuts while simultaneously thinking them ironically ridiculous. Such safe consumption of caricatured people of color reestablishes the moral superiority so often associated with whiteness, legitimizing "colorblind" racism.

CONCLUSIONS

Hip hop culture has the potential to draw attention to racism and provide disadvantaged youth with a forum in which to build solidarity and fight oppression.

While many youth are drawn to hip hop for the image, the lifestyle, and simply the music, some build the multicultural communities politicians talk about but rarely realize. However, much of commercial rap music glorifies violence and remains misogynistic. Similar to punk, there is a significant gap between the underground hip hop culture and the mainstream, commercialized music. Hip hop also demonstrates how members of subcultures "do" gender in many different ways. The meanings of gender, like race, are socially constructed and are therefore flexible and changeable. Well-meaning people of all races hope for a "color blind" society, meaning a society that, in the words of Martin Luther King, Jr., judges individuals not "by the color of their skin but by the content of their character."[14] For most of us, this seems like a worthy goal. Conscious hip hop reminds us, however, that we have not yet achieved that ideal and, moreover, to be color blind blinds us to the continuing real impacts of racism in our society.

DISCUSSION

- What is the evidence of racial segregation remaining in your school, workplace, or community?
- Why did gangsta rap and R&B rap seemingly become more popular than conscious and political rap?
- Can white participants in hip hop be as "authentic" as their black and Latino counterparts?

KEY IDEAS

Cool pose: A hypermasculine performance of gender meant to convey toughness, sexual power, confidence, and control.

Doing gender: A theory focusing on gender as an interactional process, as something we *do* continuously, rather than characteristics we inherit from biology.

Elements of hip hop culture: Include the four artistic expressions associated with hip hop—MC-ing, b-boying, graffiti, and DJ-ing.

Interactionist theory of gender: Symbolic interactionists focus on how we create and recreate the meanings of gender through our everyday actions/interactions and how we construct masculinity and femininity. Instead of fixed, biologically determined masculinity and femininity, there are many masculin*ities* and femi-ninit*ies*.

Male privilege: Unearned advantages that men have over women. Examples include being taken seriously when in positions of power and not having to worry about sexual assault.

Privilege: Unearned advantage. Privilege confers greater economic and job opportunities and improves one's overall life chances.

Race: Socially constructed categories, used to distinguish groups of people, that society considers meaningful, often based upon biological traits such as skin color, facial structure, and hair texture.

Racial ideology: The widely held beliefs about race in a given society, including explanations for racial inequality.

Racial scapegoating: The practice of blaming social problems on a racial or ethnic category, reinforcing racial stereotypes and shifting attention from root causes of the problems.

Racism: A belief system asserting that one race is inherently inferior to another.

Role: Expected behaviors associated with a status. A socially defined position in a group that includes guidelines for behavior.

Status inconsistency: When an individual occupies two or more seemingly contradictory statuses, often producing strain on the person and confusion (or worse) among others. People typically try to explain or resolve their status inconsistencies to create a coherent identity.

White flight: The migration of whites and often white-owned industry from urban to suburban areas, resulting in increased segregation, deteriorating infrastructure (for example, schools), and a scarcity of jobs in urban areas.

White privilege: The unearned advantages white people have simply by virtue of their skin color. Examples include generally better health, education, and job opportunities.

RESOURCES

The Freshest Kids: A History of the B-Boy (film, 2001)

A documentary of b-boying, from its underground roots in African American and Latino culture in the Bronx to its rise toward mainstream popularity.

Rize (film, David LaChapelle 2005)

A documentary about the "krump" dancers of Los Angeles who form a subculture around their incredibly fast dance style.

Beyond Beats and Rhymes: Masculinity in Hip Hop Culture (film, Byron Hurt 2006)

A powerful documentary about expressions of masculinity in hip hop culture.

Infamy (film, Doug Pray 2005)

A documentary examining the lives and motivations of graffiti artists from San Francisco to New York, challenging the perception that graffiti art is exclusive to hip hop culture.

Rock Steady Crew

www.rocksteadycrew.com

Web site of the longest running and arguably most influential b-boy crew.

That's the Joint: The Hip Hop Studies Reader (2nd edition)

Edited by Murray Forman and Mark Anthony Neal. 2011. New York: Routledge.

A host of authors discuss a range of topics, from history and authenticity to gender and politics.

The Real Hiphop: Battling for Knowledge, Power, and Respect in the LA Underground

By Marcyliena Morgan. 2009. Durham: Duke University Press.

An intriguing ethnography of Project Blowed, a staple of the underground LA hip hop scene, including analyses of MC "battles" and hip hop (ph)eminism. Check out the documentary *This Is the Life: How the West Was One*.

The Hiphop Archive

www.hiphoparchive.org

A research resource for hiphop scholarship featuring links to books, articles, and helpful scholars of hiphop studies.

Black Noise: Rap Music and Black Culture in Contemporary America **and** *The Hip Hop Wars: What We Talk About When We Talk About Hip Hop—And Why It Matters*

By Rose, Tricia. 1994. Hanover, NH: Wesleyan University Press; and 2008, New York: Basic Books.

Classic texts for both hip hop and subcultural studies more generally by one of the preeminent scholars of hip hop.

CHAPTER 5

⌁

Heavy Metal—Moral Panics, Satanic Scares, and Moral Entrepreneurs

Known for their long hair, dark clothing, and loathing of pop music, "metalheads" have been a fixture of the youth scene for decades. Heavy metal's history encompasses groups from glam rockers Bon Jovi and Poison to death metal bands Deicide and Morbid Angel. Once looked down upon by critics and ignored by academics, metal's popularity has spread across social classes, age groups, and the world, much to the chagrin of adults who worry over the music's impact on young fans. Ever since Ozzy Osbourne famously (and inadvertently) bit the head off of a bat on stage, creating an instant legend that mystified fans and horrified outsiders, metal culture has carried a certain mystique, its use of occult images raising the ire of parents, politicians, and religious figures alike. Authorities have accused rockers from Judas Priest to Marilyn Manson of encouraging Satanism, drug use, suicide, and promiscuous sex. Metal fans, the belief goes, are troubled, lower class kids, mostly white and male, who have a disturbing fascination with violence and destruction (Arnett 1996; Shuker 1994). At times, the thought of an army of satanic metal fans has grown into near panic, prompting opponents to call for banning heavy metal concerts and warning parents of objectionable lyrics. In this chapter, I describe the various subgenres in the heavy metal subculture, beginning with classic metal and ending with nu metal and metalcore. Next, I discuss the core themes of the metal scene before using society's response to metal as an illustration of a moral panic. The chapter ends with a discussion of the role of those responsible for campaigning against metal as moral entrepreneurs.

HEAVY METAL HISTORY

The origin of heavy metal culture has been a topic of dispute among fans and music journalists. Many point to British bands Led Zeppelin, Deep Purple, and Black Sabbath as the original metal bands, whereas others give the honor to the United States' Steppenwolf, whose song "Born to Be Wild" includes the line "heavy metal thunder" (A. Bennett 2001; Weinstein 2000). Hard rock bands such as KISS, Aerosmith, Van Halen, and AC/DC, along with classic metal bands Iron Maiden and Judas Priest, initially appealed to primarily white, working class youth. Heavy metal emerged from industrial, working class cities like Birmingham, U.K., but the music quickly became a suburban middle class phenomenon, and in the United States working class identity is less central (Denski and Sholle 1992). The music varied, but it included heavy (and LOUD) guitar riffs, intricate guitar solos, and often elaborate stage shows while the culture encouraged rebelliousness, anti-authoritarianism, and simply having a good time.

Often considered the true Godfathers of metal, Black Sabbath brought a fascination with the dark and supernatural to the newly forming scene. Other early bands adopted studded leather biker styles (Judas Priest), bluesy, working class sensibility (AC/DC), or mythological motifs (Iron Maiden). Many fans enjoyed heavy metal not only as a release from the day-to-day grind but also as an expression of anger and frustration. Like punk and hip hop, metal has fractured into a variety of subgenres that overlap with other subcultures, especially hardcore, goth, and rap. Today, metal fans are so varied that describing one coherent subculture is very difficult.

Glam rockers mixed the flair of early punk and glitter rock (New York Dolls, David Bowie) with pop music to produce a gentler, catchier sound. The makeup, colorful clothes, and impossibly big, teased hair associated with band members and fans led to the moniker "hair metal." Poison, Bon Jovi, Ratt, Warrant, and Skid Row were among the trendsetters in this scene, which became the face of popular rock until its demise in the early 1990s as grunge gained popularity. This genre, with its ballads and vaguely romantic themes, attracted more women than earlier metal and thrash (ibid.). Its focus on partying and good times (the "rock-and-roll lifestyle") contrasts thrash and death metal's more pessimistic themes. Most diehard metal fans go to great lengths to distance themselves from hair metal, contending that glam isn't metal at all. However, the success of reunion tours and the popularity of recent glam-influenced bands such as The Darkness show that the genre isn't completely dead.

Thrash metal (sometimes called speed metal), influenced in part by punk, ushered in a heavier, faster, less flamboyant sound that somehow managed to coexist with glam. Thrash metal kids defined themselves as the *opposite* of glam, that is, less frilly and more substantive (ibid.). More critical of society than glam, bands such as Metallica, Megadeth, Anthrax, and Slayer instilled in metalheads disgust for corrupt politics, conventional life, and hypocritical religion. Some thrash bands, such as Brazil's Sepultura, took an actively critical political stance, condemning war and government propaganda and promoting indigenous rights. Though they shared the long hair of their hard rock forebears, jeans, denim or leather jackets, and band shirts were the standard uniform for thrash metal.[15] It was at thrash concerts that mosh pits and slam dancing became ubiquitous. Slam dancing entails running at one another and slamming together (usually at the shoulder), making a metal concert a full-contact affair.

Death metal fans seem to have a particular fascination not just with death but with the especially revolting (to the outsider) details involved (Kahn-Harris 2004, 2007; Mudrian 2004). While goths (see Chapter 7) have an almost romantic attraction to the morbid and macabre, death metal fans embrace the disgusting, gory, and horrific aspects of death, as reflected in the bands' names: Dying Fetus, Cannibal Corpse, Carcass, Angelcorpse, Incantation, Gorguts, Bolt Thrower, Repulsion, and Carnage. The music is loud, like all metal, but often faster even than thrash, with guitars tuned down to produce a low, rumbling sound. Drummers play with two bass drums (double bass, sometimes called a blast beat), often so fast that the rhythm sounds like a machine gun. Singers grunt, screech, and growl unintelligible lyrics ranging from graphic depictions of assault and murder (Cannibal Corpse's "Stripped, Raped, and Strangled") to social commentary (Napalm Death's anti-racist "Aryanisms"; Purcell 2003). Viking metal originated in Scandinavia and pairs Norse mythology with an "epic" sound that often includes keyboards; Therion, Borknagar, and Einherjer are recent examples (see Rafalovich and Schneider 2003). Some "black metal" contains racist and anti-Semitic imagery, encouraging youth to protect their national, native (i.e., Aryan) heritage from outsiders (Burghart 1999). More often the music contains anti-Christian messages or retells mythological stories.

Like many subcultures, metal has fragmented into many more subgenres, including industrial metal, nu metal, metalcore, doom metal, deathcore, and post metal. Ministry, Nine Inch Nails, and Skinny Puppy popularized the industrial metal sound during the 1990s, crossing boundaries with industrial goth. Ultra-political Rage Against the Machine was one of the early influential bands to fuse metal, hardcore, hip hop, and funk into a new style. Nu metal, often sung in a rap-like cadence, combines the alienation and indignation of thrash with more mainstream styles, drawing fans including preppy suburban kids, goths, and skateboarders wearing oversized pants.[16] A more recent underground scene mined for the new sound has been metal-influenced hardcore. Bands such as Hatebreed, Unearth, and Killswitch Engage emerged from the hardcore scene, bringing their brutal, no-frills sound to a new audience.[17]

CORE VALUES AND THEMES

Alienation and Masculinity

Remember that in Chapter 2 I argued for the importance of examining subcultures' relationship with the larger culture in which they exist. Arnett (1996, 17) sees heavy metal "as a response to a crisis of meaning in the lives of adolescents." He argues that many youth, particularly working class youth, are alienated from their own culture. **Alienation** is a state of being isolated or disconnected, feeling outcast and oppressed.[18] As we've seen with skinhead, punk, and hip hop, many subculturists are dissatisfied with mainstream society and adopt a subcultural identity in part to have a space in which to express themselves differently or even to challenge the adult world. Metal (aside from glam) offers a bleak vision of the world and therefore appeals to disenchanted youth who may feel ostracized from their peers. Metalheads tend to take pride in their alienation, reacting to ostracism by rejecting the goals and values of society (Arnett 1996).

Heavy metal is generally considered a hypermasculine culture, but there is a range of masculinities in the scene. Glam metal seems to challenge taken-for-granted gender scripts, blending masculine and feminine styles. The record jacket for Poison's *Look What the Cat Dragged In* shows the four band members looking very androgynous with teased hair, heavy eyeliner, and bright lipstick. Yet metal more often reinforces hypermasculine themes of sexual power, domination of women, and risky behavior (Krenske and McKay 2000). Arnett (1996, 16) suggests that metal substitutes for manhood rituals in a society that fails to ritually socialize young people into adulthood: "A heavy metal concert can be seen as a substitute manhood ritual, a ritual that developed in part to fill the social vacuum left by a culture that disdains rituals." Metal concerts, with their high sensation, common enthusiasm, and imposing physical test, are similar to cultural manhood rituals, only with little to no adult guidance or supervision. American parents socialize their kids to "independence, self-sufficiency, and individualism" (ibid., 17). For some, "independence easily becomes loneliness, self-sufficiency may shade into isolation, individualism may take an alienated form" (ibid.). Slamdancing in particular is a test of manhood, a show of strength while also a ritual of bonding and solidarity.

Like some rap artists, certain heavy metal groups portray a very narrow and often negative image of women. Some death metal CD jackets display paintings of bound or tortured women. Others are sexually misogynistic; Guns N' Roses' *Appetite for Destruction* insert originally had an illustration of what appears to be a robot rape scene. Motley Crue's "Girls, Girls, Girls" portrays women as little more than sexual playthings. Thrash metal, by contrast, excludes women almost entirely, what Walser (1993) calls **female exscription**, a process that makes women absent or invisible. The music, lyrics, and videos, made by male artists for a mostly male audience, deal primarily with masculine themes, as though women were a threat to male camaraderie. For many fans of extreme metal, songs about women, partying, and living the rock-and-roll lifestyle are trivial and inauthentic compared with more "real" themes of alienation and social problems. In general, the moral outrage generated by heavy metal (with its primarily white performers and audience) is significantly less than that caused by rap (audience and performers primarily black), reflecting the ongoing power of race in our culture; some rap and heavy metal lyrics are sexist or misogynist, but racism provokes a stronger reaction about rap.

There have been a few prominent women in metal bands, including Lita Ford and Doro Pesch (formerly of Warlock; Weinstein 2000). Others included Girlschool, Vixen, Bitch, and White Zombie as well as grunge metal L7 and Babes in Toyland. The underground has more examples, such as metalcore bands Most Precious Blood and Walls of Jericho, though they remain few and far between. Entering the metal scene, demanding space in such a hypermasculine context, is a political statement. The women of metal challenge dominant gender roles, much like the women of punk and rap. They defy the stereotype of women as groupies, asserting their power in a male-dominated subculture. Still, their beauty, as much as their musical talent, is often center stage, even if their tattoos and dyed hair offer a slightly different version of femininity. Prominent metal magazine *Revolver* regularly features the "Hottest Chicks in Hard Rock" while label Century Media publishes a "Maidens of Metal" calendar showcasing artists such as Maria Brink from In This Moment or Alissa White-Gluz of The Agonist in provocative poses.

Authenticity

Metalheads have their own ways of performing authenticity. In general, they construct the rest of the world and other musicians (e.g., Britney Spears, Backstreet Boys, Justin Beiber) as fake and metal as somehow more "real." Thrash metal fans and performers considered synthesizers and keyboards inauthentic, as were music videos (that is, until Metallica's video for their song "One" was released), love ballads, and singing about "scoring chicks." "Real" metal should expose the hypocrisies of adult life. Like "true" punks or hip hoppers, "true" metalheads shouldn't care about making money or gaining fame. Yet clearly there are significant ideological differences between the various metal factions. Living the rock-and-roll lifestyle has strong appeal among some, whereas it is completely taboo among others. In virtually every metal subgenre, however, it is easier for men than for women to maintain authenticity. In fact, as metal gained popularity, new more "extreme" genres of metal emerged, in part, to reestablish the links between masculinity and authenticity (Hutcherson and Haenfler 2010)—fans frame popular metal as feminine or "gay," while more underground scenes are "brutal."

Religious/Political Injustice/Hypocrisy

Given metal's themes of alienation, the subculture can sometimes seem little more than a very loud, nihilistic way of venting anger without any real notion to challenge anything. However, metal has its own politics that serve in a way to challenge the dominant social order. All youth are quick to point out adults' hypocrisies—an adolescent told by her parents not to smoke or drink while they smoke and drink is unlikely to be swayed by the explanation, "You're not old enough." Metalheads pay particular attention to what they perceive as the contradictions in politics and organized religion. Metallica's songs "Disposable Heroes" and "One" question war, while Slayer's "Read Between the Lies" and "Jesus Saves" mock corrupt religious leaders. Often criticized by Christian organizations, metalheads point to scandals such as evangelist Jimmy Swaggart's committing adultery while preaching about others' going to hell, or to the Catholic priest child molestation scandal. Norwegian black metal bands such as Emperor and Burzum are especially notorious for criticizing Christianity, and others like Dimmu Borgir write songs dealing with demonic imagery (Rafalovich and Schneider 2003). Christianity represents not just a religious tradition but the entire moral order. The very label "black" metal contrasts "Christian notions of purity" (ibid. 2003, 14). Metalheads imagine themselves as possessing some insider knowledge of "what's really going on" in the world while people in mainstream society are the dupes of corporations and televangelists.[19]

MORAL PANICS

The history of rock and roll music includes many critics who blame the genre for a variety of social ills. Recall the worry that Elvis's gyrating pelvis on the Ed Sullivan show would induce indecent behavior or the fear that Body Count's song "Copkiller" would incite kids to kill police officers. Various authorities have held youth music and subcultures responsible for destroying values, promoting drug use, disrupting families, endorsing homosexuality, and generally corrupting youth. Establishing a causal link between metal (or hip hop, or any other music culture) and violent, anti-social, or risky behavior is very difficult. Social life is extraordinarily complex, and many factors influence individual behavior. Arnett (1996) found that kids who listen to heavy metal *do* engage in risky behaviors more often, such as drunk driving, driving fast, having sex without contraception, and using drugs. However, he argues that listening to metal does not cause these behaviors. Rather, adolescent boys who are attracted to high sensation thrills are attracted to both metal and these risky behaviors. Nevertheless, lack of scientific evidence does not stop the pressure groups and the media from suggesting a causal link between metal music and violence. Often when a sensational crime occurs, if the perpetrator listens to metal the media will continually mention this fact, as was the case in the Columbine High School shootings and the Robin Hood Hills child murders, which I discuss shortly hereafter.

At times, concern over the perceived depravity of popular culture advances to near panic, inciting calls for immediate action. A **moral panic** is when a significant number of people in a society believe that a group of "evil-doers" poses a threat to the moral order and therefore must be stopped (Goode and Ben-Yehuda 1994; S. Cohen [1972] 1993). In the early 2000s, Catholic priest sex scandals and child abduction cases continually made the news. Both of these examples had a grain of truth; some priests are pedophiles, and some children are abducted. However, in a moral panic the perceived threat far exceeds the actual danger. The media and policymakers sensationalize crime, teen gambling, killer moms, murderous postal workers, road rage, and a host of other scares beyond the realistic probabilities that any of these things might occur (Glassner 1999).

Stages of a Moral Panic (S. Cohen 1980)

1. Someone or something is defined as a threat to values or interests, often by someone in power.

2. The media depicts the threat in an easily recognizable form, amplifying the perceived danger while offering incomplete information.

3. Public concern grows rapidly as more people become aware of the threat.

4. Authorities and opinion makers issue a response, calling for swift action to quell the threat.

5. The moral panic recedes or results in social changes such as new laws or increased law enforcement.

Generally, moral panics reflect greater social anxieties. For example, the scares surrounding attacks on children (from pedophiles, killer nannies, child abductors, homicidal moms, and murderous teens) may deflect attention from the fact that our society has failed to "provide adequate education, nutrition, housing, parenting, medical services, and child care over the past couple of decades" (Glassner 1999, xxvi). A moral panic, then, often reflects some larger crisis or uncertainty that people are unable to adequately explain or solve. Two of the biggest moral panics associated with heavy metal are claims that metal encourages Satan worship and promotes suicide.

Satanism

Satanism is perhaps the longest running moral panic associated with the metal subculture. Indeed, metal bands have a history of utilizing satanic or occult images on album covers and in song lyrics. King Diamond and Ozzy Osbourne wore inverted crosses, and Black Sabbath's *Sabbath Bloody Sabbath* album jacket and Iron Maiden's song "The Number of the Beast" featured "666," a number associated with Satan. An examination of Slayer's CD covers reveals goat-headed demons, pentacles, and scenes of horror; song titles such as "South of Heaven," "Necrophiliac," and "Seasons in the Abyss" give parents little reassurance. There are many more examples from fairly mainstream metal, and death and black metal convey even more offensive (to the mainstream public) and, occasionally, satanic motifs. However, for the most part, extreme metal remains below the radar of most cultural critics, who would surely express a great deal more outrage if the genre were any more popular.

Another perceived threat from metal came in the form of subliminal backmasking, or encoding hidden messages into music discernable only when the music is played backwards. Not only were rock musicians setting a bad example, they were including in their songs subliminal messages designed to attack the listener's subconscious. Thus, for example, according to the author of *Backward Masking Unmasked: Backward Satanic Messages of Rock and Roll Exposed*, Queen's hit song "Another One Bites the Dust," when played backwards, says "Decide to smoke marijuana, marijuana, marijuana," and Led Zeppelin's song "Stairway to Heaven" played backwards says "Oh I will sing because I live with Satan" (Aranza 1983). Bands from the Beatles to the Beach Boys have been accused of attempts to brainwash kids into committing antisocial acts.

We've established that to understand subcultures we must examine the social context in which they occur. The same goes for the *response* to subcultures, including moral panics. Moral panics about Satanism tend to occur among fundamentalist Christians with relatively little education who live in rural areas (Victor 1993). Santanic scares typically take hold in places suffering economic recession and/or where people perceive a decline in traditional religious and family values (ibid.). When people experience rapid social change and no longer feel completely in control of their lives they may scapegoat their fears onto another group.

Rather than simply a personification of evil, to metalheads Satan is a metaphor for everything society rejects; therefore, what better way to alienate and offend adult society than to flaunt satanic images (Walser 1993)? Just as punks who wore swastikas were not necessarily Nazis, metalheads who sport inverted crosses or pentagrams are likely not actually Satanists. Satan is a symbol of rebellion and open disdain for mainstream society.

A greater, and more real (though still very small) threat comes from a minority of black metal fans who adopt not just Satanic practices but ultra-nationalist, racist beliefs akin to supremacist skinheads (Kahn-Harris 2007; Moynihan and Søderland 1998). Again, it is important to avoid painting the black metal scene with too broad a brush; the majority of fans are neither nationalist nor racist. However, in Scandinavia especially, a few have participated in church burnings and racist organizations, and even committed murder (Kahn-Harris 2004; Burghart 1999).

Suicide

In the 1980s the United States Congress held hearings to investigate the potential of heavy metal to cause anti-social behavior and even suicide. In 1985, a lawsuit alleged that Ozzy Osbourne's song "Suicide Solution" prompted a young man to kill himself, despite Osbourne's contention that the song carries a message *against* alcohol abuse rather than *for* suicide. Judas Priest also faced allegations of inserting subliminal messages into their music, prompting two young men to commit suicide. Finally, Slayer faced legal action claiming that the violent themes in their music led three fans to commit murder (Rafalovich and Schneider 2003). These cases typically end up going nowhere, yet they reflect the larger and ongoing fears regarding metal music.

Establishing that heavy metal actually *causes* suicide is very difficult. However, researchers have shown that heavy metal fans are at increased risk of feeling suicidal, especially females (Sheel and Westefeld 1999). In other words, kids who listen to heavy metal may be at greater risk of attempting suicide, but the music and culture do not cause suicidal behavior. Rather, alienated kids who have family, school, or other problems may turn to metal as an outlet for their frustrations (Gaines 1991; Arnett 1996). The same feelings that predispose people toward suicide may also attract them to metal. In fact, metalheads report that listening to their music makes them feel *better*, not worse: "Heavy metal music characteristically has the effect of *calming them down*, of purging their anger rather than inflaming it" (Arnett 1996, 81; emphasis in original). Listening to metal is a cathartic experience for youth (Arnett 1991), and most metalheads are not suicidal (Sheel and Westefeld 1999).

Folk Devils—The West Memphis Three

In 1993, authorities found three young boys brutally murdered in the Robin Hood Hills area of West Memphis, Arkansas. Three young men—Damien Echols, Jessie Misskelley, and Jason Baldwin—stood trial and were convicted for the crimes. Some of the evidence against them, particularly Echols, included the fact that they listened to heavy metal, read books about magic and witchcraft, and dressed in dark clothing. Other evidence aside, the prosecution used the three's enjoyment of heavy metal and fascination with the occult to paint them as malicious Satan worshipers. The grieving community, needing some explanation for such heinous crimes, believed the murders were part of a satanic ritual, making the West Memphis Three into modern-day folk devils. A **folk devil** is someone who embodies evil and is held responsible for the suffering of a community. They serve as "visible reminders of what we should not be" and often become scapegoats for other social problems (S. Cohen [1972] 1993, 10). A folk devil is not necessarily a specific person (e.g., Marilyn Manson) but a role, such as black metal fan or skinhead. Members of deviant subcultures make ideal folk devils because of their often "spectacular" appearance (they are easily identified), their disdain for conventional ideals (which creates an "us" vs. "them" differentiation), and their relative lack of social power (it is difficult for subculturists to dispute exaggerated claims about them). The West Memphis Three precisely fit this profile. Gangsta rappers, goths, and (in England) football hooligans have all been folk devils. In Norway, Varg Virkernes, a fixture in the black metal scene and at one time a self-described Satanist, was convicted of murder, transforming black metal fans, most of whom are entirely peaceful, into folk devils. Despite little empirical evidence to support claims that metal music is responsible for the social ills for which it is blamed, moral panics persist, due largely to the efforts of moral entrepreneurs.

West Memphis Three Go Free

Based upon new DNA evidence and a variety of problems with the original case, the West Memphis Three were released from prison in 2011 after each accepted an "Alford" plea, an agreement professing their innocence while acknowledging the prosecution had enough evidence to convict. They served over eighteen years in prison and continue working for complete exoneration.

MORAL ENTREPRENEURS

After the 1999 Columbine High School massacre in Littleton, Colorado, frightened and confused parents blamed heavy metal rocker (and folk devil) Marilyn Manson for inciting hatred and violence. With an album titled "Antichrist Superstar," a gender-bending persona, and an anti-authoritarian attitude, Manson has consistently been a source of controversy. An organization called Citizens for Peace and Respect, including local pastors, held protests denouncing Manson and encouraging Denver authorities to cancel Manson's 2001 OzzFest appearance, despite little evidence that the killers were fans of his music. In addition to holding meetings and vigils, they convinced Colorado Governor Bill Owens and Congressman Tom Tancredo to call for barring Manson's performance. Manson, of course, refused to cancel his appearance and allegedly read passages from the Bible onstage (rather than ripping them up, as he had in the past).

Citizens for Peace and Respect are not the first group to organize against "moral decay," nor will they be the last. They are examples of **moral entrepreneurs**, people who bring attention to a problem, create rules, label deviants, and then try to have the rules enforced (Becker 1963). Recall from Chapter 1 that deviance is socially constructed rather than an individual characteristic and that people or groups *label* some actions deviant. **Labeling theory** suggests that actions or people are deviant only when society *labels* them deviant. Metal performers are not inherently deviant; rather, moral entrepreneurs label them, their music, and their behaviors deviant. Some adults believe that society is in moral decline and that greater enforcement of morality is necessary. They perceive (correctly or incorrectly—it's irrelevant) a world of increasing teen pregnancy, drug use, and crime, a world losing its rules and traditions where sex is rampant and kids are out of control. They initiate **moral entrepreneurial campaigns**, also called **moral crusades**, to convince politicians and the public to take immediate action against the tide of filth and restore values and decency to society. The first step in such a campaign is to raise awareness of the problem and convince a significant segment of the public that there *is* a problem. Most people, for example, never would have considered heavy-metal-induced Satanism as a big threat to their communities were it not for media exposure prompted by moral entrepreneurs. In the second stage of a moral campaign, entrepreneurs set about converting others to their point of view. They call upon "experts" (often with marginal credentials), celebrities, and religious leaders to both legitimize and popularize their cause with the public. In manufacturing the satanic scare, religious leaders and religious studies professors proved useful allies (Walser 1993). Once the public is on board, the campaign can turn to creating and enforcing new rules.

Moral crusades require both rule creators and rule enforcers (Becker 1963). **Rule creators** perceive a social problem and create new social rules or laws to redress the problem. In the labeling theory of deviance, they are the ones defining and labeling deviant acts. They typically hold strong convictions and can fall on either end of the political spectrum; on the left, rule creators might seek laws expanding animal rights while more right-leaning groups might push for laws prohibiting same-sex marriage. Regarding metal, the Parent Music Resource Center successfully pressured the Recording Industry Association of America to require labeling of records containing "explicit content." Many moral crusaders are not simply trying to enforce their own morals on others; they truly believe that if others' adopt their morals and follow their rules everyone will be better off. Kids, according to some rule creators, will lead better lives if they don't smoke, drink alcohol, or, in the case of music, listen to heavy metal. Likewise, Prohibitionists believed that outlawing alcohol would improve lives.

New rules are useless without a means of enforcement. **Rule enforcers** implement the new rules, monitor those to whom the rules apply, and sanction rule breakers. Police and other organizations were necessary to enforce the Eighteenth Amendment prohibiting the sale of alcohol. A successful moral crusade may require existing agencies to enforce the new rules or necessitate the creation of a new enforcement agency (ibid.). The moral panic of satanic cults created a minor industry of cult experts, anti-satanist religious groups, and monitoring agencies.

Parent Music Resource Center

The Parent Music Resource Center (PMRC) was perhaps the most influential national U.S. organization of moral entrepreneurs dedicated to protecting children from immoral music. Formed in 1985 by wives of government elites, including Tipper Gore, wife of Tennessee Senator and future Vice President Al Gore, the center vowed to educate parents about disturbing content in popular music. In actuality, they were more of a political pressure group than an educational center. Claiming that heavy metal glorified violence, drug use, suicide, and promiscuous sex, the PMRC used its considerable political clout to call for Congressional hearings investigating rock. Eventually their pressure forced the recording industry to adopt Parental Advisory labels, small black stickers placed on tapes, CDs, and records containing explicit lyrics (Walser 1993). Although the PMRC found a variety of music objectionable (from Madonna and Cyndi Lauper to Prince and Sheena Easton), it reserved its most heated criticisms for rap and heavy metal.

The PMRC provoked a response from metalheads (among others), who saw the group as just another corrupt organization focused on enforcing their own brand of morality while ignoring larger issues (e.g., poverty). Predictably, many artists framed the PMRC as promoting censorship. Megadeth's song "Hook in Mouth" invoked images of the PMRC as fascist puppet-masters bent on thought control, and Jello Biafra, a target of several moral crusades beginning during his time with the Dead Kennedys, spoke out against the so-called "Tipper stickers."

Symbolic Politics

Other important questions we can ask about moral crusades are "Who initiates them?" and "Who benefits from them?" One theory holds that moral panics emerge from the general public—the **grassroots**—while another contends that **elites** manufacture moral crusades to generate fear among the public, making them easier to control and distracting them from larger social problems (Goode and Ben-Yahuda 1994). Still another explanation identifies **interest groups**, which may reflect real public concerns but also may work in their own interests, as the main force behind moral entrepreneurial campaigns (ibid.). For example, perhaps the public (the grassroots) stands to gain from a crusade against obscenity in music and television—the Parents Television Council has launched a variety of campaigns against TV shows (e.g. MTV's short-lived teen soap opera *Skins*) believed to be harmful to kids. However, interest groups such as religious and political organizations also have something to gain; churches may gain supporters and moral capital, politicians may gain votes and money to run their campaigns. The important insight is that moral entrepreneurs may have agendas apart from their stated goals. A politician declaring a "war on crime" may or may not genuinely wish to help "save" a community from criminals, but she or he undoubtedly weighs the political support to be gained from taking a tough stance on crime.

Despite the best efforts of moral entrepreneurs such as the PMRC, few attempts to reign in musicians' freedom of speech have succeeded. According to one theory, attempts at censorship are actually **symbolic politics** designed to promote politicians' popularity rather than actually change anything (Edelman 1977). It may be that politicians and interest groups construct "political spectacles" around heavy metal more for their own ends than in a sincere effort to make a difference (Purcell 2003). Symbolic politics appeal to citizens' concerns and fears, usually using emotional expressions of outrage, oversimplified or ambiguous arguments, and half-truths (Edelman 1988). Politicians talk tough, call for hearings, and hold press conferences expressing their moral outrage at the moral degradation in popular media, knowing all the while that little will change. They may or may not sincerely hold the convictions they espouse; either way, any legislation is likely to change little. Take the Janet Jackson "wardrobe malfunction" during the 2004 Super Bowl in which Justin Timberlake tore loose a piece of Jackson's costume, exposing her breast to a national audience numbering in the tens of millions. The morality of their actions aside, the political uproar after the incident was sensational. Michael Powell, head of the Federal Communications Commission, called the exposure a "classless, crass, and deplorable stunt" and immediately opened an investigation. Television pundits and radio commentators demanded that the FCC clamp down on the entertainment industry. Politicians, Democrat and Republican alike, gain favor by assuming the moral high ground, but in actuality they enact little enforceable legislation. Political commentators thrill their audiences with titillating scandal but rarely present systematic research to back their claims. Perhaps these periodic moral outrages are little more than political drama meant to curry constituent favor and audience market share?

Having relatively little political power, deviant subcultures often become the scapegoats for larger social issues. Thus, rather than focus on how homophobia in schools or the extraordinary prevalence of guns in U.S. society contributes to youth violence, it is politically convenient to attack Marilyn Manson's music as the culprit. The National Rifle Association, a powerful political lobby that vehemently opposes gun control, contributes to many politicians' political campaigns and wields significant clout in Washington, D.C. Many Marilyn Manson fans are too young to vote, let alone to make extraordinary campaign contributions. With little to counter negative portrayals of metalheads, the general public, for the most part uninformed about subcultures, hears what it wants to believe: that violence is the result of weird groups and strange music rather than deeper, more complex social problems. Ironically, many metal fans are savvy enough to recognize symbolic politics for what they are, further fueling their alienation from the political system (Purcell 2003).

CONCLUSIONS

Metalheads have been the focus of moral entrepreneurial campaigns and have served as modern-day folk devils despite the fact that the vast majority of metalheads neither engage in "devil worship" nor commit suicide (Walser 1993). Any particular moral panic eventually dies away or is replaced by a newer, likely more sensational scare—consider scares around raves and ecstasy; *Beavis and Butthead* and *South Park*; and computer games and "Internet addiction." In a strange turn of events, Ozzy Osbourne, once the PMRC's major villain, had his own reality TV show, appeared in Pepsi commercials, and was invited to the White House by President George W. Bush (to the chagrin of both die-hard fans and right-wing Christians). Moral panics, like deviance, are socially constructed and maintained. Today's folk devil may be tomorrow's mainstream television show.

DISCUSSION

- Describe a contemporary moral panic or moral entrepreneurial campaign. Who are the key moral entrepreneurs involved? What is the basis of their claims?
- Discuss a person or group cast as a modern folk devil, a scapegoat for some broader social problem. How has the media contributed to the negative imagery surrounding this person or group?
- How did politicians use symbolic politics in the last election cycle to win electoral support?
- Do you think musicians should be held responsible for the behavior of those who listen to lyrics that purportedly advocate violence or other harm?

KEY IDEAS

Alienation: A state of being isolated or disconnected, feeling outcast and/or oppressed.

Elite theory of moral panics: Moral panics emerge from political, religious, wealthy, or other elites in an effort to control and distract the public from other, more pressing, issues and to uphold and consolidate power.

Female exscription: The exclusion of women from either part or all of a subculture. The absence of women in subcultural production and consumption.

Folk devil: An individual or group who embodies evil and often becomes a scapegoat for other social problems. Folk devils function as symbols for deviance and warnings for what we should not become.

Grassroots theory of moral panics: The notion that moral panics emerge from genuine concern and initiative among the general public, rather than from self-interested elites.

Interest group theory of moral panics: The notion that moral panics emerge from pressure by interest groups that gain grassroots support.

Moral entrepreneurs: People who bring attention to a perceived problem, create rules, label deviants, and then try to have the rules enforced.

Moral entrepreneurial campaign/moral crusade: An ongoing effort by moral entrepreneurs to fight deviant behavior and groups, restoring "morality" by enacting new rules. Often associated with a moral panic.

Moral panic: When a significant number of people in a society believe that a group of "evil-doers" poses a threat to the moral order and therefore must be stopped.

Rule creators: Moral entrepreneurs who take the initiative to create new social rules.

Rule enforcers: Authorities who enforce the rules created by rule creators in a moral entrepreneurial campaign.

Symbolic politics: Political messages that appeal to citizens' concerns and fears, usually using emotional expressions of outrage, oversimplified or ambiguous arguments, and half-truths, while actually changing relatively little.

RESOURCES

Extreme Metal: Music and Culture on the Edge

By Keith Kahn-Harris. 2007. Oxford, UK: Berg Publishers.

The definitive study of extreme metal, examining the metal community and its themes of death, war, the occult, and sometimes violence.

True Norwegian Black Metal

By Peter Beste. 2008. VICE Books.

A book of beautiful photographs featuring black metal musicians.

Metal Rules the Globe: Heavy Metal Music Around the Globe

Edited by Jeremy Wallach, Harris M. Berger, and Paul D. Greene. 2011. Durham, NC: Duke University Press.

A collection of articles about metal all over the world, featuring some of the foremost scholars of metal discussing gender, race, class, globalization, consumerism and other topics.

MetalUnderground.com

www.metalunderground.com

Site with news and information about many varieties of metal.

Metal Edge **magazine**

www.metaledgemag.com

Available in print or online, this magazine covers all things metal.

The Decline of Western Civilization Part II: The Metal Years (film, Penelope Spheeris 1988)

A documentary on the 1980s metal scene, featuring Ozzy Ozbourne, Megadeth, and various hair metal bands.

Paradise Lost: The Child Murders at Robin Hood Hills (film, Joe Berlinger and Bruce Sinofsky 1996)

A documentary chronicling the case of the West Memphis Three, three outcast teenage boys convicted of killing younger boys. A great illustration of a moral entrepreneurial campaign, folk devils, and moral panic.

Metal: A Headbanger's Journey (film, Sam Dunn and Scot McFadyen 2005)

Anthropologist (and metal fan) Sam Dunn examines heavy metal in this documentary featuring members of Slayer, Iron Maiden, Motorhead, White Zombie, and many more.

CHAPTER 6

↻

Virginity Pledgers—Religion, Sexual Identity, and Positive Deviance

"Sex sells," goes the old saying, and sex marketed to youth seems to be selling quite well. Spend a few minutes watching MTV or strolling down the magazine aisle at the market and you'll get an eyeful of suggestive looks, sensual poses, and barely covered bodies. Bare midriffs and bellybutton rings prompt parents to worry, politicians to lecture, and religious leaders to moralize against the decadence of pop culture. Despite the clichés, not all teens are into sex, drugs, and rock-n-roll, and some focus their energies toward more spiritual pursuits. While many youth subcultures are ambivalent or even hostile toward organized religion, Christianity has spread beyond church youth groups to a variety of subcultures. Christian rock music is a burgeoning business, with artists such as P.O.D., Switchfoot, Underoath, and MxPx playing heavy music while looking like indie rockers. Perhaps one of the most widespread Christian youth movements has been the "virginity pledge" movement in which teens make a public pledge to wait until marriage to have sex. Originating in the early 1990s with the Christian Sex Education Project and the Southern Baptist Church, abstinence programs have spread around the world, with pledge groups popping up in schools, colleges, and various religious denominations. Youth can now find pledge communities online—The Silver Ring Thing has a Facebook page and Twitter feed—and can even make their promise on the Web. University groups such as Princeton's Anscombe Society and Harvard's True Love Revolution challenge the popular perception of sexually promiscuous undergrads. Just as straight edge makes it cool to say no to drugs and alcohol, virginity pledgers make saying "no" to sex admirable rather than prudish or geeky. And as straight edgers oppose peer pressure to drink and smoke, virginity pledgers fight pressures to have intercourse. Sex, pledgers argue, should be a romantic expression of love reserved for married couples.

Virginity pledgers may seem a bit out of place in this book. After all, they seem to thrive on *following* the rules, not breaking them. Given adults' involvement in pledge organizations, they don't seem particularly *subcultural* either. Yet if premarital sex has become the norm, perhaps it's deviant to wait until marriage to have sex? And judging by pledgers' commitment to replacing what they perceive as a "hook up" culture with a "courtship" culture, in some ways perhaps they engage in subcultural resistance. In this chapter, we'll examine the cultural context that shapes pledgers' core values and we'll look at how sexuality becomes part of one's identity. Then we'll consider pledging as an example of positive deviance and end with a discussion of religion and social control theory.

SOCIETAL CONTEXT OF VIRGINITY PLEDGERS

A Resurgence of Cultural Conservatism

Virginity pledging emerged in the midst of a growing movement of conservative Christians that began asserting its cultural and political power in the 1980s. What some saw as the excesses of the 1960s and 1970s bolstered a resurgence of cultural conservatism. While the movement pursues many agendas, its central issues often revolve around controlling sex: making abortion and stem cell research illegal; promoting sexual abstinence for teens; banning gay marriage; and regulating sexual content in music and the media. For cultural conservatives, celebrity sex tapes and *Girls Gone Wild* videos indicate an immoral culture and a decline in "family values." The lyrics, CD covers, and music videos of much of pop music are also considered offensive and a bad influence on kids. Finally, many conservatives perceive that U.S. culture is generally in decline and traditional religious and moral values have been supplanted by irreverence, irresponsibility, and promiscuity (W. Bennett 1994).

Virginity pledging also reflects changes in the politics of sex education. When Republicans took control of Congress in 1994 and the Presidency in 2000, the movement toward "abstinence only" sex education gained political ground. Even though the teen pregnancy rate had steadily declined through the 1990s,[20] the George W. Bush administration ushered in a shift in focus from "safe sex"—using condoms to avoid pregnancy and AIDS and other STDs—to abstinence-based programs emphasizing that the only safe sex is sex within marriage.[21] In 2010, the Obama administration implemented plans to fund a variety of sex ed programs based upon their proven effectiveness, prompting outcry from social conservatives. While many schools institutionalize abstinence-based education, churches have supported pledge programs with significant success—about 10 percent of boys and 16 percent of girls have taken some sort of virginity pledge (Murray and Aguayo 2008). Far from being settled, the controversy over whether schools should focus on safe sex or "abstinence only" sex education rages on.

Virginity Pledgers' Core Values

A 2005 federal survey found that just under half of U.S. kids engaged in sexual intercourse, a decline since the early 1990s (Bigg 2006). However, other studies reveal that each generation of youth is having sex earlier, with nearly two-thirds of contemporary youth having had vaginal intercourse by age eighteen and only 16 percent of young adults between eighteen and twenty-three remain virgins (Regnerus and Uecker 2011). Even fewer remain virgins on their wedding night (Laumann, Gagnon, Michael, and Michaels 1994).[22] So while it's a myth that most younger teenagers are having sex, very few people wait until marriage for their first sexual encounter. Regardless of how many teens are actually having sex, pledgers perceive themselves as going against the grain—and those who *do* abstain until marriage are clearly in the minority.

Most pledge groups claim that abstinence is the only "foolproof" way to prevent STDs and unplanned pregnancy and that premarital sex is unhealthy for both the body and the mind. The vast majority connect their pledge to religious values, finding strength in their faith communities. Pledge programs frame abstinence as a commitment to one's self, one's parents, and one's God. Thus, more than a practical way to stay healthy and avoid pregnancy, pledging becomes a meaningful identity in its own right, a way to set oneself apart.

Pledge Organizations—The Silver Ring Thing, True Love Waits, and More

Virginity pledgers differ from many other youth subcultures in that they have strong ties to organizations run by adults. Many religious groups have taken up the fight against teen sex, creating networks of youth committed to abstinence. The Silver Ring Thing (SRT; www.SilverRingThing.com), founded in 1996 by Christian youth minister Denny Pattyn, seeks to "create a cultural shift in America. We want to see the concept of abstinence be the norm rather than the exception." Members promise to wait for sex until marriage, wearing a silver ring to symbolize their vow. The ring serves as a visible marker of "the faith decision and vow pledged to God Almighty" and membership in the SRT collective identity. The organization travels nationwide, putting on events featuring music, drama, laser lights, comedy, and videos, and in the course of the event, SRT staff register new pledgers. Much like members of a twelve-step program (such as Alcoholics Anonymous), they choose "accountability partners" (of the same gender, who have also made the pledge) with whom they can meet at least once a week, be "painfully honest," and feel comfortable discussing their struggles against "temptation." They are well established online, featuring a Podcast, MySpace and Facebook pages, online newsletter, mailing list, and instant messaging.

Sponsored by Lifeway Christian Resources and associated with the Southern Baptist Convention, the True Love Waits (www.truelovewaits.com) program also utilizes positive peer pressure to encourage abstinence. Members often wear TLW rings or wristbands and sign "covenant cards" with the following pledge: "Believing that true love waits, I make a commitment to God, myself, my family, my friends, my future mate, and my future children to a lifetime of purity including sexual abstinence from this day until the day I enter a biblical marriage relationship."[23] Other abstinence programs abound. Focus on the Family, based in Colorado Springs, Colorado, one of the largest conservative Christian organizations in the world, also has programs directed primarily toward youth. They print youth-oriented magazines filled with stylish, hip, and presumably sexually abstinent kids, squeezing confessions of faith in between reviews of Christian rock music. Project Reality promotes secular abstinence education in public schools, creating curricula for kids of all ages, while the Not Me, Not Now media campaign uses radio, billboards, posters, and TV to advertise abstinence to youth. While most parents support these groups' principles, some are wary of replacing safe sex education with abstinence-only programs. The Silver Ring Thing, for example, has generated some controversy for claiming that condoms do not work.

SEXUALITY AND SEXUAL IDENTITY

As you've probably noticed, society sends mixed and often contradictory messages about sexuality. Teens see scantily clad, hypersexualized performers on TV and read about sex tips in *Cosmopolitan* magazine while simultaneously learning about STDs, the "sin" of premarital sex, and "abstinence only" in their sex ed classes. The results are seemingly clashing views about sex: on one hand, sex is pleasurable, natural, and "cool." On the other, sex is fearful, immoral, and "dirty." Sex is simultaneously private and in need of public regulation.

Just like race and gender, the meanings of sexuality are socially constructed rather than fixed and universal. An interactionist perspective demands that we ask how the meanings of sexuality emerge and how society labels sexualities—which expressions of sexuality does society value, and which does it stigmatize? How do people "perform" their sexualities? How do the meanings of sexuality change in different contexts? These types of questions reveal how a culture defines sexuality. **Sexuality** is "the ways we experience and express ourselves as sexual beings" (Rathus, Nevid, and Fichner-Rathus 2000). More than defining sexual behavior, sexuality encompasses the socially constructed meanings of sex and gender, including the culturally specific norms, beliefs, traditions, and taboos related to sex.

Like other abstainers, such as vegans and straight edgers, virginity pledgers define themselves by what they *do not* do (Mullaney 2006)—abstinence becomes part of their identity. Whether one believes sexual attraction is based solely on genetics or some combination of biology and socialization, **sexual identities** are socially constructed. "Gay," "straight," and "bisexual" identities have meanings that change and shift over time (Plante 2006). Is one gay simply for having a same-sex sexual encounter? Not necessarily, as some self-identified heterosexual men cruise for casual sex with other men; they consider themselves straight men who just happen to occasionally have sex with other men (Tewksbury 1996; Doll et al. 1992). Sexual acts are therefore separate from sexual identity—someone who identifies as straight may not be sexually active at all. Even the "virgin" identity, which seems rather clear cut, is open to interpretation. Is one a virgin after oral (but not vaginal) sex? Anal sex? Many teens seem to think so. Some abstinence programs, such as the Silver Ring Thing, allow "second virginity" for those who previously had sexual intercourse, an opportunity to reclaim the virgin identity despite previous sexual activity. One can thus be a "born-again virgin" or "secondary virgin" (see, e.g., Rosenbaum 2006; Keller 1999). So you see, what "counts" as sex and what "virginity" and "abstinence" mean are open to interpretation—we learn the meanings of sex from our parents, peers, sex ed teachers, the media, and so on, but those meanings are fluid and often contradictory. In promoting *their* meanings of sexuality, virginity pledge groups seek to minimize ambiguity and encourage young people to connect their sexual and religious identities. Yet many youth still hold conflicting views on what constitutes abstinence.

Sexual Scripts

In the past, especially, sex was viewed as subversive or rebellious, and subcultures were viewed as promiscuous havens for deviant sexual behavior. Subcultures have often pushed the boundaries of accepted sexuality—the hippies' "free love" of the 1960s and 1970s came as a shock after the more conservative 1950s, and lesbian and gay subcultures questioned the notion of sex as a procreative act between two married, heterosexual individuals. Teen sex is still framed as a social problem, and those who are sexually active risk being labeled deviant.

"Deviant" sexuality is any sexual practice deemed strange, unacceptable, unlawful, or unnatural. To understand "deviant" sexuality, we must identify how society defines acceptable sexual behavior. Imagine for a moment the idealized sexual encounter. Who is involved? How old are they? What are they doing, and when and where are they doing it? Why are they having sex? You probably imagined one man and one woman, of similar ages, probably relatively young and attractive (say, in their 20s), of the same race, going out on a date of some kind, ending up in the bedroom, engaging in foreplay, having consensual missionary-style vaginal intercourse, climaxing (both partners), and perhaps finishing with cuddling, smoking a cigarette, or some other post-sex bonding. Your own imagination might come up with a slightly different scenario, but there is undoubtedly a standard **sexual script**, or set of norms we learn that outlines the boundaries of an ideal sexual encounter (Gagnon and Simon 1973). You might not agree with this script, or you might find other scenarios more erotic, yet we often compare sexual activity to this fairly narrow standard. Clearly, this leaves a whole range of behavior at the margins. Different sexual positions, mild spanking or bondage, and mutual masturbation are exotic or freaky and thus, for many people, deviant. Viewing pornography online, though widespread, is deviant in many people's minds. And of course remaining a virgin into one's thirties, forties, or beyond is, in its own way, deviant, as demonstrated by the mockery made of an older virgin in the film *The 40 Year Old Virgin*.

Even though we all learn the basics of our cultural sexual script, the script continually changes. Is marriage part of the script? Or, if not marriage, at least love? Or are one night stands more or less acceptable, as many TV shows seem to imply? Again, you can quickly see that social meanings of sex change. In the past, sex (ideally) was for married couples in order to procreate. Now, Western societies tend to have a more liberal view of sex; even if people claim sex should be reserved for marriage, they acknowledge that most people have premarital sex. Yet *promiscuous* sex (especially for women) and sex between same-sex partners is still considered deviant. In the course of resisting premarital, or deviant, sex, virginity pledgers reinforce the idealized sexual script. They identify premarital sex as a problem and create an ideology explaining the pitfalls of sex.

Many subcultures have stretched the definitions of the dominant sexual script. You may have noticed in particular that the sexual script we constructed automatically excludes lesbians and gay men. That makes same-sex sexual activity deviant and any sexual identities outside the straight/heterosexual standard deviant identities. **Heterocentrism** is the notion that heterosexuality is "normal" and "natural" while homosexuality is "abnormal." Being straight requires no explanation because we take heterosexuality for granted. Lesbians and gay men, however, face constant questions and criticisms for their sexual identity, such as "What 'made' you gay?" Virtually our entire society is organized around the assumption that people are straight. **Compulsory heterosexuality** suggests that society actually pressures people toward heterosexuality. From very early on, kids learn to be straight as their parents guide them toward acceptable (straight) sexuality—imagine a father joking with his son about pursuing sex with girls or a mother asking her daughter if she has a boyfriend. Most of us are socialized, by our families and peers and through the media, as if we are and should be straight.

Not only is heterosexuality the norm; it is also considered superior. Youth who "come out" and identify as lesbian, gay, or bisexual often face **heterosexism**, or prejudice and discrimination against homosexuals. According to the National Mental Health Association, harassment of gay youth, including name calling, teasing, threats, and actual physical violence, is commonplace in schools.[24] Such prejudice rests on **homophobia**, or the fear, stereotyping, or even hatred of homosexuals or homosexuality. **Heterosexual privileges**, or privileges and opportunities straight people have that lesbians and gay men do not (similar to white privilege discussed in Chapter 4), include holding hands in public without fear of reprisal, marriage and all the accompanying rights, and not having to worry about being verbally assaulted or physically attacked due to one's sexual identity.

Rather than challenge the traditional meanings of sexuality, virginity pledgers construct an identity based upon conventional gender roles, straight sexuality, purity, and religious tradition. Pledge programs take heterosexuality for granted and promote compulsory heterosexuality. Some avoid the topic of homosexuality altogether while others reinforce the notion that same-sex relationships are sinful.

Does Pledging Work?

Evaluating the effectiveness of abstinence programs is extremely difficult, because teens do not always provide reliable information about their sexual lives (Hollander 2006). Proving that such programs actually "cause" virginity is problematic (Constantine and Braverman 2004), and the issue is very politically charged. People tend to interpret studies in ways that support their own political agendas. The conservative Heritage Foundation claims that pledging produces many beneficial outcomes, such as pledgers being 40 percent less likely to have children prior to marriage (Rector, Johnson, and Marshall 2004). Meanwhile, the liberal National

Organization for Women is critical of abstinence-only programs, claiming that they increase unprotected sex and misrepresent facts about the effectiveness of condoms.

So do virginity pledge groups work? The best answer is sometimes, but only for a period of time, under certain conditions, and not without some unintended consequences. Bearman and Brückner (2001) found that virginity pledgers are much less likely to have sex than their peers who do not pledge. Pledging does delay first intercourse, at least for a while. Most people eventually have premarital sex, but pledging can help kids resist the pressure to have sex early in adolescence. However, the pledge works primarily for youth aged sixteen to seventeen and not so well for those eighteen and older. The average pledger delays sex by eighteen months,[25] though 88 percent end up breaking their pledges before marriage.[26] Also, pledgers abstain only if they are surrounded by *some* pledgers but not too many. If more than 30 percent of teens in a school pledge, pledging is much less effective. In order for the pledger identity to be meaningful, it has to be a minority. Once the subculture becomes too mainstream, it loses some of its power. Another study contends that youth who make a *private* abstinence pledge to themselves remain abstinent longer than those who make a formal *public* pledge (Bersamin, Walker, Waiters, Fisher, and Grube 2005). Finally, those who break their promise are one-third less likely to use contraception the first time they have sex, potentially risking pregnancy and exposure to sexually transmitted diseases (Brückner and Bearman 2005). So all the effort that went into avoiding the potentially negative outcomes of sex can be erased because pledgers are suspicious of or don't have access to condoms.

Congressional Study Finds Programs Ineffective

A 2007 Congressionally ordered study found that students in abstinence-only sex ed programs were equally likely to have sex while they are teenagers as those who did not. Studying both participants and a control group of nonparticipants in such programs, the study showed that both groups had similar rates of abstinence and began engaging in sexual intercourse at about the same age. The study also showed similar rates of unprotected sex in each group. Critics of the study claim it examined only a fraction of the abstinence programs available, inferring that the results may not be representative.[27]

The pledge can become so much a part of one's identity that youth rewrite their sexual history to fit with their current pledge status. Rosenbaum (2006) found that 53 percent of pledgers who eventually have premarital sex deny ever having made a pledge. Kids who previously had sex but then made an abstinence pledge were four times more likely to deny ever having had sex than those who did not pledge. Apparently, identity does not always dictate behavior—behavior can actually shape identity.

POSITIVE DEVIANCE

Even though we've established that deviance is socially constructed, the word still typically has negative connotations: strange, weird, antisocial, nontraditional, and undesirable. Sociologists also often think of deviance in the negative sense, meaning behaviors and attributes that fail to conform to prevailing norms and trends. Yet we can all think of times when standing out from the crowd is a good thing, when challenging convention is rewarded and rebels are revered. For example, people who push for social change are often labeled deviant, but may eventually gain heroic status. Opponents of the civil rights movement labeled Martin Luther King, Jr., and his fellow activists "outside agitators," even "communists." As he upset the balance of power, King deviated from the norm, and his detractors vilified him. Yet we now celebrate civil rights activists as heroes and pioneers. The same could be said of women suffragettes or European civilians who opposed the Nazis by hiding Jews. Virginity pledgers live out many dominant cultural virtues: the sanctity of (heterosexual) marriage, sexual self-control, fidelity, religious faithfulness. Yet if premarital sex has in many ways become the norm, pledgers deviate from the norm, only in what many would call a "positive" way. In my work on the straight edge movement (Haenfler 2006) I note how, in many ways, these clean-living youth are overconforming to middle class values of self-control, sexual purity, and personal responsibility. Virginity pledgers follow this same pattern. In fact, organizations such as Atlanta-based Revolution Abstinence see themselves as seeking to "revive the world" and resisting the "world's view to determine how we should live."[28]

There has been an ongoing debate among sociologists who study deviance as to whether "positive" deviance is a useful concept or an oxymoron (Goode 1991). **Positive deviance** describes attributes or behaviors that surpass normal expectations and are evaluated favorably by a reference group. Take, for example, "overachievers" or "brown-nosers." They also deviate from the norm, yet they do so by *overconforming* to teachers' and parents' expectations. While adults may label them the "good kids," they still stand out, or deviate, from the norm. Supporters of the concept claim that if deviance, in part, means deviation from the norm, then our definition of deviance should encompass *all* types of deviance, whether positively or negatively judged by society. Opponents counter that including overconformity as deviance makes the concept too broad—if virtually anything (and anyone) can be deviant, the concept of deviance becomes useless (Best 2004). Plus, the reactions from authority figures to overconformity and nonconformity are often very different (Best and Luckenbill 1982; Goode 1994).

A. Heckert and D. M. Heckert (2002) have created a typology of deviance that incorporates both normative standards and how people react to deviance; their analysis examines both the "objective" deviant behavior or condition and the "subjective" reactions from others. In other words, they examine both how behavior compares to society's expectations and how people react when someone falls short of or exceeds those expectations. These different types of deviance, including negative deviance, rate-busting, deviance admiration, and positive deviance, are useful in bridging the debate over positive deviance.

Negative Deviance

"Negative deviance is any type of behavior or condition that the majority of a given group regards as unacceptable *and* that evokes a collective response of negative type or would evoke a collective negative response if detected" (ibid., 459, adapted from Tittle and Paternoster 2000). Sexual contact between adults and children is an example of negative deviance in the United States and many other cultures, as is the unprovoked killing of another person.

Rate-Busting

Rate-busting is when someone overconforms or surpasses norms but is judged negatively for doing so. Students who score much higher than average on an exam ("curve-busters") surpass their professor's expectations but risk hard feelings from other students. Workers on an assembly line who work harder or faster than others are rate-busting by overconforming to the company's norms, but the other workers will likely react negatively.

Deviance Admiration

Deviance admiration refers to nonconformity that others judge positively. A whistleblower who reports corruption in her or his corporation would be breaking the norms of loyalty to the employer but might be hailed as a brave, righteous person in the media. Sometimes outlaws earn admiration if, for example, people see them as defying an unjust system.

Positive Deviance

As described in the beginning of this section, positive deviance entails overconformity that is judged positively, exceeding society's expectations in ways that people generally admire. Extraordinary acts of charity and self-sacrifice fall into this category. Another example of positive deviance is very attractive people—those who, by society's standards, exceed the norms of appearance.

When applied to virginity pledgers, Heckert and Heckert's typology shows just how much deviance depends upon context; as they suggest, "The same behavior and conditions can result in either positive or negative evaluations, or both simultaneously" (2002, 468). If everyone in a given context expects that teens will have sex, they may respond to pledgers with deviance admiration—the kids are not conforming and others judge them positively. However, if pledgers are simply upholding the abstinence expectations of their community, we could call their behavior positive deviance—they are overconforming by following the prevailing norm *and* by making their pledge public. If we look to pledgers' nonpledging peer groups, we might draw different conclusions. Other teens might judge pledgers negatively as rate-busters, mocking their "goodness" or believing they are "holier than thou." Thus these categories, while useful, still require that we understand the context in which behaviors are being judged.

SOCIAL CONTROL THEORY OF DEVIANCE

Like most societies, the United States has tried to regulate and control sex by passing a variety of laws: statutory rape laws and child abuse laws, for example, are meant to dissuade adults from having sex with minors, and until relatively recently several states still had anti-sodomy laws designed to criminalize homosexual sex. The assumption is that people have impulses that need to be controlled. The **social control theory of deviance** (Hirschi 1969) presumes that some activities labeled deviant are actually tempting and even enjoyable to many people. People generally seek their own short-term gratification, but we are socialized to control our impulses. In fact, rather than asking why people are deviant, we might ask why people follow rules that curb their own selfish gratification. Those with low self-control are more likely to engage in deviant or criminal behavior (Gottfredson and Hirschi 1990). For example, activities that many adults enjoy, such as drinking, sex, smoking, and gambling, are prohibited to youth. However, because youth might also enjoy such activities, adults feel they must *control* adolescents' impulses. Without learning self-control, more youth would engage in deviant behavior. In fact, according to this theory, social control, or more specifically people's "bond" to society, is the main factor keeping many people from being deviant. Strong social attachments dissuade people from breaking the rules. Many factors can serve as agents of social control: parents, teachers, peers, coaches, extracurricular activities, jobs, and other responsibilities.

Whether or not someone engages in deviance depends at least in part on their attachments to others, their involvement in legitimate society, and their investment in their nondeviant identity. For Hirschi (1969), there are four elements of people's social bonds: attachment, commitment, involvement, and belief. **Attachment** is the degree to which an individual has relationships with people who (explicitly or implicitly) promote normative behavior, such as being married or part of a family. Weak attachment to others means fewer people to disappoint or betray through deviance. Likewise, strong attachment means more people to let down by deviant acts. **Commitment** entails being committed to society's rules because you have access to the means of achieving a bright future, such as a good education and/or a career. If you feel like society offers you good opportunities and ample chances to get ahead and lead a meaningful life, why jeopardize that with deviant behavior? Believing that the costs of deviance outweigh the potential risks promotes conformity—if you are worried that engaging in deviance might threaten your career, you might choose a different course of action. **Involvement** in "conventional" activities such as work, sports, or extracurricular clubs keeps many people out of trouble—they simply do not have the time and energy to devote to deviant pursuits. Raising children is especially time intensive and explains in part why most mothers are unlikely to engage in criminal activity. **Belief** in conventional social values and authority figures also promotes conformity and inhibits deviance. The less you believe in the rules, the more likely you are to violate them.

For a variety of reasons, young people, especially young men, are most likely to be deviant and to commit the most crime. Social control theory suggests that part of the reason is that young people have less attachment to their communities, fewer commitments, less involvement in "adult" responsibilities, and are less likely to genuinely believe in the social values many people take for granted.

In the case of virginity pledgers, most have an *attachment* to their families, religious communities, and their fellow abstainers. Having a church, youth group, and peers that will look down upon you for having premarital sex increases the cost of having sex compared to someone without such connections. Most pledgers also have a *commitment* to society, likely feeling they have bright futures and in fact that premarital sex may imperil their futures. They (and many other youth) are taught that an unplanned pregnancy or an STD could hurt their chances of going to college and starting a career, getting married, and beginning a family. For some, *involvement* in church, family, and youth group activities (as well as other typical activities) keeps them too busy to "hang out" and associate with kids who might encourage deviant behavior. Finally, and perhaps most importantly, pledgers *believe* in the ideal of reserving sex for married couples and they generally believe in the adults who support them (such as their religious leaders and leaders of abstinence organizations). Yet these beliefs, in the absence of the other elements of social control, would likely not be enough to sustain pledgers' commitments. Their supportive communities hold them accountable. However, even those communities are not enough to keep most pledgers from having sex in the long term— sex, after all, can be enjoyable and hardly seems deviant to many youth.

CONCLUSION

Sex is perhaps the scariest, most exciting, and most contentious part of growing up. Virginity pledgers counter the "sex, drugs, and rock-n-roll" image many people have of youth subcultures by making a public commitment to postpone sex until marriage. They exemplify positive deviance, showing that sometimes society rewards, rather than stigmatizes, standing out from the crowd. However, pledgers also feel like their peers stigmatize *virginity* and so attempt to reframe abstinence as cool, as *resistance* to cultural norms. They illustrate that even something as seemingly straightforward as sexual identity is actually socially constructed and filled with different meanings: straight, gay, and virgin have more flexible and fluid meanings than we might think. We can't take the meanings of sexuality for granted any more than we can the constructions of deviance. It makes you wonder, should you have children, how will predominate meanings of sexuality have changed by the time they are teens?

Virginity pledgers' strong religious beliefs and affiliations also set them apart from most other groups in this book. While most punks, skinheads, and heavy metal kids question organized religion, for pledgers faith reinforces their beliefs about premarital sex. The social control theory of deviance raises the idea that deviance can be pleasurable, people are often impulsive, and without supportive social networks and a belief in the rules, many will engage in deviant behaviors. Religious organizations may, for a time, serve as agents of social control. Yet the fact that most pledgers do not wait until marriage to have sex shows that managing young people's sexuality is no easy task.

DISCUSSION

- How would you describe the sexual "climate" in your high school or on your campus? Do you think abstinence programs are helpful or harmful?
- What are some examples of heterocentrism in your school, workplace, and community?
- What is the evidence that the dominant sexual script has changed in the last thirty years? What is the evidence of resistance to such change?
- Describe some examples of how the cultural script is different in other countries.

KEY IDEAS

Compulsory heterosexuality: The notion that heterosexuality is pushed or enforced by society rather than being simply a natural inclination. We are intentionally socialized toward heterosexuality.

Deviance admiration: Nonconformity that others judge positively.

"Deviant" sexuality: Any sexual practice socially defined as strange, unacceptable, unlawful, or unnatural. Despite a widespread cultural belief in "natural" (heterosexual) sexuality, the meanings of sexuality are socially constructed.

Heterocentrism: The notion that heterosexuality is "normal" and "natural" whereas homosexuality is "abnormal." We generally take heterosexuality for granted.

Heterosexism: Prejudice and discrimination against homosexuals.

Heterosexual privilege: Privileges and opportunities straight people have that lesbians and gay men do not.

Homophobia: Fear, stereotyping, or even hatred of homosexuals or homosexuality.

Negative deviance: Behavior that breaks generally agreed upon social norms and evokes a negative collective response from most of society.

Positive deviance: Overconformity that society generally judges positively; exceeding society's expectations in ways that people generally admire.

Rate-busting: Overconformity that society generally judges negatively.

Sexuality: The culturally defined ways in which we express and experience ourselves as sexual beings. The socially constructed meanings of sex and gender, including the norms, beliefs, traditions, and taboos related to sex.

Sexual identity: How people name their sexual attractions and experience of sexuality. Sexual identities, including the labels "gay," "straight," and "virgin," are socially constructed.

Social control theory of deviance: A theory suggesting that people are generally selfish and impulsive but learn self-control. Those who fail to learn self-control are most likely to engage in deviant or criminal behavior. People with strong social networks and bonds to others are less likely to break social norms.

Attachment—degree to which an individual has relationships with people who (explicitly or implicitly) promote normative behavior.

Commitment—obeying society's rules because you have access to the means of achieving a good future, such as educational opportunities and a career.

Involvement—participation in "conventional" activities (work, social clubs, raising children) raises the costs of deviant behavior, making such behavior less likely.

Belief—believing in conventional social values and authority figures promotes conformity and inhibits deviance.

RESOURCES

Body Piercing Saved My Life: Inside the Phenomenon of Christian Rock

By Andrew Beaujon. 2006. Cambridge, MA: Da Capo Press.

A journalist's look at the seemingly improbable combination of rock music and Christianity.

Forbidden Fruit: Sex & Religion in the Lives of American Teenagers

By Mark D Regnerus. 2009. New York: Oxford.

An empirical examination of the connections between religion and sex among youth, including a chapter specifically on virginity pledges.

Righteous: Dispatches from the Evangelical Youth Movement

By Lauren Sandler. 2006. New York: Viking.

Examines the Christian "counterculture," including how youth meld religion, pop culture, and politics.

Wannabes, Goths, and Christians: The Boundaries of Sex, Style, and Status

By Amy C. Wilkins. 2008. Chicago: University of Chicago Press.

An ethnographic comparison of three youth groups, including their beliefs about and practice of sexuality.

SilverRingThing

www.silverringthing.com

Site for one of the largest and most popular virginity pledge organizations.

True Love Waits

www.truelovewaits.com

Another popular pledge organization.

~/&

CHAPTER 7

Goth—Stigma and Stigma Management

In 2003, at the urging of U.S. Rep. Sam Graves, the federal U.S. government gave Blue Springs, Missouri, a $273,000 grant to study goths in order to prevent violence to themselves or others.[29] The grant came during the ongoing aftermath of the 1999 Columbine High School massacre in Littleton, Colorado, in which two young men who commonly dressed in black clothing and trenchcoats killed fifteen people, including themselves. Mistakenly identified by the media and authorities as goths, the incident fueled hysteria around subcultures, sparking a moral entrepreneurial campaign to monitor and manage countercultural youth (Kilpatrick 2004). Although most school shooters have been average-looking, fairly conventional boys rather than members of subcultures, the public, desperate for answers, points to music, media, and alternative culture as the culprits behind youth violence. Just as the hippies, skinheads, and metalheads mystified their elders and came to symbolize everything wrong with society, so current subcultures like goth signify the decline of decency and moral values.

Segments of society have always stigmatized subculturists for their appearance and values, and goths especially have faced more than their share of misunderstanding and mistrust. In this chapter I give some background into the history of goth and its many forms. Then I explain how members manage being a part of a stigmatized identity before moving to a discussion of gender in the goth scene, particularly its focus on androgyny. The chapter ends with a discussion of how goth is organized into loosely connected scenes.

INTRODUCING GOTH

Rather than popping up out of nowhere, new subcultures often emerge from the ashes of the old, recycling some aspects of previous scenes and replacing others. Goth emerged in the early 1980s in Britain from what was left of the original punk movement (Hodkinson 2002). Performers such as David Bowie, Joy Division, and Siouxsie and the Banshees provided early inspiration for what would become goth-themed music (Goodlad and Bibby 2007). Siouxsie Sioux set the tone for goth style with her black hair and heavy makeup, but the Bauhaus song "Bela

Lugosi's Dead" was the most influential song in the fledgling scene.[30] Its melancholic, dreary sound and lyrics about the undead foreshadowed a variety of other favorite goth bands including The Mission, Southern Death Cult, and especially the influential Sisters of Mercy. The scene gained in popularity until the mid-1990s with bands such as Lycia and Faith and the Muse, but eventually popular interest declined. However, a strong scene exists today, and while goth music has branched into various styles, much of it maintains a dark, foreboding vibe with deep vocals and horror-influenced lyrics. Goth has overlapped with a variety of other music scenes (Introvigne 2002). Early punk bands such as The Damned and the Cramps were influences, as were the Misfits, who wore skulls, black clothing, dark eye makeup, and dyed black hair and often sang about gruesome topics such as murder. Toward 2000, goth-punk band AFI merged a gothic look with a pop punk sound, showing that even decades later the punk–goth connection lives on. Finnish "love metal" band HIM has also appropriated goth style, as has Italy's Lacuna Coil and Theatres des Vampires. Perhaps there is no such thing as a "new" subculture, as each group emerges in a social context influenced by those who came before.

Goth's distinguishing feature is its focus on death and the macabre (ghastly, ghoulish). Members embody "glamorous, and usually feminine, forms of the somber, the sinister, and the macabre" (Hodkinson 2004, 131). In the Western cultures in which goth is most prominent, death is a taboo subject to be feared and avoided. The goth scene is a space where participants can safely play with death and have fun with the darker sides of human existence. Contrary to public perception, most goths are neither obsessively depressed nor perpetually grumpy. In fact, most lead relatively healthy, normal lives.

Like members of most youth scenes, goths revel in their difference, constructing themselves as "freaks" who consciously reject the mainstream. Yet despite their efforts at uniqueness, they are not necessarily so different from many of their peers: "they scare adults, command social distance from their peers, and create a community in which they get to claim membership, but also get to hang out, develop intimate relationships, and have sex" (Wilkins 2005, 2). They push no political agenda, insisting only on respect for individuality and a tolerance for diversity, and they claim no single religious affiliation, with some being completely secular and other pursuing various spiritual paths.

Goths are perhaps most known for their dark, grim style characterized by black clothing, black hair, black eyeliner, and, well, pretty much black everything. While some may be virtually indistinguishable from their peers, many use (black) makeup to highlight the lips and eyes, starkly contrasting a pale face (sometimes accentuated with white foundation), creating a pallid, skull-like appearance. Both sexes wear makeup, often including painting the fingernails black. Piercings of all kinds are prevalent, as are fishnet stockings and shirts. Religious symbols are popular, particularly the Christian cross and Egyptian Ankh, though valued more in an ironic sense rather than for their intended religious meanings. Goths insist there is no singular way to define goth, and they dislike stereotypes that pigeonhole them into pre-packaged caricatures.[31] While there is no overarching or mandatory style of goth, these common themes consistently reoccur.

In addition to being a music-based scene, goth draws influences from popular culture as well, especially horror fiction and films. Anne Rice's series of romantic novels featuring Lestat, a charming but brooding vampire, have been an inspiration for many goths. Movies such as *Bram Stoker's Dracula* and *Interview With a Vampire* (based on Rice's book) exemplify dark yet sexy and romantic characters. *The Crow* and *The Matrix* featured black leather costumes, industrial music, and characters with pale countenances, and Tim Burton's animated film *The Nightmare Before Christmas* offers a macabre take on a joyful holiday—Jack, the gaunt, skeleton-like main character, has become an icon among some goths. Other Burton films, such as *Edward Scissorhands, Beetlejuice, Sleepy Hollow,* and *The Corpse Bride*, all tales of misunderstood outsiders, resonate with many goths, and *The Rocky Horror Picture Show* is a cult classic with great appeal.

Pinning down one coherent goth style or ideology is difficult, as goths come in many shapes and sizes and hold many different beliefs. Beyond a general fascination with the darker side of life (and death), goths have many interests. Many goths feel an affinity for the past and enjoy enacting an anachronistic version of goth. Anachronism describes something that comes from or seemingly belongs in a different time period. Romantic goths draw inspiration from the past; imagine an undead lord and lady from nineteenth-century England. Women wear Victorian dresses or corsets with lace and flowing skirts while men sport Edwardian coats with ruffled cuffs. Cyber goths (sometimes overlapping with cyberpunks), on the other hand, inspired by films such as *The Matrix*, look to the future, wearing more futuristic clothing and enjoying science fiction. Dark sunglasses, neon accessories, and large-soled shoes are common, as is a general interest in technology. Cyber clubs play more electronic dance music and less gothic rock and metal. That goths look to both the past and the future for inspiration shows the diversity of the scene.

In the 1990s other goths ventured into a more industrial style, following Trent Reznor's project Nine Inch Nails, wearing metal clasps and Doc Marten boots. Industrial rock music features heavy, thumping beats, often at breakneck speeds. Popular industrial bands, past and present, with a goth following include KMFDM, Skinny Puppy, Ministry, The Birthday Massacre, and Combichrist. "Fetish" goths sport dog collars, rubber pants, and bondage gear. While some goths wanted nothing to do with metal, others bridged the gap with Type O Negative, Marilyn Manson, and black metal bands mentioned in Chapter 5.

A minority of goths take a stronger fascination with vampires, wearing fangs and dribbling fake blood down their chins. More traditional goths tend to find the practice silly at best and playing into popular stereotypes at worst (Hodkinson 2002, 46). Finally, another faction of goths combine their gothic style with club culture, accenting their black attire with brighter colors and listening to music with less melancholy and faster beats. Sometimes called "candy goths," their cheery appearance belies the ironic combination of macabre and childlike innocence.

STIGMA

Despite their diverse interests and styles, goths typically share a common experience of feeling like outsiders, in one way or another. After the Columbine shootings the group faced increasing stigma from school administrators, parents, and even law enforcement. Perhaps you have read Nathaniel Hawthorne's novel *The Scarlet Letter*, in which authorities mark Hester Prynne, an adulterous woman in seventeenth-century Boston, with a red letter "A," signifying shame and disgrace to the public. People henceforth treat her with suspicion and hostility, causing her great trouble. The scarlet letter is a symbol of the *stigma* she carries for violating the norms of the community. Such a stigmatized identity carries sanctions, making life uncomfortable or even unbearable. Like Hester Prynne, goths are often stigmatized by the rest of the society, reinforcing their outsider status.

Erving Goffman (1963) wrote about stigma as a social phenomenon rather than simply an individual trait. A **stigma** is a discrediting attribute or mark of disgrace that leads others to see us as untrustworthy, incompetent, or tainted. Stigmas can change our entire self-concept and identity. Goffman identified three main categories of stigma: physical disfigurements (such as missing an ear); individual character flaws (like drug addiction); and membership in a "tainted" group (for example, based upon race, religion, or ethnicity). There are many contemporary examples of stigmatized characteristics and identities: gay men with AIDS (Sandstrom 1990) and women with STDs (Nack 2000); teenage pregnancy; eating disorders; people with physical disabilities; ex-convicts; people who receive welfare; and both rapists and rape victims, to name but a few. People of color, Jews, and lesbians and gay men face stigmas based upon stereotypes. Mental illness, though increasingly understood as a medical condition, is still generally stigmatized. In one way or another, we *all* walk the line between stigma and "normalcy," managing others' impressions of us and avoiding stigmatized labels.

For Goffman, people with a stigmatized identity are either "the discreditable" or "the discredited." The **discreditable** include people with deviant characteristics they are able to hide (such as sexual fetishists), while the **discredited** have either been revealed or are unable to conceal their stigma (such as people who use a wheelchair). Sometimes the discreditable become the discredited when their deviance is uncovered. For example, corrupt politicians who take bribes from lobbyists quickly lose public support when their dealings come to light. A goth who hides her or his goth identity at work is discreditable but when spotted in gothic attire by a coworker becomes discredited.

Remember that stigma, like deviance in general, is socially constructed, that is, it is based upon socially created meanings rather than universal and absolute rules. A stigmatizing characteristic in one culture might be completely normal in another. Stretched earlobes signify beauty among some tribal cultures but are discrediting in others. Teen pregnancy is the norm in some cultures but is frowned upon in the United States and stigmatized as a social problem. Often stigmas entail stereotypes and falsehoods based on relatively trivial characteristics. For example, being born with red hair has socially constructed (and stigmatized) meanings, sometimes of beauty and sexiness, but often of strangeness or awkwardness (D. M. Heckert and Best 1997). Sometimes stigma is related to gender. For women, being a redhead can be sexy, whereas for men it's considered rather unsexy.

Some theorists propose that powerful people or groups (often moral entrepreneurs) stigmatize less powerful groups for political or economic gain, even promoting a culture of fear to take minds off of more significant responsibilities/ problems (Edelman 1988; Glassner 1999). A **culture of fear** describes a society in which people regularly suffer a variety of worries emerging from the media, moral entrepreneurs, advocacy groups, and political and religious leaders. Killer mold, shark attacks, cyber-predators, murderous moms, drug addicts, identity thieves, diseased food, and aggressive bees are just a few threats we feel a need to guard against. The sensationalism with which the media reports social problems (such as crime) ensures that fears often far outweigh the actual risks. Take school shootings, for example. Even when violence in schools is declining, media reports of an event often leave people believing an isolated event is part of a growing trend and that homicidal kids are everywhere (Glassner 1999). A critical, or conflict, perspective suggests that perhaps moral panics serve to distract the public from other, potentially more meaningful, problems (Edelman 1988). Recall from Chapter 1 that the **conflict theory of deviance** suggests that powerful groups define deviance to serve their own interests, including stigmatizing and controlling less powerful groups. It is easier for adults to create school dress codes and other rules targeted toward goths than to examine larger social problems behind school violence. For example, if one were to weigh the relative social costs of extreme poverty versus heavy metal, it would be difficult to argue that metal plays a greater role in social disorder, crime, malnutrition, or premature death than poverty. Likewise, blaming goths or the much-maligned Marilyn Manson for school shootings takes the focus off of the preponderance of guns in U.S. society and a general uneasiness about the deficiency of social support for children. Yet, as Rep. Graves demonstrates, politicians frequently stoke public fears (and thereby gain support and votes) by blaming stigmatized groups for any number of social "problems," whether "moral decay" or the decline in "family values." Thus it is important to note that power often plays a significant role in the determination of which groups and characteristics are stigmatized and which are not. Goths, having relatively little individual or collective power, make easy scapegoats, serving as folk devils in a culture of fear.

STIGMA MANAGEMENT TECHNIQUES

Once stigmatized, a person faces the work of somehow managing the stigma, developing strategies for interacting with others that minimize teasing, shunning, violence, or other unwanted sanctions. Perhaps you have tried to cover up acne with makeup or other skin products, avoided associating with "unpopular" people, or bought stylish clothes to appear as if you are of a higher social class than that to which you belong. All of these are examples of stigma management.

Stigma management is the process of avoiding, concealing, or masking a stigmatized identity. Assuming that most people have ties to conventional society and desire to avoid shame and judgment, they must somehow neutralize their stigma and/or justify their deviance (Sykes and Matza 1957). We often suggest to others that we have a higher or more "positive" status than we actually do have. Goffman and others have identified a number of stigma management techniques.

Stigma Management Techniques

- **Normalization:** We use normalization in an effort to avoid a stigmatized label by hiding our deviant acts or attributes and maintaining a conventional presentation of self. For example, an intellectual might hide his love of professional wrestling or NASCAR by saying it is a "guilty pleasure" for fear of being viewed as lowbrow by his intellectual friends.

- **Neutralization:** Sometimes we accept our actions being labeled deviant but give an explanation why we should not be labeled deviant for engaging in the act. Imagine an environmental activist who drives a gas-guzzling car pointing out that she was given the car or explaining that she very rarely drives. She knows her environmentalist friends might see her actions as deviant and hypocritical, so she readies a response to neutralize the stigma.

- **Passing:** Passing involves putting forth an appearance or identity that implies we have different characteristics from our actual status, so we avoid being stigmatized by others. Examples include gays and lesbians passing as straight or people hiding an illness or disease.

- **Covering:** Covering requires changing aspects of our appearance or presentation of self to disguise a characteristic that will elicit a negative response from people. Covering includes concealing facial blemishes with makeup or making excuses for an alcoholic family member's behavior.

- **Insulating:** Insulating involves avoiding stigma by carefully limiting our interactions or affiliations with others. We put others (such as family, friends, members of a support group) between us and the stigmatized identity. An example might be a goth who only socializes with other goths to avoid being put down by others. A member of the College Democrats might associate primarily with members of liberal student groups.

- **Distancing:** Distancing is a way of avoiding stigma by separating ourselves from roles, associations, or institutions that imply stigmatized identities. For example, kids who want to avoid being labeled a "nerd" might try not to look too smart by shunning groups labeled geeky or intelligent. When parents warn their kids to stay away from certain groups, they are worried their kids will be "guilty by association."

- **Embracement:** As the name suggests, embracement is a strategy of openly claiming a stigmatized characteristic, fashioning it into a positive identity. A lesbian activist and a member of the National Association for the Advancement of Fat Acceptance have each embraced their stigmatized identity.

We all practice stigma management at one time or another, but goths and adherents of many subcultures engage in it consistently. A goth might *pass* as a "normal" at work by wearing conventional clothes, making sure to *cover* tattoos. Clearly many subculturists *embrace* their stigmatized identity, as when goths proudly display their style in public, often reframing the stigma as a symbol of pride and defiance. They also seek to maintain status among their subcultural peers. Thus a goth may *distance* herself from jocks to maintain her status as an outsider. A black metal kid who goes to church might *neutralize* to his friends by claiming his parents force him to go. Finally, many people *insulate* themselves from goths to avoid all of the stigmas we've discussed.

We manage stigma and communicate our "normal" status through **symbolic imagery**, the verbal and nonverbal cues we use to establish our normalcy. Goffman (1963) claimed that we employ three types of symbolic imagery—prestige symbols, stigma symbols, and disidentifiers. **Prestige symbols** convey socially desirable traits like being honorable, wealthy, or honest and draw attention away from a stigmatized attribute. For example, a woman with unusually large feet might wear expensive, glamorous jewelry to focus attention away from her feet. After the 9/11 attacks, especially, politicians and newscasters wore U.S. flag pins to communicate their patriotism, a socially desirable trait in the best of times but especially relevant during the buildup to the invasions of Afghanistan and Iraq. In addition to employing prestige symbols, we also try to avoid **stigma symbols** that draw unwanted attention to a stigmatized attribute. An elderly man may resist using a cane for fear of being seen as weak or infirm. A Southerner at a New York high society event may hide her accent to avoid negative assumptions associated with being from the South. We also use **disidentifiers** to distract people from noticing stigma, helping us pass or cover. Imagine someone earning poverty-level wages who wears expensive name-brand clothing—the stylish clothes mask the person's true social class.

In the goth scene, maintaining a goth Web site or wearing a particularly creative and unique piece of jewelry could be prestige symbols. Spiders, pentagrams, inverted crosses, and pagan symbols are common accessories, and less conventional items such as hose clamps and dog collars show up from time to time. Self-described "authentic" goths tend to frown upon mass-produced goth accessories available at Hot Topic, making such things stigma symbols in the scene and calling the trend "mallgoth." Other goths, occasionally labeled "Tuesday goths" by their more committed counterparts, dress up for the club on Tuesday night but resume their "straight" or "vanilla" appearance as they return to their conventional lives. Such goths might employ disidentifiers like conservative or colorful clothing to conceal their deviant identity to their coworkers and nongoth friends.

Being an "outsider," embracing a stigmatized identity, can be empowering—clearly no one *has* to be goth; they *choose* this stigmatized identity for any number of reasons. Yet managing stigma often comes at great personal cost. The **challenges of stigma management** can include strained relationships and the stress of being "in the closet." Sometimes subculturists feel pinched between the demands of the scene and their work or family lives. Trying to sustain one's "scene cred" while avoiding stigmas outside the scene can be tough. Yet other, more "full-time," goths may question Tuesday goths' and mallgoths' authenticity and commitment to the scene. Ultimately this tension results in many people leaving youth scenes.

GENDER-BENDING AND SEXUAL PLAY

Previous chapters showed how cultures create unwritten "rules" of gender, dividing masculine and feminine behaviors, and that those who bend or break norms of gender and sexuality often face especially harsh sanctions. In your own school you may have witnessed how kids treated boys labeled "too feminine" or girls labeled "too masculine." Consequently, we put forth a masculine or feminine performance to avoid being judged "gay" or "girly" as boys or as a "butch" or "dyke" as girls. Some people join subcultures, including goth, in part to challenge or avoid rigid mainstream notions of what it means to be men and women. Goth in particular creates a space for experimenting with gender and sexual identities (Wilkins 2004).

Contrary to many subcultures, goth appears to have nearly equal numbers of men and women (Gunn 2007). The scene is much more open to women than the hardcore, metal, and skinhead scenes. Goths claim to value androgyny, promoting an "ideology of genderlessness" (Brill 2008, 37) that they view as more tolerant and enlightened than the mainstream. **Androgyny** involves displaying both feminine and masculine characteristics, yet the goth scene extends this luxury almost exclusively to men. Many goth men engage in **gender-bending**, or playing with what it means to be a man or woman, challenging conventional gender expectations. As we saw with punk and with some female rappers, subcultures can challenge the accepted norms of femininity and masculinity. Goth's generally feminine aesthetic created a space for men to express themselves in ways considered taboo by the larger culture (Hodkinson 2002). Wearing makeup and long hair, having a quiet, soft-spoken, or demure demeanor, and occasionally wearing skirts, women's tank tops, and fishnet are clear example of gender-bending, as is the value placed upon less masculine (muscular) physiques. Some goth men even adopt girlish personas such as wearing pigtails or carrying a stuffed animal (Wilkins 2005). Whereas the dominant masculine script calls for men to avoid showing emotions considered feminine, the goth scene fosters broader emotional expression and connection between males.

Goth women appreciate being in a setting where unwanted advances from men are less common. They advocate respect of one another's personal space and frown on the unannounced touching and even groping sometimes common at other clubs. Yet the goth scene provides women with a space to resist "passive" femininity and engage in "active sexuality" (Wilkins 2004). Like straight edge women, goth women believe their scene affords them greater independence from men and control over their sexuality. They feel sexy despite looking and dressing somewhat differently than what is typically seen as sexy. Goth women also report feeling more free to experiment with their sexuality, including having multiple partners without being negatively judged. Some goths engage in polyamory, the practice of forming meaningful, open, intimate, honest, and ideally loving sexual relationships between more than two people (ibid.). While girls are typically believed and expected to have less sexual desire than boys, goth women tend to be more open about their sexual desires and enjoyment of sex.

However, goths' version of gender egalitarianism still, in some ways, essentializes masculine and feminine roles: "The compulsion for women to dress sexily and to be sexually available, the continued objectification of women as recipients of predatory and critical male and female gazes, and the maintenance of gendered double standards in individual sexual relationships" (ibid, 329). While goths reward male androgyny, "hyperfemininity" is the norm for women, encouraging a "cult of femininity for both sexes" (Brill 2008, 41). The men rebel while the women strive for beauty, albeit with a darker edge. The women may feel like they are making a "free choice" to wear corsets to clubs, choosing to perform femininity in their own way. But the fact that many, if not most, women perform a "sexy" femininity shows that choosing how we perform our gender is not truly a free choice (Lorber 1994; A. Levy 2005), and sexual freedom for women may benefit men more as they have greater access to women without having to relinquish any power. On top of that, in focusing on sexual freedom, goth women fail to challenge broader gender inequalities such as employment or family issues (Wilkins 2004). All of this shows how male privilege and sexual double standards are deeply embedded in our culture and, yes, our subcultures. So is their resistance meaningful or illusory? Is the freedom to dress sexy really freedom? This is a very difficult question, and one that other subcultures have wrestled with as well.

GOTH SCENES

Both scholars and subculturists commonly describe subcultures as "scenes" (J. Irwin 1977; Straw 1991; A. Bennett and Kahn-Harris 2004), often referring to a subculture based in a specific location, although post-subculture theory suggests that *scene* connotes a diffuse, often temporary social grouping with porous boundaries. Your town or city may have a variety of scenes, from slam-poetry and indie rock, to gaming and jazz. You might even talk about the local "bar scene" or "frat scene." But, like the term "subculture," the meaning of scene is not always clear, especially when so much subcultural interaction takes place online and between different geographical locations—the "punk scene," for example, transcends any one town, state, and even country (see Haenfler 2006). Therefore, a scene encompasses much more than location, and being part of a scene does not necessarily require face-to-face contact (Straw 1991). **Local scenes**, or consistent groupings formed around a specific location, exist within translocal scenes, which are more geographically dispersed. **Translocal scenes** are connected "rather abstractly, through shared tastes...and quite concretely through social and economic networks" (Kruse 1993, 33). The abstract connections include *identity* and *tastes*. Goths, for example, likely feel more connected to goths in other cities and regions than to nongoths in their local area—there is a shared identity that transcends place. Part of that shared identity comes from common and familiar tastes. While each local goth scene has its own idiosyncrasies, the music, clothes, and style are similar from place to place and are even consistent between international scenes. A goth visiting another country will often recognize a fellow goth and feel a connection.

Translocal scenes are also tied together through *concrete* connections, especially travel, commerce, and media (Hodkinson 2002). Subculturists often travel to different scenes, such as Grateful Dead and Phish fans whose commitment to following their favorite bands created subcultures in themselves—Deadheads and Phans/Phishheads. The Whitby Gothic Weekend, a twice-yearly music festival in England, brings together fans from all over Britain and beyond, including bands from abroad. As goths travel, they share styles and develop translocal friendship networks. Commerce also plays a large role in fostering translocal community. Music and clothing retailers contribute to scene consistency by establishing and perpetuating the basic stylistic elements of goth identity. CD compilations featuring bands from various regions and countries expose goths to the diversity of the scene while associating bands under the goth genre. Finally, the media, including online discussion groups, zines, and flyers, connect members of the translocal scene and document goth history. As with many subcultures, the latest networking tool for goths has been the Internet (Mercer 2002; Hodkinson 2003). Hundreds of goth sites, both locally and translocally oriented, provide forums for goth interaction. Someone from small-town Iowa may not have the opportunity to attend goth clubs, but she or he can buy goth music and fashions online, join a discussion forum, and order goth zines.

The importance of translocal scenes in a "globalizing" world does not mean that local scenes are relics of the past. Indeed, many subculturists still experience their scene primarily in their local areas (A. Bennett 2000). Virtual connections often facilitate future face-to-face meetings rather than eliminating such interaction, and the Web is a primary resource for "off-line lifestyle" (Hodkinson 2002, 182). Furthermore, many youth take pride in their "hometown" scene, and local scenes often develop distinct reputations and histories of their own. Straight edge and hardcore kids often connect their city to their scene, as in "New York Hardcore" or "Boston Straight Edge" (Haenfler 2006). However, in increasingly mobile, technologically advanced, hypermediated societies, thinking of scenes in purely local terms doesn't capture the complexity in any subculture. With a little research, you would discover goths in Brazil, Australia, Japan, Italy, South Africa, and dozens of other countries.[32] While each of these scenes certainly has its own flavor, they also have a good deal in common. They share identity tastes through concrete connections such as the Internet and music.

CONCLUSION

Goth has endured factionalizing, fluctuating popularity, and decades of social changes to become one of the longest running contemporary subcultures. Goths have been stigmatized for their grim appearances and macabre interests and occasionally have been used as modern-day folk devils, pieces of a culture of fear around youth violence. Goths manage their stigma through a variety of techniques, forming communities within the transnational goth scene where difference is a source of pride. Their uncommon attitudes regarding gender, sexuality, and death challenge some very deep-seated cultural beliefs, making them particularly easy targets for moral entrepreneurs.

We are all prone to judging others, and we have all been judged. Most of us can remember a time when we were teased or excluded for looking different, having the "wrong" clothes, or not belonging to the cool group. Studying stigma reminds us that the characteristics upon which we are judged are socially constructed—our interpretations of subcultural styles and practices are neither fixed nor God-given. Thinking sociologically about stigmatized groups can help us question who sets the "rules," who benefits by stigmatizing a group, and how stigma feeds the larger culture of fear surrounding youth.

DISCUSSION

- Discuss some examples of formerly stigmatized identities, beliefs, or behaviors that have since gained greater acceptance. What changed?
- Which stigma management techniques have you used in order to manage others' impression of you?
- How are goths' and other subculturists' challenges to conventional displays of gender and sexuality used by moral entrepreneurs to contribute to a "culture of fear" around sex?

KEY IDEAS

Androgyny: The simultaneous presentation of both feminine and masculine characteristics.

Culture of fear: A society in which people worry about a variety of social problems fueled by the media. Fears often far outweigh the actual risks. The constant warnings about various threats that are outside individual control lead to a state of generalized fear in which people feel insecure and ill-equipped to control their lives.

The discreditable: People with stigmatized characteristics they are able to hide, at least for the time being.

The discredited: People who are unable to conceal their stigmatized characteristic or whose deviance has been revealed.

Disidentifier: Symbolic imagery used to distract people from noticing stigma, helping us pass or cover.

Gender-bending: Challenging the dominant conventions of masculine and feminine appearance, fashion, and behavior, often with the goals of both personal satisfaction and political statement.

Local scenes: Consistent social groups tied to a specific location, such as the Birmingham goth scene.

Prestige symbol: Symbolic imagery that conveys socially desirable traits like being honorable, wealthy, or honest. A fancy sports car could be a prestige symbol.

Stigma: A discrediting attribute or mark of disgrace that leads others to see us as untrustworthy, incompetent, or tainted. Goffman's three main categories of stigma include physical disfigurements, individual character flaws, and membership in a "tainted" group.

Stigma management: The process of avoiding, concealing, or masking a stigmatized identity. Common stigma management techniques include normalization, neutralization, passing, covering, insulating, distancing, and embracement.

Stigma symbol: Symbolic imagery that draws unwanted attention to a stigmatized attribute. We generally seek to avoid stigma symbols.

Symbolic imagery: The verbal and nonverbal cues we use to communicate our "normal" status, including prestige symbols, stigma symbols, and disidentifiers.

Translocal scenes: Social groups connected by shared interests, tastes, styles, and economic and communication networks rather than through geographical proximity.

RESOURCES

Goth Culture: Gender, Sexuality and Style

By Dunja Brill. 2008. Oxford: Berg.

Very interesting insider research focused especially on the gender and sexual dynamics of the goth scene.

Goth: Identity, Style and Subculture

By Paul Hodkinson. 2002. Oxford: Berg.

A great study of goths conducted and written by an insider.

Goths: A Guide to an American Subculture

By Micah L. Issitt. 2011. Santa Barbara, CA: Greenwood.

A brief introduction to goth, particularly in the U.S. context.

Goth's Dark Empire

By Carol Siegel. 2005. Bloomington, IN: Indiana University Press.

Another interesting study of goth culture, particularly its resistance to contemporary sexual norms.

Goth: Undead Subculture

Edited by Lauren M. E. Goodlad and Michael Bibby. 2007. Durham and London: Duke University Press.

A collection of scholarly articles by academics from a variety of disciplines.

VampireFreaks.com

http://vampirefreaks.com

A comprehensive site for all things dark and gloomy, featuring member profiles, music pages, clothing stores, forums, and pictures.

Goth.net

www.goth.net

Another site full of active discussion forums, art, and writing by goths.

CHAPTER **8**

∽

Gamers, Hackers, and Facebook— Computer Cultures, Virtual Community, and Postmodern Identity

If you are a typical college-age person, you might have difficulty recalling a time before video games, downloaded music, and DVDs, let alone a time before personal computers. From smartphones and iTunes to video games and the Internet, computers play a role in nearly every aspect of our lives. New technologies have spawned new subcultures and given established subcultures a new arena in which to interact. Immersive fantasy games such as *World of Warcraft* allow players to become heroes in fanciful realms, and *Second Life* enables residents to own virtual land, run virtual businesses, and even attend virtual concerts performed by real-life musicians. Message boards and e-mail lists connect music fans, help social activists network, and bring together people of every possible interest, from bird watching to sports. Blogs enable amateur journalists a forum to write (or rant) about politics, religion, and pop culture, and chat rooms serve as virtual cafes where people can socialize or cruise for a date. Auction sites, such as Ebay, make buying and selling nearly anything a mere mouse click away. Whether it's Xbox Online, Facebook, Twitter, Google+, foursquare, or MySpace, many of us spend an increasing amount of our lives online, forging meaningful communities and online identities.

Subcultures have taken full advantage of these digital spaces, expanding our notion of "scene" from physical spaces to online communities. For example, punks, skaters, and hip hoppers all congregate online in addition to face-to-face gatherings. Others, such as gamers and fic writers, interact *primarily* online; some subculturists may rarely (if ever) find themselves in a physical scene, raising questions about authenticity, identity, and subcultural capital. The Internet also fosters new opportunities for deviance and especially for moral entrepreneurs to make claims regarding the purported dangers of online interaction and "Internet addiction."

In this chapter, we examine two virtual cultures: massively multiplayer online role-playing games (MMORPGs) and computer hacking. Then we look at the facets of virtual community and online profile sites such as MySpace and Facebook before discussing other elements of virtual scenes, such as economy, communication, and geography. The chapter ends by examining virtual identity and what all this technology and online interaction means for our sense of self.

VIRTUAL SUBCULTURES AND SCENES

Hundreds of millions of people around the world use the Internet, many of them for the pleasure and emotional support of socializing online (Hornsby 2005). Civic organizations, activists, political junkies, and a myriad of other groups form groups on the 'net. Here we'll discuss one of the original online subcultures, hackers, and one of the fastest growing, players of online video games.

Hacker Culture

Popular movies have portrayed computer hackers either as pranksters—*WarGames* (1983), *Hackers* (1995)—or as rebellious heroes—*Sneakers* (1992), *The Net* (1995), *The Matrix* (1999; D. Thomas 2002). Computer developers and software companies are the "good guys" while hackers are dangerous renegades out to undermine national security, steal your identity, or rob your online bank account. Quite to the contrary, most underground hackers do not fit the villain stereotype, and many expose computer bugs and software loopholes that ultimately benefit all computer users (S. Levy 2001).

According to anthropologist and media scholar Gabriella Coleman, "A 'hacker' is a technologist with a love for computing and a 'hack' is a clever technical solution arrived through a non-obvious means" (Coleman 2010). This broad definition includes advocates of free and open-source software and gamers who modify their PCs or Xboxes to activists who sabotage big banks or government agencies. Most hacking is legal, a way for computer enthusiasts to satisfy their curiosity; some hackers, however, thrive on disrupting our cultural reliance on secrecy (D. Thomas 2002). Secrecy encompasses everything from corporate trade secrets to the dozen passwords you likely have for everything from your bank account to your Facebook page. Hackers challenge (or threaten, depending on your perspective) the secrecy underlying so much of our virtual lives while often meticulously hiding their own identities.

Hackers trace their roots to phone "phreaking" in the 1950s, in which "phreakers" would mimic the frequencies used to conduct phone calls, often with the intent of gaining free access. Early hacker cultures thrived at university computer labs such as MIT and Harvard, and underground hacker culture has always been mostly a suburban, white, boy culture (D. Thomas 2002). "Old school" hackers, the hackers of the 1960s and 1970s, held a utopian view of technology—computers would make the world a better place to live in, and freely sharing information and technology, rather than keeping it a secret, would lead to human liberation. New school hackers, sometimes called cyberpunks or "crackers," appreciate the benefits of the computer age but have a much grimmer outlook regarding the possibilities of technology. Computers, rather than tools for liberation, can be used to dominate and control. Corporations, for example, continually gather consumer data in an effort to create demand for their products; politicians use pollsters to determine how best to sell their policies to constituents; governments use surveillance technology to monitor their citizens. This tension between the costs and benefits of technology is clear in the trilogy of *Matrix* movies, which set the main character, a cyberpunk hacker named Neo, against a computer system that employs virtual reality to pacify and enslave humans. In a show of resistance, contemporary hackers use technology to "outsmart the system," holding on to the old hacker ideal that the free and open exchange of ideas can benefit humankind (D. Thomas 2002, 42). The 1983 film *WarGames*, in which a young computer enthusiast inadvertently begins the countdown to nuclear war and then saves the day, marks the transition from the old school to the new breed of hacker: Technology can be dangerous, but those who know how to tame it can be heroes.

As with MMORPGs, in the hacker world a loose social order emerges. Newspaper stories of hackers defacing Web sites and breaking into computers for no apparent reason might make hackers appear anarchistic, randomly acting on their own behalf without any governing rules or norms. While it's true that hackers come from a variety of political leanings and that most hackers mistrust authority, the hacker subculture still produces norms, even a "moral code." As Steven Levy wrote in 1984, the old school hacker code revolved around six themes (as summarized in D. Thomas 2002, 10):

- "Access to computers—and anything which might teach you something about the way the world works—should be unlimited and total."
- "All information should be free."
- "Mistrust Authority—Promote Decentralization."
- "Hackers should be judged by their hacking, not bogus criteria such as degrees, age, race, or position."
- "You can create art and beauty on a computer."
- "Computers can change your life for the better."

Like any subculture, hackers are a diverse bunch with different motivations and goals, some seeking to resist or challenge the social structures in which they find themselves. Some hackers see themselves as cultural warriors in the battle for free and open information—monopolies on information must be overthrown, and power must be taken back from the media (D. Thomas 2002). They are often part of the "free software movement" that advocates for "open source" software which makes code available to (and thus modifiable by) everyone. A prominent example is the Firefox Web browser. Other hackers have more selfish motives, seeking financial gain or merely to cause mischief. "White hat" hackers seek out holes in security systems in order to repair them, while "black hat" hackers seek the same flaws to exploit them (ibid.). Lacking conventional markers of style and authenticity, hackers use technical savvy as a mark of status, drawing a distinction between a "true hack" and a "derivative hack." A true hack requires the hacker to have extensive technical knowledge, discovering a security hole and working through the hack using trial and error. A derivative hacker is when someone with little technical expertise uses a program written by another hacker to exploit a weakness in a system. Hackers hold true hacks in greater esteem as a more authentic expression of the hacker ethos, while derivative hacks are viewed as trivial at best and dangerous at worst, as when amateurs damage a system and give hackers a bad name.

Casting hackers as either heroes or villains oversimplifies their Trickster role, alternately helping or hindering people and refusing to be confined by one particular ideology or set of rules. They may pull pranks such as "Rickrolling" in one instance, and engage in seemingly political protest the next. "Anonymous" and "antisec," diffuse networks of geeks and hackers, defaced police Web sites with an anti-police rap video in response to officials' attempts to reign in the Occupy Wall Street protests of 2011 (Norton 2011). They also "d0xed," or released sensitive information such as passwords, membership lists, and internal documents, as well as leaking Facebook accounts and passwords in response to a police crackdown on Occupy Boston. Thus, rather than being viewed in strictly destructive terms, some hacking should be examined as political action (Coleman 2011).

"Anonymous 101: Introduction to the Lulz"

By Quinn Norton for *Wired* magazine, November 8, 2011.
A fascinating introduction to the world of the Anonymous hacker culture. Best known for their often comical protests against the Church of Scientology, Anonymous combines pranks with politics.
www.wired.com/threatlevel/2011/11/anonymous-101

Popular portrayals of computer hackers in many ways symbolize society's ambivalence about technology in general. On one hand, we enjoy watching movies at home online or on DVD, texting and instant messaging our friends, and listening to MP3s on an iPod. On the other hand, many people also understand that technology created the nuclear bomb and other instruments of warfare, television and Internet advertising foster hyperconsumption, and having email may create more work rather than saving time. Rather than unequivocally making life easier, technology often comes with unintended consequences.

Massive Multiplayer Online Role Playing Games

Since rudimentary 1950s–'60s video games such as tic tac toe, *Tennis for Two*, and *Spacewar!* the video game industry has grown exponentially, taking in billions of dollars a year in the United States and rivaling the film industry in profitability. Whether you grew up with Atari, Nintendo, Playstation, Xbox, or Wii, video games have become ubiquitous in contemporary youth culture. Some players have even gone professional, securing sponsorships and competing in tournaments as part of a pro circuit. The latest surge in video game popularity has been Massively Multiplayer Online Role Playing Games (MMORPGs) such as *Everquest, Star Wars: The Old Republic, World of Warcraft, Runescape, Ultima Online, Eve Online,* and *Dungeons and Dragons Online. World of Warcraft* alone has over ten million subscriptions worldwide, including players in the United States, Korea, New Zealand, China, Australia, United Kingdom, Singapore, France, Germany, and Spain.[33] In each of these games, players create a virtual persona called an avatar, character, or "toon." Unlike more conventional video games in which players assume a role created by the game designers (for example, you play Lara Croft in *Tomb Raider*, the Master Chief in *Halo*, or Marcus Fenix in *Gears of War*), MMORPG enthusiasts create and customize their own characters, including abilities, skills, appearance, profession, possessions or weapons, and names. Most games charge a monthly subscription fee of around $15, making the most popular games big business.

These games have roots in the table-top, "pen and paper" fantasy role-playing games such as *Dungeons and Dragons* in which a group of players create characters who adventure in a world created and described by a "game master" according to a set of rules that govern possibilities in the game (Kelly 2004).[34] Players and game master use their imaginations to create a "shared fantasy" in which almost anything can happen, rolling dice to determine if they successfully accomplish tasks such as attacking a monster with a sword or sneaking past a guard undetected (Fine 2002). While MMORPGs require no dice, and replace the game master with faceless game developers, the notion of a party of adventurers questing in a fantasy world populated by mythical creatures remains.

After creating a character, players enter a vast virtual world of spectacular geographies and fantastic opponents. They explore the terrain, meet non-player (computer controlled) characters (NPCs), and undertake perilous quests. While players can play "solo," most band together, forming groups in which each member performs a specialized role.[35] Quests require gamers to travel across the world, gather/collect magical items, deliver messages, and slay mythical beasts. Each quest confers rewards in the form of money characters can spend on new items and ability upgrades, equipment they can use or sell, and experience points (XP) that advance the character in level. Players begin the game at level one and gradually increase their rank—most games have a maximum level between fifty and eighty-five. With each advancement characters gain new abilities, and players can customize spells, abilities, and new equipment according to their own preferences. These games have become wildly popular not only with teenage boys but with a fairly wide cross-section of people. While women make up approximately half of all online gamers (including games like bingo), they comprise *at most* 20 to 30 percent of all MMORPG players in the United States; in the most popular game, *World of Warcraft*, women make up about 16 percent of players[36] (T. Taylor 2006; Griffiths, Davies, and Chappell 2004). The average player's age is about twenty-six, with male players tending to be younger (average age 25.7 years) and females older (average age 31.7; Yee 2006). Many female players play with a romantic partner and tend to be motivated more by the social aspects of the game than by achievement. Thus, *Second Life*, a game built around social interaction (as opposed to fighting and so on) has nearly a fifty-fifty gender split.[37]

Gaming Goes Big

As of 2012, millions of people around the world, both kids and adults, spent time in a virtual universe. A few of the more popular online MMORPGs include[38]

World of Warcraft

Runescape

Lineage I and II

Final Fantasy XI

Eve Online

Everquest II

Lord of the Rings Online

Star Wars: The Old Republic

Dungeons and Dragons Online

Warhammer Online

Despite the lack of face-to-face contact, norms, values, and a sort of social order emerge in every MMORPG. Some players "role play" their characters, creating an in-game personality and speaking and acting accordingly. They craft a virtual self that may or may not reflect their own presentation of self. Just as in the non-virtual world, players exist in a status hierarchy and in organizational structures. A "noob" (also called a n00b, nub, or newbie), a novice player new to the game who has yet to develop her/his playing skills and master the game mechanics, is at the bottom of the status ladder. Calling someone a noob for making a mistake can be a playful joke or a serious insult, depending upon the relationship, and the definition of the situation, between the interacting players. "Power gamers" are "hard-core" gamers who play a great deal (sometimes eight or more hours at a time), advancing in the game very quickly and focusing primarily on increasing their character's statistics, completing difficult high-level quests, and acquiring rare and powerful items. Being the first player to conquer a difficult opponent, complete a challenging quest, gain a rare artifact, or reach the highest level confers status. More casual gamers often accuse power gamers of taking the fun out of the game by being so instrumental, competitive, and goal oriented that gaining levels and power become more impor-tant than having fun. To some, power gaming and "grinding," or slogging through tedious and monotonous tasks to gain rewards, looks and feels like work (T. Taylor 2006). Casual gamers see such play styles as somehow less legitimate, while power gamers maintain that their style of play is both legitimate and fun.[39]

One of the main ways in which the MMORPG virtual community is organized is through guilds. Guilds are associations of players that, ideally, help one another by sharing information, cooperating on difficult quests, and pooling resources (such as rare items and weapons). For some players, guilds become their virtual families; indeed, some favor their guild families over their real-life relationships (Kelly 2004). They often have their own Web sites where members schedule play times, offer services, and simply chat about the game or real life. More established guilds purchase and maintain guild halls and have guild uniforms (called "tabards" in *World of Warcraft*). Different types of guilds reflect differing orientations to the game. "Family guilds" operate more for casual gamers and, as the label suggests, try to be a flexible support system for members. "Raid guilds," on the other hand, typically have higher expectations of members, catering to power gamers and demanding significant time, commitment, and loyalty from guildmates. Within any guild there are leaders, officers, and rank-and-file members. Leaders have the ability to invite, promote, demote, or even banish other players within the guild. Thus a virtual social order emerges in which different organizations establish norms and expectations for members.

MMORPGs focus increasingly on Player vs. Player (PvP) combat, in which players either duel one another individually or fight as members of various factions—for example, the "Horde" vs. the "Alliance" in *World of Warcraft*. Players gain honor points and are ranked on PvP boards, providing yet another way to gain prestige in the gaming world.

The MMORPG community has expanded far beyond the games themselves. Hundreds of Web sites, such as OGaming and Thottbot, provide discussion forums, quest descriptions and hints, and opportunities to give game designers feedback about the game itself. Sony Online Entertainment (SOE), publisher of *Everquest I* and *II* and the *Star Wars* games, holds a Fan Faire, a convention bringing gamers together in real space for several days of presentations, panels, and, yes, online gaming (T. Taylor 2006).

Reports of players becoming addicted to the games have generated concern among players' parents and family members and have led some psychologists to diagnose "Computer Addiction, Internet Addictive Disorder, or Cyberaddiction," fueling a moral panic.[40] Similar to online gambling addiction, gaming addicts reportedly neglect work, school studies, and personal relationships as they become consumed by gaming. A Yahoo group called World of Warcraft Widows brings together people who have "lost" a family member to WoW. The propensity of some gamers to overindulge is not terribly difficult to explain. Part of the appeal of MMORPGs is the opportunity to take risks and make daily progress without any of the risks and drawbacks of real life (Kelly 2004). The games are immersive and goal oriented, and characters can achieve riches and fame while the occasional death suffered along the way is at most a minor setback. What's more, many players feel they are part of a meaningful community.

VIRTUAL COMMUNITY—FACEBOOK, MYSPACE, AND MORE

If I were to ask you to tell me about your community, you would most likely describe the physical space and people in your neighborhood, town, or city. We tend to think of community in narrow terms and almost always tie community to geography, a physical place. In the information age, however, we need a broader definition. A **community** is a social network of people who somehow interact and have something in common such as geographic place (e.g., a university community), common interests (e.g., the poker community), distinct identity (e.g., the Latino and gay communities), or shared values (e.g., the Baptist community). Though we typically think of it in terms of place, a community is not explicitly tied to one location but is instead another way of identifying people who claim an identity, such as "the lesbian community," "the African American community," or "the Pagan community." Community can bring people with similar interests together, as in "the mountain biking community" or "the peace community." The Internet, especially, calls into question the idea that community is necessarily connected to a physical location.

Chances are you are one of the millions of people who have created a personal online profile page using MySpace, Facebook, or a similar social networking site. Facebook has over 800 million users worldwide. Each of these sites encourages users to post personal information such as favorite music, movies, and activities as well as pictures, blogs, videos, and songs. Members can customize their sites and form and join groups based upon similar interests—anything from horror films to indie rock music. Many users are young adults in the United States and Europe, though the sites have spread to many countries and attracted people of all age groups. Users appreciate the opportunity to reconnect with old friends and to make new ones. In fact, given that you can immediately "screen" users' age, interests, and motivation (for example to make friends or find a date), profile sites are an *efficient* way to make friends.

In 1983 novelist William Gibson coined the term "**cyberspace**," which has since come to describe the virtual, computerized realm of Web pages, chat rooms, emails, video games, and blogs.[41] **Virtual communities** are communities of people who regularly interact and form ongoing relationships primarily via the Internet (Rheingold 2000). People who interact online are not automatically part of a community—virtual community entails more than surfing Web sites, making a Facebook page, reading emails, or engaging in brief chats on bulletin boards. Just because someone plays an MMORPG does not necessarily mean they are part of a virtual community; after all, you could theoretically play the game and never chat with another human player. On the other hand, someone who regularly plays an MMORPG with the same people (as part of a guild, for example), gets to know them a bit beyond playing the game, and develops personal relationships in the game is part of a community.

In postindustrial society we have more freedom to choose our communities. Before the advent of advanced communication technologies, affordable travel opportunities, and job mobility, people were more or less restricted to their local or regional communities—their hometown, with its churches, schools, and civic organizations. Now, to a certain extent, we can select the communities we are drawn to (Hewitt 2000). Our loyalties may be divided among many different communities, and we can leave and join communities relatively easily. Think about the myriad interest groups and subcultures that connect people online. You like goldfish? Chat with other enthusiasts at www.koivet.com. Enjoy bird watching? If you can't locate members of the Audubon Society (or if you can find them, but don't *like* them), join a bird-watching listserv. The main idea is this: Community, now more than ever, is flexible and less tied to *geography*.

Every subculture in this book has a virtual presence. In fact, some participants, be they goths, straight edgers, or virginity pledgers, experience their subculture primarily or even *exclusively* through the Internet (see Williams 2003). The Web changes the nature of subcultures, potentially expanding community, but in a different form. If you can buy your favorite underground music for less money online, maybe you'll frequent your local independent record store less often, and eventually what was once perhaps a hub of a local scene might fade away.

Subcultures have typically relied upon physical spaces in which members can get together: clubs, record stores, skate parks, street corners, pubs, alternative fashion boutiques, and so on. You can think of these spaces as part of the **subcultural geography**, the terrain in which youth congregate and live the subculture day to day. Virtual subcultures have their own geographies, or digital hangouts that bring together participants from all over the world. Kendall (2002) likens chat rooms/MUDs to virtual pubs, "neighborhood" hangouts where regulars meet and gossip (Kendall 2002). Correll (1995) claims that members of the Lesbian Café BBS (bulletin board system) talked about their virtual space as if it were a physical place in which they interacted. Instead of dropping by the neighborhood pub after work to have a laugh and catch up on news, many of us are logging in to virtual communities, often several times a day (and often *during* work!).

As virtual worlds complete with continents, cities, stores, forests, canyons, rivers, taverns, and public transportation, MMORPGs expand how we understand subcultural geographies. Walking through a virtual city in a MMORPG isn't that far removed from strolling through a nonvirtual city. There are a variety of neighborhoods (often *ethnic* neighborhoods based on in-game races) with shops, market stalls, hotels, fruit vendors, pet stores, bars, schools (training centers), and temples. Stray dogs and cats, police (guards), preachers, and citizens roam the streets. In *Everquest II*, most players rent and maintain their own apartments that they can decorate with paintings, bookcases (and books), pets, and a variety of furniture including a bed, table, and storage units. Guilds form their own guild halls in which some hold virtual gatherings and guild meetings. In *Star Wars Galaxies*, players can build their own cities, forming a charter, electing a mayor and other officials, erecting buildings, and collecting taxes. In *The Sims* online, people from twenty different countries establish virtual households, families, and careers. A newsletter, player blogs, an online news feed, and a Sims podcast keep people connected even though their real-life geographies may keep them thousands of miles apart.

Many people are skeptical of virtual communities, sometimes called "**computer-mediated communities**" to emphasize how interaction takes place via, or through, computers. In addition to concerns about online sexual predators, identity thieves, and other criminals they worry that computers will make us more isolated—the more we're "plugged in" the less we're interacting face to face (Nie and Erbring 2000). We all know the stereotype of the isolated computer nerd who substitutes virtual friendships for "real" ones, implying that virtual communities are less "authentic" than face-to-face relationships (D. Miller and Slater 2000). While the differences between face-to-face and virtual communities pose meaningful sociological questions, we should be cautious in assuming that new technologies automatically undermine community and wary of moral panics about "gaming addiction." After all, people initially had the same worries that the telephone would impede rather than help build genuine community. Critics claim video games promote unhealthy lifestyles, disrupt families, and inhibit community. But as gaming scholar and economist Edward Castronova (2008, ix) suggests, "the lifestyles of the real world are already unhealthy...the real world pulls families apart,...makes people give their time to huge soulless organizations rather than themselves...and isolates us and takes away all sense of personal meaning and significance." Perhaps games and other "synthetic worlds" have something to teach us about the rest of our lives.

ELEMENTS OF THE VIRTUAL SCENE

All of the standard elements of nonvirtual subcultures, from style and status hierarchy to jargon and gender ideology, have their equivalents in the virtual world. Although we do not have enough space to cover them all, a few are especially interesting in the way they transcend the virtual/nonvirtual divide.

The Virtual Economy

While the underground subcultural economy still exists, most scenes have taken their DIY businesses online. Auction sites like eBay and Craigslist allow DJs to buy and sell records, goths to shop for corsets, and gamers to exchange games. While these types of transactions all involve buying and selling something tangible, the latest development has MMORPG players exchanging "real" money for "virtual" goods.

Online auction sites blend with MMORPGs when players sell and bid on game items: armor, weapons, characters, and virtual money, be it gold pieces or credits (Castronova 2005). In addition to completing quests, MMORPG players can adopt professions such as carpenter, engineer, chef/provisioner, alchemist, architect, and enchanter. In these roles, players create virtual products (such as boots, houses, backpacks, and weapons), which they then exchange "face to face" with other players or via an auction system run by the game. However, some players exchange real currency for virtual currency and spend real money for items that do not exist outside of cyberspace. In 2004, an avid gamer paid $26,500 for an island in "Entropia," a virtual fantasy land.[42] Another invested $100,000 on a space station he plans to develop into condos, a mall, a stadium, and a biodome.[43] The only thing "real" about this transaction was the thousands of dollars the gamers spent. Sound crazy? Some of these virtual real estate developers are making good money on their investments and some gamers, especially in China, make a living selling virtual goods.

Geek and Gamer Language—Netspeak, l33t sp33k, txtspk

Just like any subculture, virtual cultures have produced their own languages. If I were to show you "/ooc 24 wiz lfg AQ3 pst," would you understand that I am communicating an "out of character" message, playing a "24th level wizard," am "looking for a group" to complete "armor quest 3," and would like you to "please send a tell" to me if I can join your group? Do the acronyms "ROFL," "brb," "afk," "lol," "mt," "pwn," or "lmao" mean anything to you? To online gamers and members of other virtual communities they mean "rolling on the floor laughing," "be right back," "away from keyboard," "laughing out loud," "mis-tell" (or "main tank," depending on context), "owned/pwned," and "laughing my ass off," respectively. Just as nonvirtual subcultures create and use their own vocabulary, virtual subcultures like hackers employ their own dialect consisting of shorthand words, acronyms, and computer jargon, sometimes called "l33t" speak, short for elite where the numeral "1" substitutes for the letter "l" and "3" for "e."[44] More commonly known as netspeak or text speak, abbreviated words and acronyms are now interwoven into daily language, Twitter, and text messaging (though automatic spellers have perhaps lessened the use of text shorthand). Words are symbols that convey meaning, and text becomes part of symbolic interaction. Knowledge of gaming-specific acronyms and ability to decipher text speak separate insiders from outsiders, contributing to a sense of community for those "in the know."

In real life, we use much more than words to communicate our intended meaning. Normal communication cues such as voice tone, facial expressions, gestures, and posture help us convey the meanings we want to accompany our words. Online talking with text alone leaves a lot of room for misinterpretation and misunderstanding, requiring other ways of conveying emotion and meaning. Many of you have probably used "emoticons" ("CONventions for expressing EMOTIons") to add feeling and emphasis to email messages (Hornsby 2005). Thus, as you surely know, :) and :(become smiley faces that can indicate a whole range of feelings, depending on the context: excitement, happiness, contentment. Likewise ;) is a winking smiley and connotes a shared joke, sarcasm, teasing, flirting, or similar meaning. In the MMORPG world, players can enact emotion and a presentation of self through their avatars. Toons dance, bow, smirk, threaten, flirt, scowl, cheer, clap, and blow kisses at the direction of their player-puppet masters.

Online language is no longer confined to virtual settings, as email shorthand and 1eet speak have moved to the nonvirtual world. In the last several years I have noticed (often with dismay) an increasing number of student papers including text message writing—"u" substituted for "you" and "b4" for "before." The sheer numbers of people playing online games ensures the blending of texting and talking, with gamers exclaiming "Woot!!" (typed as w00t! in online gaming) to express joy in real life, "gee gee" (for gg, or good game) to congratulate, and calling each other noobs (for newbie, or newcomer) as a joking insult. Language, both virtual and nonvirtual, is fluid and will continue to evolve as the virtual and nonvirtual worlds overlap.

Virtual Gender and Nerd Masculinity

Long considered the domain of adolescent boys, video games often represent women in very sexualized ways. The hit series of *Tomb Raider* games is one of the few with a female protagonist; yet with her tiny waist and enormous breasts she hardly represents the typical female form. Another extremely popular series, *Grand Theft Auto*, has been maligned for the way players can direct the thuggish main character to commit violence against women. To regain health, players direct the main character to pay for sex with a female prostitute—afterwards players can beat and rob her to regain the money they just spent. To claim that video games are the source of real-life degradation of women is a simplistic attempt by moral entrepreneurs to create a moral panic or engage in symbolic politics; video games make an easy scapegoat for larger social problems, including sexism and violence against women. Nevertheless, in the context of a sexist culture, games that often depict violent men as tough and admirable heroes and women as seminaked sexual objects do perpetuate stereotypical gender representations and roles.

Despite the sexist depictions of women in games and the male-dominated tech world, computer culture has long been associated with geeks and nerds—the "computer geek" is a cultural icon. The "nerd" status serves a purpose in youth culture as one of the identities that other groups define themselves against. Jocks, for example, are almost always defined in part against the stereotypical nerd—jocks are popular, strong, self-confident, and attractive to the opposite sex, while nerds are unpopular, weak, shy, and asexual. In a sense, nerd "connotes a lack of masculinity," particularly dating/sexual incompetence and little athletic ability (Kendall 2002, 80).

As with the goths discussed in Chapter 7, some self-described nerds proudly claim (or reclaim) their deviant status, embracing the nerd identity (Wright 1996). As with all deviance, meaning depends upon context—calling someone a nerd can be a demeaning slur or a show of affection and solidarity (among nerds). Technical expertise becomes a mark of superiority to more popular kids, particularly for male nerds. Female nerds face a more difficult situation; being stereotyped as unattractive has more negative consequences for women than for men. Computer programming has traditionally been thoroughly male dominated, making fitting into the "boys' club" a challenge for many young women. In addition, women who do manage to break into the boys' club risk being viewed as somehow less feminine or perhaps even intimidating to men because of their perceived intelligence and expertise (Seymour and Hewitt 1999). Still, some women gamers take "a strong sense of pleasure in surprising male players with their competence and skill" as well as satisfaction from the technical mastery of a game or computer hardware (Kennedy 2011, 207). While women gamers may not have an explicitly feminist agenda, they contest dominant meanings of gender.

Nerd masculinity encompasses both a critique and reinforcement of hegemonic masculinity. Like straight edgers, self-described nerds and geeks are often sharply critical of the stereotypical young male bent on sexual conquest of women and domination of other men. Yet nerds and geeks, like skinheads, punks, and others who question what it means to be a man, do not fully resist hegemonic masculinity. For example, players in MMORPGs regularly talk trash as if they were on the basketball court or football field. They also talk about women as sexual objects even as they tease one another about their lack of experience with women and refuse to adopt the "asshole" persona necessary, in their minds, to be attractive to women (Kendall 2002). In virtual competitive games, players often express dominance and power, claiming to have "owned" (often typed pwned in-game) the other team and hurling insults at opposing players or less-skilled teammates. Many games reward players for high kill counts and set up online rankings—a kid who could never hold his own in gym class or on the football field could be the king of *Halo* or *Call of Duty* rankings—virtual status, to be sure, but appealing nonetheless.

The Trolls Among Us

Perhaps you have encountered, in a game, message board, or even on YouTube, someone whose sole purpose is seemingly to be offensive, disruptive, or provocative. Such "trolls" as they are called, range from merry pranksters to cruel bullies, alternately making fake dating posts on Craigslist and mocking suicide victims to evoke "lulz" (a derivation of lol) by "disrupting another's emotional equilibrium." In this revealing essay, reporter Mattathias Schwartz investigates the world of Internet trolls. www.nytimes.com/2008/03/magazine/03trolls-t.html?pagewanted=all

---

POSTMODERN IDENTITY AND THE VIRTUAL SELF

Most of us have, at one time or another, dreamed of being someone we are not—maybe a movie star, professional athlete, revolutionary, or supermodel. Virtual worlds may help us live out these dreams as, in a sense, we can all be rich, powerful, and beautiful, even achieving a measure of fame. We have the opportunity to recreate and remake, to an extent, who we are. In chat rooms we can express a different personality, in online games we can gender-bend by playing a toon of the opposite sex, and in the *Simms* we can pick up people in clubs and take them back to our virtual mansions. All of these possibilities raise questions about how we think of our "self" and our identities. Online games, especially, offer an opportunity to construct a self relatively free from some of the constraints of the material world (Crowe and Bradford 2007). Players choose their appearance, associations, professions, and so on. Yet it is important not to overemphasize the freedom offered in online forums. Participants bring with them their knowledge and experience from the material world. While opportunities to experiment with identity abound, status hierarchies emerge nonetheless. Players value some identities and expressions of self more than others. Having the most rare, expensive, or difficult-to-acquire armor becomes a status symbol in game, much as a sports car might in the material world—the difference is a players' assumption that anyone can have the armor with considerable effort.

We tend to think of our personal identity as coherent, ongoing, and stable—we might periodically abandon an identity (such as student) or adopt a new identity (such as becoming a parent), but ultimately we are who we are. Symbolic interactionists take a much more fluid and social view of the self. The **self** is a *process* including one's thoughts, feelings, and choices as well as being something we *do* rather than simply *are* (Sandstrom, Martin, and Fine 2006). Our self emerges in interaction with others. Rather than packing a coherent self with us from time to time and place to place, we express our self (or many selves) depending upon the context of a particular interaction. Sociologists disagree to what extent the self continually changes, and virtual interaction has added another complex piece to the puzzle.

In diverse, mobile, technologically advanced, rapidly changing societies is it possible to construct a stable and coherent self? Rather than having one relatively stable identity, we have multiple identities, some only briefly. Think of your own life. You might have many different selves, one you express at work, one for your family, and another for your sorority. **Postmodern identity** is temporary, unstable, and fluid. Rather than being deeply personal and unified, the self is a relational and fragmented (Gergen 1991). People assume a variety of seemingly contradictory identities, such as an athlete who is also a band geek, a religious preacher who loves gory horror films, or a porn star happily married with a family. Rather than being tied to a consistent, stable "self," we bring a different, flexible self, so to speak, to each context (Zurcher 1977).

Changing computer and communication technologies are central to many theories of the self (see Agger 2004). Think about the ways you can communicate that differ from when your grandparents were your age: fax machines, email, cell phones, video conferencing, and voice mail. Now consider the technologies you may take for granted that people two generations ago could only dream of: satellite and cable TV, iPads, laptop computers. These technologies enable hackers, MMORPG players, and personal profile users to literally construct virtual selves unfettered by the same rules that apply to face-to-face relationships. The **virtual self** is "the person connected to the world and to others through electronic means such as the Internet, television, and cell phones" (Agger 2004, 1). It is a state of being, created and experienced through technology. Perhaps people feel more comfortable exploring and enacting taboo identities in the anonymity of cyberspace? Thus a shy, reserved, even socially awkward person can be outgoing, boisterous, and charming in the online world. You can never be sure when someone's online identity matches their offline characteristics and when they are **masquerading**, or pretending to be something they are not (Turkle 1997; Kendall 2002). How do you determine someone's authenticity if you can't even reliably determine their age, sex, race, or real-life actions (Williams 2003)?

CONCLUSIONS

We are in a state of profound ambivalence about technology. We love the comforts and conveniences it affords us, but we are wary of its dangers, as films like *2001: A Space Odyssey*, *The Matrix*, and *Terminator* demonstrate. As more and more people "plug in" to the Web, new moral panics arise: Internet stalkers, porn and video game addiction, and identity thieves. Yet for all the panic, many of us cannot wait to upgrade our cell phones, iPods, and Facebook pages, injecting a bit more of ourselves into the virtual universe.

The latest communication technologies are still so new that we continue to make a false distinction between "virtual" and "real" life, as if online experience is somehow secondary, less meaningful, and less real than face-to-face interaction (Chee, Vieta, and Smith 2006). Instead, we should be asking how (and *if*) virtual scenes differ from nonvirtual and, more importantly, how they overlap. Hackers, MMORPGs, chat rooms, blogs, and personal profile/networking sites force us to ask how the Internet might change our very conceptualization of subcultures/scenes. They show us how the boundaries between what we see as virtual and real are blurry (T. Taylor 2006; Castronova 2005). People meet online and then agree to meet offline, but they also meet offline and subsequently get together online. Our communities, and our identities, transcend the virtual–real divide.

DISCUSSION

- What are the unintended consequences of social networking sites and mobile phones?
- Are online relationships as "real" as non-virtual relationships? Why or why not?
- Do you think people can become "addicted" to the Internet? To online games?
- How do virtual spaces both "free" people from the constraints of race, class, and gender and reinforce inequalities in new ways?

KEY IDEAS

Blog: (Derived from "Weblog.") A Web site of chronologically organized news, commentary, or personal journal entries. In some ways, blogs are virtual zines, or e-Zines, which allow readers to post comments and engage in dialogue.

Community: A social network of people who somehow interact and have something in common such as geographic place, common interests, distinct identity, or shared values. Community is not necessarily long-term, stable, or tied to a physical space.

Computer-mediated communities: Another phrase describing virtual and online communities. Communities in which the primary mode of interaction is via computer.

Cyberspace: The virtual, computerized realm of Web pages, chat rooms, emails, video games, and blogs. The totality of online "space."

Masquerading: Assuming an online identity significantly different from one's real life identity, such as switching gender or race.

Nerd masculinity: Encompasses both a critique and a reinforcement of hegemonic masculinity.

Postmodern identity: A sense of self that is temporary, fragmented, unstable, fluid, and sometimes contradictory.

Self: According to symbolic interactionists, the self is a *process* including one's thoughts, feelings, and choices. It is something we *do* rather than simply *are*, and it emerges in interaction with others.

Subcultural geographies: Virtual spaces, both textual and three-dimensional, in which people interact online.

Virtual community: Communities of people who regularly interact and form ongoing relationships primarily via the Internet.

Virtual self: A sense of selfhood experienced primarily online. May differ and overlap with other (offline) senses of self.

RESOURCES

My Life as a Night Elf Priest: An Anthropological Account of World of Warcraft

By Bonnie Nardi. 2010. Ann Arbor: University of Michigan Press.

An ethnography of gamers that explores many topics related to MMORPGs.

Digital Culture, Play, and Identity: A World of Warcraft Reader

Edited by Hilde G. Corneliussen and Jill Walker Rettberg. 2008. Cambridge: MIT Press.

A collection of scholarly essays related to World of Warcraft.

Synthetic Worlds: The Business and Culture of Online Games (2nd edition)

By Edward Castronova. 2006. Chicago: University of Chicago Press.

A scholarly analysis of online gaming, especially virtual economies.

Play Between Worlds: Exploring Online Game Culture

By T. L. Taylor. 2006. Cambridge: MIT Press.

An interesting study of online gaming including material on power gamers, women gamers, and offline life.

Second Skin (film, Juan Carlos Pineiro-Escoriaza 2008)

Documentary exploring the lives of several hardcore gamers, guilds and their leaders, Chinese gold farmers, and the question of gaming "addiction."

Frag (film, Mike Pasley 2008)

This documentary delves into the world of competitive video gaming, revealing how some youth attempt to turn their hobby into a professional career. Watchable on YouTube.

The King of Kong (film, Seth Gordon 2008)

A documentary following the exploits of two gamers vying for the title of world's greatest Donkey Kong player.

Geek Girls Unite: How Fangirls, Bookworms, Indie Chicks, and Other Misfits are Taking Over the World.

By Leslie Simon. 2011. New York: It Books.

A fun look at fangirls, music, literary, and film geeks, challenging the notion that only boys can reclaim the "geek" label.

CHAPTER 9

↙♄

Riot Grrrls and Fic Writers—Girls Take on the Media

Walk down the newsstand aisle in your local supermarket and you will likely see a section with a variety of teen magazines for girls, each offering variations on the same themes of beauty, fashion, and sexuality. *CosmoGirl's* "Guy Guide" teaches girls how to "Never be a boring kisser!" and how to "Impress your boyfriend's friends!: 3 tips to get approval from his friends." If they get stuck, readers can go online to "Ask a Model" for fashion or relationship help. *ElleGirl's* online site offers "Free Dress Up Games, Beauty Tips Secrets, Celebrity fashion, and more at ELLEgirl.com." *Teen Vogue* offers a 30-day Back-to-School Makeover, featuring the "latest fall gear," "beauty tips," and "workout videos." *Seventeen* magazine coaches young women on how to attain "hot abs" while the "All You issue!" provides "Makeup for your skin tone, hair ideas for your texture, clothes for your shape." While such magazines claim a desire to empower young women and occasionally feature stories about volunteering or politics, they focus primarily on beauty, fashion, exercise, and celebrities, leaving the impression of girls preoccupied with makeup, clothes, dieting, and attracting (and pleasing) boyfriends. Meanwhile, magazines geared primarily toward boys and men showcase automobiles (*Lowrider*), gaming (*Game Informer*), sports (*Sports Illustrated*), and music (*Revolver*).

In contrast to the beauty-obsessed teen magazines, stories of "bad girls" permeate the news media. A 2005 *Newsweek* article captured the worry: "Bad Girls Go Wild—A Rise in Girl-on-Girl Violence Is Making Headlines Nationwide and Prompting Scientists to Ask Why." Girls, it seems, are catching up to boys in their propensity to harass their peers. In 2008, an online video of six teenage Florida girls beating a female classmate provoked a spate of stories about female bullies and stoked fears of "girl gangs." Movies such as *Mean Girls* and *Heathers* portray girls as gossiping, vindictive, and backbiting or revenge-seeking, violent criminals, while books like *Queen Bees and Wannabes* and *Odd Girl Out* further the image of girls as competitive, judgmental, nasty, and popularity obsessed. The fascination with girl violence constitutes a moral panic based upon media hype, given that rates of girl-on-girl violence are not increasing (Chesney-Lind and K. Irwin 2008).

These contradictory images of girls illustrate the ongoing cultural confusion about gender, as girls and women increasingly play sports, drive race cars, and run businesses yet are expected to continue displaying "feminine" qualities. Consequently, the media often portray girls in fairly narrow terms, reinforcing false dichotomies of meanness/kindness, virginity/promiscuity, and competition/cooperation (ibid.). In this chapter, I explore two subcultures—Riot Grrrl and fan fiction—in which girls and women have taken control of their representations by making *their own* media, in the process subverting gender norms and demonstrating the complexities of girlhood.

WHERE ARE ALL THE GIRLS?

By now you've learned that girls face a variety of challenges, not only in larger society but in the various subcultures I've discussed in this book. While girls are involved in all of the subcultures I describe, they often seem less visible than the boys, and Skinhead, punk, metal, and hip hop all marginalize women in their own ways, despite sometimes professing inclusiveness. Explanations for the seeming lack of girls in Birmingham subcultural studies include: biased male researchers either did not study women or wrote about them in derogatory terms; women were present but less visible than boys; the "costs," or stigmas, of belonging to a subculture are greater for girls than for boys; girls have less disposable income than boys to spend on subcultural props such as motorbikes or cars; parents give girls less freedom to participate in subcultures than they give boys; and girls have different ways of socializing in groups (McRobbie and Garber 1976). Perhaps subcultures offer little appeal to girls? Mike Brake (1980) claims that subcultures foster a **cult of masculinity,** a space for boys (especially working class boys) to gain status by exalting masculinity when they can't gain power, status, and prestige in other arenas. As a result, subcultures are typically male-dominated and masculinist, revolving around masculine concerns, interests, and norms, glorifying traits commonly associated with maleness such as toughness, daring, and delinquency while denigrating everything "feminine." Girls in these spaces suffer the same "**structured secondariness**" they do in other spheres, present but marginalized, consuming fans instead of creative participants.

Early research by McRobbie and Garber (1976) showed that girls participate in a **bedroom culture** of pop star fandom in which small groups of "teenyboppers" listen to pop music, experiment with makeup, collect records, flip through teen magazines, and gaze at pinups of their favorite (male) music, movie, and TV stars. Rather than joining spectacular subcultures on the streets—risking social sanctions and the ire of parents—many girls found friendship and fun at home where they could put off real sexual pressures and avoid judgment from boys while building female solidarity and safely fantasizing about famous young men. In the 1970s, girls daydreamed about singer/actor David Cassidy; in the 1980s it was Kirk Cameron and Tom Cruise. Later "boy bands," such as New Kids on the Block, Boyz II Men, Backstreet Boys, and 'N Sync seemed sweet and nonthreatening while still being edgy and sexy. Although stereotyped as passive, shallow trend-followers, teenyboppers used their music fandom to set themselves apart from other girls, parents, and teachers, actively defining themselves as different. The research on teenyboppers casts girls as media *consumers* rather than *producers*, even though they produced letters, scrapbooks, and newsletters about their idols (Kearney 2006). In fact, girls have made great strides in producing alternative media, challenging mainstream depictions of women while creating supportive communities.

Media production has been a source of empowerment for many young women. Research on adolescent girls reveals their struggles in a variety of arenas (Gilligan 1982; Pipher 1995). As they enter the teenage years, girls tend to experience a drop in self-esteem, negative feelings about their bodies, and a lack of sexual agency. Further, girls lose their "voice" or opportunities to discuss their problems and concerns, actively create their own cultures, or express their opposition to the pressures young women face. Yet girls are far from meek wallflowers, passively observing from the sidelines as their male peers gain status on the football field or in the mosh pit. The Riot Grrrl movement inspired a generation of young women to express themselves creatively and paved the way for powerful female characters in popular culture, while fan fiction writers, the majority of whom are women, challenge taken-for-granted gender norms while upending heterocentrist sexuality.

Riot Grrrl

Under the slogan "Revolution Girl Style Now!" Riot Grrrl emerged from a remarkable fusion of punk and feminism. Punk's early history included many women—bands such as X, the Germs, The Slits, and X-Ray Specs are just a few examples of groups with women musicians or singers. Punk claimed to challenge mainstream ideas about gender, and early punk provided kids with the opportunity to play with their gender identities. It allowed, even encouraged, girls to abandon feminine standards of beauty, express their anger, and claim a space in the counterculture. However, punk, and especially hardcore, increasingly became male-dominated; by the mid-1980s women were relatively scarce (Leblanc 1999). In 1991, women in Washington, D.C., and Olympia, Washington, were fed up with the exclusivity and male dominance of the scene. Women such as Bikini Kill's Kathleen Hanna combined the punk ethos with feminist politics and sought to reassert women's presence in alternative music via a new movement called Riot Grrrl (Gottlieb and Wald 1994; Turner 2001). The name emerged when Molly Neuman and Allison Wolfe of the band Bratmobile created a zine called *Riot Grrrl* to give voice to girls' anger and to confront sexism in both the music scene and larger society. These initial efforts spawned a variety of zines in which young women found a political voice, bringing feminism to a new generation of girls (Comstock 2001; Schilt 2003a, 2004). Bikini Kill's song "Double Dare Ya" dared girls to "Do what you want," "Be who you will," and "stand up for your rights."

Music was only one part of the Riot Grrrl movement. In D.C., members of Bratmobile and Bikini Kill held weekly gatherings for punk girls similar to feminist consciousness-raising groups of the past (Kearney 2006). These events helped forge a supportive all-female community while creating a forum for girls to strategize resistance to patriarchal oppression. The first major gathering of Riot Grrrls occurred in August of 1991 at the International Pop Underground Convention in Washington, D.C. (Aapola, Gonick, and Harris 2005). An all-female bill on the first night, dubbed "Love Rock Revolution Girl Style Now," showcased bands such as Bikini Kill, L7, Bratmobile, and Heavens to Betsy. In 1992, Washington, D.C., hosted the first Riot Grrrl "convention," featuring not only music but discussions of racism, domestic violence, body image, and rape (Kearney 2006). Soon, Riot Grrrl groups emerged throughout the United States, and mainstream media outlets such as *Sassy* magazine took notice. Though less prevalent than it once was, Riot Grrrl's legacy continues to inspire young women in the "creation of a place for women, defined by women, that allows women to unite and support each other" (Turner 2001, 54). Riot Grrrl inspired other bands, including Sleater-Kinney and Le Tigre, as well as whole generation of young, feminist Web designers, bloggers, and zine writers.

Fandom and Fan Fiction

There is a good chance you are, or have been, a fan of something, whether sports teams, movie stars, TV shows, or music. In addition to watching your favorite team (for example), perhaps you collected t-shirts, posters, or other team paraphernalia, or maybe you visited Web sites to learn about your favorite players. Often ridiculed, some fans develop strong emotional attachments to their team/show/band, seeking ever new ways to enjoy their fascination with others. A **fandom**, or **fan culture**, is a community built around shared enjoyment of a movie, book, band, TV show, comic book, hobby, sport, celebrity, or other piece of popular culture (Gray, Sandvoss, and Harrington 2007). Fantasy, science fiction, and horror have produced some of the most well-known fan cultures, including *Star Trek, Star Wars, Xena: Warrior Princess,* Tolkien/*Lord of the Rings, Buffy the Vampire Slayer, Harry Potter, True Blood, Supernatural,* and *Twilight,* though crime dramas such as *NCIS* and *Law and Order* have followings as well. Many fans consume products not directly tied to the original object of fandom, accumulating action figures or other collectors' items. Others attend fan conventions ("cons") and engage in "cosplay," dressing the part of their favorite characters—the Star Wars themed 501st Legion (www.501stlegion.org) being a prime example (see Lancaster 2001). Still others perform "filk" music—science fiction and fantasy folk music commonly themed around one of the sci-fi worlds I've just mentioned.

Mainstream media often stigmatize fans (perhaps especially science fiction fans) as abnormal, nerdy, obsessed, even crazy, leading purposeless lives on society's margins (Jensen 1992). Common passions and potential ridicule from outsiders build solidarity among fans, who often form intense bonds with one another (Bury 2005). Similar to gamers and leetspeak (e.g., n00b), fans communicate via **fanspeak**, using a common set of expressions and "insider knowledge" to distinguish themselves from nonfans. Fans also thrive on knowing the minutiae of their fandom: Tolkien fans might know the histories of various nations in Middle Earth; Harry Potter fans might be able to recite the ingredients to a polyjuice potion; and a few Star Trek fans have learned to speak the language of the show's premier alien race, the Klingons.

Fan fiction, also called "**fic**," involves unauthorized stories based upon characters in a fandom, written by fans for fans and shared rather than sold. While fic writing has a long history, the contemporary fic era really took off with *Star Trek* in the 1970s (Pugh 2004). In the past, fic writers created print fanzines to showcase their stories, but today a variety of Web sites serve as fanfic hubs, archiving fics in searchable databases. While anyone is welcome as an equal, **big name fans** (BNFs)—fic writers who gain a following of their own—have more prestige in the fic world. Although men have traditionally dominated the film, television, and publishing worlds, the vast majority of fic writers are women, making it an important domain for women's creativity and resistance (Bury 2005).

MEDIA CONSUMERS AND PRODUCERS

Critics of mass media and popular culture have often portrayed audiences as uncritical consumers, even "dupes" that passively absorb professionally created TV shows, magazines, movies, comic books, music, and so on. Fans, then, were the ultimate media consumers, turning their enjoyment into an almost irrational obsession. After all, how else can one explain the popularity of professional wrestling, an incredibly lucrative "sport" in which the audience knows the combat and outcome are completely staged? On the surface, girls, especially, seem to be media consumers rather than producers. Magazines targeted toward girls and women focus overwhelmingly on beauty and fashion, encouraging girls to see their bodies as "projects" to improve upon (Brumberg 1997). Even *Seventeen*'s "Body Peace" project—designed to help girls be "at peace" with their bodies—makes self-improvement central to girls' lives.

Since the 1990s, some media scholars have challenged such negative images of audiences and fans, examining fandom from fans' point of view. Henry Jenkins (2006) contrasts consumer culture with **participatory culture**—rather than being passive consumers or spectators of media created by a cultural elite, many people actively contribute to pop culture, appropriating cultural products for their own uses. For example, instead of uncritically consuming media, female fic writers "poach" from mainstream media, taking ideas and creatively recasting them in new forms to serve different interests (Jenkins 1992). Participatory culture forces us to rethink stereotypes of fans as ridiculous followers or hopeless dorks. Instead, they participate in the creative process, build meaningful communities, and democratize the media. Thus, participatory culture also demonstrates the politics of subcultures and media production. Making media is a form of power, a type of resistance (Jenkins 2006). Riot Grrrls used DIY media to advance a feminist political agenda in punk and rock music scenes. Rather than being the alienated dupes portrayed in the press, fans "develop a sense of personal control or influence over the object of fandom" and create subcultures reflective of their values (C. Harris 1998, 6).

Fan

"One becomes a 'fan' not by being a regular viewer of a particular program but by translating that viewing into some kind of cultural activity, by sharing feelings and thoughts about the program content with friends, by joining a 'community' of other fans who share common interests. For fans, consumption naturally sparks production, reading generates writing, until the terms seem logically inseparable."
—Henry Jenkins (2006, 41)

THE GIRLS WILL HAVE THEIR SAY

As we've learned from punk and hip hop, many girls use participation in subcultures as an opportunity to subvert gender norms, defying standards of beauty and challenging feminine ideals. Even when they are male-dominated, subcultures can offer girls opportunities for self-expression unavailable to them in conventional settings (Leblanc 1999). Subcultural media, especially, provide young women with opportunities to shape images of girls and bend the rules of femininity in meaningful ways.

Riot Grrrls, Feminism, and Anti-consumerism

In the 1990s and 2000s, the numbers of girls making zines, films, and Web sites rose dramatically (Kearney 2006). One of the first Riot Grrrl zines, *Bikini Kill: A Color and Activity Book*, encouraged girls to join bands both for fun and "To make fun of and thus disrupt the powers that be" (Kearney 2006, 61). Riot Grrrls used both zines and music to call attention to a variety of issues and social problems confronting women, including puberty, self-esteem, and sexism as well as domestic violence, sexual abuse, sexual harassment, and rape. Riot Grrrl zines connected an underground network of young feminist women, creating a new "geography" that transcended any one particular place (Leonard 1998). Exemplifying the personal as political, zines gave voice to girls' joys and concerns, providing a *girl-generated* tool of resistance during a time when many girls experience declining self-confidence and increasing body-consciousness (Schilt 2003a). Other Riot Grrrl zines, such as *Jigsaw*, *Girl Germs*, and *Gunk*, tackled not only the sexism but also the racism in the music scene.

Riot Grrrls embraced feminist ideals but challenged patriarchy and oppression in their own way, combining a "girlish aesthetic" with expressions of "rage, bitterness and political acuity" (Aapola et al. 2005, 20). Some mixed combat boots and spiked belts with lipstick and dresses, while others scrawled "rape," "slut," or "whore" on their bodies with black marker. Even the moniker "Grrrls" was an ironic reclaiming of a denigrated identity meant to "show their rebellion and rage against traditional values" (Archer 1998). Feminists avoided using the term "girls" in reference to adult women, preferring "women" and "young women" because "girls" connotes childhood, naivety, innocence, immaturity, and even weakness, giving men, in particular, license to take women less seriously. By contrast, males in their late teens or twenties are rarely called "boys." However, a new generation of feminists, including Riot Grrrls, reclaimed the term "girl," changing it to a political identity with the added connotation of anger and fierceness. Rather than rejecting girlhood outright, Riot Grrrls ironically combined the traditionally feminine—skirts, heels, and makeup—with the feminist, cherishing the innocence of girlhood (before body image and other insecurities) while promoting feminist politics. The nostalgia for an idealized girlhood, represented on record covers and insert art by childish drawings or child-hood photos of band members, offered a stark contrast to songs about darker topics such as incest and violence and, in the context of punk rock, poked fun at the "music industry's infantilizing representation of adult female sexuality" that so often cast women as bimbos fawning over male rock stars (Wald 1998, 598).

While music and zines were Riot Grrrls' primary media, their bodies became canvases for their message. The terms "slut" and "whore" written on a woman's body were a shocking method of confrontation designed to encourage debate (Leonard 1997). Reclaiming pejorative words such as "queer" and "bitch" is part of gender and sexual politics (Butler 1997), and Riot Grrrls threw such labels back at the society that so often used them to degrade women. The word "slut" has a long history of policing women's behavior and sexual expression, connoting not only sexual behavior but social class and cleanliness: "The history of 'slut' demon-strates a number of things; that historically women have often been seen in terms of their sexual relations to men, and often as a source of pollution; that the term is not only an indicator of gender, but of class; and that it is used by and between women, as well as by men of women" (Attwood 2007, 235). In other words, both men and women have used "slut" to stigmatize women and thus control them. Self-labeling as a slut defuses the word's power, symbolizing a refusal to be policed or controlled, from a woman who enjoys sex and is in charge of her sexuality.

In addition to challenging gender oppression, Riot Grrrls, like their DIY punk and feminist forebears, sought to resist consumerist capitalism. Previously, girls and women, especially, had been viewed as uncritical media *consumers* rather than *producers*—think masses of screeching, sobbing teenyboppers pulling at their hair while Elvis or The Beatles performed, or girls huddled around a magazine article about pop star Justin Bieber. Riot Grrrl's DIY roots fed a disdain for mass-produced pop culture, especially when it reduced girls to shoppers and groupies. As an anti-consumerist movement Riot Grrrls encouraged young women to make their own media, on their own terms. Thus they disdained major record labels to avoid com-promising their vision or having to "package" themselves for a wider audience. Riot Grrrls were "**culture jammers**," interrupting, mocking, and replacing commercial media and advertising messages with art and satire. The beauty and fashion indus-tries were among their central targets. Riot Grrrls created zines in part "to either resist or oppose representations of gender, sexuality, class, race, and age found in mainstream culture" (Kearney 1998, 300). They were not the first contemporary feminists to question sexist media and art or to reclaim the term "girls." Since 1985, a women's activist group called the Guerrilla Girls has used poster campaigns and street theater (sometimes wearing gorilla masks) to challenge women's exclusion from museums and galleries, Hollywood's stereotypical portrayals of women, and racist practices in both.

The digital age provides girls with even greater opportunities to produce media. **New media** includes interactive digital, computerized, and networked technologies most often associated with the Internet. The emergence of new media has further democratized media production, especially for middle and upper class girls. The Internet, for example, has accelerated girls' opportunities to culture jam; "jammer girls" "seek choice, change, place, and media that celebrate the individual, physical, and intellectual qualities of girl-ness, and encourage speaking out about the damage done to girls by the steady stream of commercial messages" (Merskin 2006). As access to computer technology spreads, girls dissatisfied or disgusted with narrow media representations can create their own. The very notion of girls engaging with media technology is radical. Kearney (2006, 12) writes,

> by engaging with the technologies and practices of media production, [girls] are actively subverting the traditional sex/gender system that has kept female cultural practices confined to consumerism, beauty, and the domestic sphere for decades. When girls invest in the role of media producer, stereotypical notions of girlhood and girls' culture are altered radically, and so is the popular understanding of media production, an activity historically constructed as adult- and male-dominated.

Riot Grrrl zine culture persists, but online zines (and blogs, discussion forums, etc.) thrive. Taking charge of their portrayals is a form of power, as is taking an active role in media production. Grrrl culture has segued into **gURL culture**, diverse communities of computer-savvy girls who frequent and contribute to girl-centered sites. Just as zines helped pro-feminist punks network, so too does gURL culture connect young women around a variety of enjoyments and problems. For example, members of www.gurl.com can create their own "bedroom" (the site's name for profile), read frank forums on sex education, ask questions about body image, and find resources regarding eating disorders, birth control, sexual assault, depression, suicide, and other issues. For "cybergurls," new media bring a whole new dimension to bedroom culture—"The Internet allows young women to actively manipulate the borders between public and private, inside and outside, to attempt to manage expression without exploitation, and resistance without appropriation" (A. Harris 2004, 162).

Virtual Sexualities in Fic

Fan fiction has become a significant forum for women's creativity and an important way women use new media. Fic sites provide young women with a forum in which to explore sexual themes in a community that is relatively free from male judgment. As both Riot Grrrls and female hip hop artists showed, girls face a sexual double standard, expected to be sexually available but not *too* interested in sex. Straight men fantasize about seductive women but often prefer real-life women who are less sexually aggressive. A straight boy who shows an interest in pornography is "just being a boy," while a girl with such an interest is deviant, even "slutty." Often marginalized by both the science fiction media industry and fan community, girls and women have turned to fan fiction as a forum for creative expression and a source of community and support. Fic writing is a form of resistance (Jenkins 2006) to both the media industry and dominant beliefs regarding gender and sexuality.

While some fandoms are mixed-gender, many fic communities are woman-centered, and others are women-only (Bury 2005), allowing participants the freedom to discuss their favorite male characters, explore sexual themes, and express fantasies and desire without interference and judgment by men. Some fic writers—many of them straight, bisexual, or lesbian women—produce erotic stories (Lee 2007). The erotic fic genre "Plot? What Plot?" (PWP), also called "Porn Without Plot," may lack a coherent narrative or even a connection to the larger canonical universe, focusing purely on sexual encounters between characters. A "**ship**" (short for relationship) or "**ficship**" involves a relationship between two characters and is often designated by combining the characters' names; Severus Snape and Harry Potter fics become "Snarry." While stories featuring dalliances between straight characters (say, Han Solo and Princess Leia from *Star Wars* or Scully and Mulder from *The X Files*) are common, many explore same-sex relationships. Writers call this genre of fanfic "**slash**": "Slash is...a genre of fanfic that posits a homoerotic relationship between two characters, usually male" (Lee 2007, 88). The name comes from the slash in the pairings, for example Kirk/Spock (or K/S) from *Star Trek* or Harry/Ron from *Harry Potter*. Slash can be extremely sexual, sweetly romantic, or both at the same time. Comic books, TV series, movies, and even cartoons inspire slash fiction. A romantic and often sexually explicit branch of Japanese manga comics and anime cartoons called *hentai* by Westerners has also inspired slash, with *yaoi* (pronounced yah-oh-ee) pairing two males and *yuri* two females.

Slash Genres

Part of the "subculturalness" of fic is insider knowledge of different fic genres:

- Alternative universe (AU): stories set outside the "official" fictional universe or storyline
- Actor slash: involves the actors, not their characters
- Angst: emphasizes characters' emotional relationships
- Hurt/comfort (h/c): one character comforts another injured/anguished character
- Issue: stories with a political slant, such as gay marriage
- First time: the first sexual encounter between the characters
- BDSM: bondage, domination, sadism, and masochism
- Non-con: involve non-consensual sex

SOURCE: Bury 2005, 72

There is no single motivation behind women writing slash. One fan explains that many fans, women included, connect and empathize with the "hero," who often happens to be male (Green, Jenkins, and Jenkins 1998). It follows then that when writing fic, women would rather take the role of the hero than many of the female characters—they may not identify with female archetypes such as the damsel in distress or the sexy seductress. As for the hero's love interest, the hero's "buddy" is convenient because he has an emotional bond with the hero and their relationship is more or less egalitarian and "real," as opposed to sexist or motivated by simple biological (and straight) sexual desire. Perhaps women want intimate, emotional relationships between equals but find them difficult to imagine in a heterosexual context (Bury 2005). However, this explanation is incomplete, as many slash fics include domination and/or sadomasochism. Additionally, women who write slash can safely and anonymously explore a range of taboo sexual fantasies free from the "cultural constraints" on women in everyday life (Green et al. 1998, 16–17). Other women do not necessarily identify with the characters, instead enjoying the power of controlling male characters or the opportunity to create "a new genre that more perfectly expresses their own social visions and fantasies" (ibid., 34). Part of the enjoyment of slash, part of the *fantasy*, lies in the unknown, in *not* being able to fully identify with the characters. And others enjoy slash simply for the raw sexual pleasure, echoing Riot Grrrls' demand that women's desire is natural and good rather than shameful or promiscuous.

Women who write slash "queer" sexuality by challenging widely accepted sexual norms. **Queer theories** question the notion of fixed gender and sexual identities as well as the divisions between "normal" and "deviant" sexualities. Masculinity and femininity are socially constructed; as you've already learned, there are many masculini*ties* and feminini*ties*. Likewise, "gay" and "straight" are too restrictive to encompass the range of sexual identities, let alone sexual behaviors. And perhaps "female" and "male" are too static as well, as intersexed and transsexual individuals make evident. Slash fiction "queers" both sexuality and gender roles by upending the taken-for-granted assumptions that go along with being straight/bisexual/gay, masculine/feminine, even female/male. Romantic slash places men in emotionally vulnerable situations, highlighting men's empathy and compassion. Writers of "gender switch" (also called genderfuck) fic place a character in an opposite-sex body, for example having Harry Potter wake up in a female body. Such play destabilizes the idea that biological sex is permanent, also suggesting that biology does not determine gender. In queering popularly accepted stories and characters, slash challenges beliefs in "normal" sexuality and "natural" identities while highlighting the fluidity of sex and gender. Most "buddy movies" such as *Bad Boys* or *Rush Hour* place straight male characters in emotionally (even sexually) charged situations while upholding the basics of straight hegemonic masculinity. A ficcer who translates that sexual tension and male camaraderie into actual sex and romantic emotion queers the dominant sexual and gender paradigms. Some see this practice as explicitly feminist and/or political; others do not (Bury 2005). Regardless, slash provides a subcultural space in which women can express sexualities that are considered deviant or even taboo in other media forms.

GIRL POWER—POLITICS OR PAYDAY?

Just as Riot Grrrls articulated a new feminist politics, and ficcers (re)wrote sexualities, images of strong women and girls infiltrated the media, seemingly affirming self-confident, ambitious, even powerful girls and women. *Xena: Warrior Princess, Buffy the Vampire Slayer, The Hunger Games*, and *Dollhouse* featured intelligent, resourceful, physically powerful female characters that often outwitted or out-fought their male nemeses. The *Powerpuff Girls* cartoon pitted three superheroic kindergarten girls against various foes, pairing "cute" little girls with sometimes-brutal violence. Girl power, once a feminist, anti-consumerist rallying cry, became yet another marketing device. Clothing designers have taken the Riot Grrrl practice of writing on the body, emblazoning "Playgirl," "Vixen," "Bitch," and "Porn Star" on feminine apparel. And even as the Internet has fueled girls' cultural production it has served as a space for tattooed and pierced "alternative" girls to pose nude at SuicideGirls.com. As with previous youth movements, corporate interests co-opted and commercialized Grrrl power and women's "new" sexual expressiveness for financial gain. Even as many Riot Grrrls studiously avoided media coverage for fear of being misrepresented, by the mid-1990s the media had co-opted "grrrl" to stand for any seemingly independent, "alternative" young woman, from major label musicians such as Courtney Love and Natalie Merchant to athletes and computer-savvy girls (Jacques 2001). A wave of "angry women in rock," including Alanis Morissette and Fiona Apple, gained radio play in the 1990s, and British pop group Spice Girls appropriated girl power!, mass marketing feminine assertiveness and strength but muting the underlying feminist politics (Schilt 2003b). Do such developments further the cause of empowering girls and young women, or do they signal the death of a truly resistant grrrl power?

While girl power may have been co-opted, one could argue that it also increased the visibility of girls and women making media. The very act of making music, Web sites, and zines is an act of resistance for many girls. As you have learned, interpretations of any particular artist or cultural product vary. For some, Lada Gaga may be "just" a good pop singer; for others, she serves as an empowering inspiration. When Gwen Stefani of the band No Doubt sings "Just a Girl," she may be properly "packaged" to be palatable to a mainstream audience, but the lyrics playfully mock patronizing men who curtail women's rights under the guise of protecting women: " 'Cause I'm just a girl / little 'ol me / Don't let me out of your sight / I'm just a girl, all pretty and petite / So don't let me have any rights." Even the *Powerpuff Girls* can serve as a site of feminist resistance within the superhero genre (Hains 2004). Still, stripped of its feminist consciousness and call to *action*, girl power loses much of its potential to inspire girls to make *their own* media—it's easier to imagine playing in Bikini Kill than being the next pop superstar (Schilt 2003b). As you will learn in the final chapter, mass-marketed, commercialized rebellion may depoliticize a subculture, but it also sows the seeds of the next underground movement.

CONCLUSIONS

What impact might Riot Grrrl have had? While corporate advertisers may have co-opted girl power, the era also produced many noteworthy feminist-inspired media. Having begun as a small DIY production, *Bust* magazine—"For women with something to get off their chests"—combines articles on cooking and crafts with profiles of inspiring women. The more political *Bitch* magazine offers a "feminist response to pop culture," challenging "the sexist and narrow-minded media diet that we all—intentionally or not—consume." *Latinitas*, a Web zine created by and for young Hispanic women, seeks "To empower Latina youth through media and technology." And, of course, these print magazines have online versions as well, providing forums for women to respond to articles and make their own contributions. Additionally, grrrl power has coincided with, inspired, or reinforced other women's scenes. The revival of roller derby, a contact sport played on roller skates and reflecting queer and feminist sensibilities about the body and sexuality, combines athleticism with genderplay as competitors often dress in revealing "uniforms" and adopt monikers such as James Blonde and Auntie Climax. Contemporary burlesque, or neo-burlesque, involves women who often do not fit dominant beauty standards performing partial strip-tease with flamboyant costumes and campy flair. Ficcers, in queering popular characters for their own ends, challenge heteronormativity, and the very act of girls occupying a technological space is meaningful. As subcultures, both grrrls and ficcers show that far from being marginalized spectators or passive consumers, girls are increasingly proactive, particularly in new media. They demonstrate that many of today's girls and women, benefitting from previous generations' feminisms, transcend the good girl/bad girl dichotomies foisted upon them by the media, resisting narrow portrayals of femininity by creating their own (Merskin 2006).

DISCUSSION

- Do contemporary scenes such as Riot Grrrl, roller derby, burlesque, and Suicide Girls offer women a space to control, assert, or "reclaim" their sexual agency, or do they continue the sexist exploitation of women?
- How are the challenges that young women face today similar to and different from those faced by women of previous generations?
- Are subcultures such as Riot Grrrl still *necessary*?

KEY IDEAS

Bedroom culture: A girl-centered fandom involving listening to music, collecting posters and magazines, and fantasizing about young pop culture icons. Bedroom culture resulted from girls' limited opportunities to participate in other subcultures, but also served as a temporary refuge from sexual pressures and as a way for girls to set themselves apart from their peers.

Cult of masculinity: The theory that subcultures are spaces for boys (especially working class boys) to gain status by exalting masculinity since they can't gain power, status, and prestige in other arenas. As a result, subcultures are typically male-dominated and masculinist, revolving around masculine concerns, interests, and norms, glorifying traits commonly associated with maleness such as toughness, daring, and delinquency while denigrating everything "feminine."

Culture jamming: A range of activities seeking to satirize hegemonic popular culture. Culture jammers may have any number of motivations, personal and/or political, including challenging commercialism and advertising.

Cybergurls: Computer-savvy girls who use new media to express themselves creatively, often forming online communities with other girls.

Fandom/fan cultures: A community built around shared enjoyment of and emotional connection to a movie, book, band, TV show, comic book, hobby, sport, celebrity, or other piece of popular culture.

Fan fiction: Unauthorized, fan-written stories using characters or settings from an original work of fiction.

Fanspeak: Insider knowledge (such as humor or factoids) and ways of speaking that are particular to specific fandoms.

Fic: Short for "fan fiction" and another name for a work of fan fiction (i.e., a fic). Fic writers are also known as "ficcers."

Ficship: A **fic** highlighting a relation**ship** between two characters, such as Snarry (Snape/Harry). Fans of a particular ficship might identify as "shippers."

New media: The theory that modern media—especially, but not exclusively, the Internet—is an arena of interactive participation and ongoing construction rather than a static entity simply consumed by viewers.

Participatory culture: The theory that people actively contribute to pop culture, appropriating cultural products for their own uses rather than being passive consumers or spectators of media created by a cultural elite.

Queer theory: A body of theory that emerged from feminist theory and gay and lesbian studies and that questions the idea of fixed gender and sexual identities as well as the divisions between "normal" and "deviant" sexualities.

Slash: A genre of fan fiction pairing two or more same-sex characters in romantic and/or sexual relationships.

Unstructured secondariness: Describes conditions in which women or other minorities are present but informally marginalized in a social setting.

RESOURCES

Fanfic sites

livejournal.com

fanfiction.net

skyehawke.com

Trekkies (film, Roger Nygard 1999)

A documentary of *Star Trek* fandom, including interviews with fans and journeys through fan conventions.

Don't Need You: The Herstory of Riot Grrrl (film, Kerri Koch 2005)

Featuring archival footage and interviews with many of the early Riot Grrrls, this DIY film traces the impact of the movement from its origins to the present day.

Rise Above: The Tribe 8 Documentary (film, Tracy Flannigan 2006)

An award-winning documentary about lesbian/queercore band Tribe 8, featuring live performances and interviews but also the political motivations behind the band.

Fan Fiction and Fan Communities in the Age of the Internet: New Essays

Edited by Karen Hellekson and Kristina Busse. 2006. Jefferson, NC: McFarland. A collection of essays by fans/scholars includes a history of media fandom, list of fan terms, and discussions of gender and sexuality in fan fiction.

About-face

www.about-face.org

Recognizing the "toxic media environment" that encourages girls' and women's low self-esteem, body anxiety, and other problems, About-face names the worst media offenders and provides resources for girls and women to fight back.

Guerrilla Girls

www.guerrillagirls.com

A site about some of the original feminist culture jammers.

CosmoGirl

www.cosmogirl.com

An example of a conventional site popular with teenage girls.

Latinitas

www.latinitasmagazine.com

Online magazine targeted toward empowering Latina youth.

CHAPTER 10

Questions and Conclusions— Resistance, Commodification, and Growing Up

Whether or not we are part of a subculture, learning about them teaches us something about ourselves and our social worlds. If you've read carefully, you have some sense of how society constructs deviance and normalcy, labels deviants, and sanctions rule breakers. You've learned about various theories of deviant behavior and that those who society labels deviant are not necessarily psychologically flawed or morally bankrupt. You understand how subcultures both challenge and reinforce dominant gender, race, class, and sexual relations. We've covered a lot of ground, but a few questions remain. Do subcultures, after all, end up resisting anything? What happens when big business commodifies youth culture, and can subcultures resist being bought? Is the term "subculture" still useful, or have distinct subcultures dissolved? And finally, where do subculturists go when they grow up?

DO SUBCULTURES RESIST THE "MAINSTREAM"?

Ask just about any participant in a subculture why they are involved and they will likely give you some version of the same story: "I want to be an individual"; "I don't fit in with the popular kids"; or "I want to be different from mainstream society." Some even profess hatred or disgust toward "normal" kids and the mainstream in general, swearing they will resist ever becoming like their (boring/domineering/wage-slave) parents. For generations, youth have divided up the world into the cool and the uncool or, back in the day, "hip" vs. "square" and have then gone to great lengths to prove they are hip and not square. Whatever the current language, the point is that subcultural youth claim they want something different and want to resist what they see as the negative and conformist aspects of dominant society.

As I stated in the Introduction, early subculture researchers were especially interested in "spectacular" youth style and its meaning. Even though CCCS scholars were sympathetic to the struggles of working class youth, they questioned whether subcultures were little more than symbolic, ritualistic protests that really didn't change much and often even inadvertently reinforced the dominant social class structure (Hall and Jefferson 1976; Willis 1977; Hebdige 1979). Are subcultures all style and no substance, so to speak? Some theorists suggest that youth subcultures are fairly apolitical (e.g., Polhemus 1998 Muggleton 2000), more interested in consuming a lifestyle than challenging the status quo—youth just want to have fun! After all, what are club hoppers, emo kids, and nu metal goths really resisting? Perhaps we shouldn't even be thinking of subcultures in terms of resistance.

In my own work, I show that current theoretical explanations of resistance are too narrow to capture the multitude of *meanings, sites,* and *methods* of resistance (Haenfler 2004c). Subculturists construct many different meanings around their lifestyles, both individual and collective. Collectively, skinheads resisted what they saw as the decline of working class culture and opportunity; but an individual skin may have more personal reasons for involvement. Coming out as a gay skinhead or queer punk may have significant *individual* meaning. Subculturists engage in resistance at many different sites besides the government or class structure. For some kids, parents become targets of resistance; for others, peers, teachers, the opposite sex, or media conglomerates become targets. Finally, youth employ many methods of resistance, both personal and political. In some contexts, dressing differently may be a powerful statement. Same-sex couples holding hands in public can be a form of resistance, as can promoting a vegetarian lifestyle. Rather than thinking of it in traditionally political terms—protesting the government or engaging in class politics—or in purely symbolic terms—fashion and style—we need a broader conceptualization of resistance. To really understand resistance we need to know something about subculturists' subjective experiences (Leblanc 1999). Subcultures simultaneously reinforce and resist both mainstream and youth culture, yet ultimately, as the Riot Grrrls demonstrate, they can create a meaningful space of resistance that transcends a subculture's style.

Some theorists in the post-subcultures tradition are reexamining the political potential of subcultures (see Muggleton and Weinzierl 2003).[45] Subcultures and social movements are not necessarily distinct phenomena, and cultural and political changes are not mutually exclusive. To say that subcultures are "inherently" radical or always hedonistic and politically disengaged oversimplifies the issue. Some youth belong to overtly political subcultures such as certain feminist, animal rights, queer, and anarchist groups. Others, such as those who identify with the "global justice" movement, might align their lifestyles with their values by shopping for fairly traded goods and avoiding big-box chain retailers or companies with poor human rights records. Most combine alternative lifestyles with political action. A feminist punk might challenge traditionally feminine standards of beauty day to day ("cultural" resistance) while also occasionally lobbying for reproductive rights (a "political" challenge). Some subculturists engage the political process more directly. Punks have used their DIY skills and independent media networks to engage in social movements, including Rock Against Racism in 1970s' Britain; peace, nuclear freeze, and anti-apartheid in 1980s' U.S. hardcore; and feminism in the 1990s' Riot Grrrl scene (Moore and Roberts 2009). On the other end of the political spectrum, right-wing movements in Germany capitalize on commercialized subculture identities to organize youth into both voting blocks and violent gangs; rather than stifling political potential, commercialization helps gather support (Deicke 2007).

So, while resistance is not an essential aspect of every subculture, the potential for subcultural resistance is there, though not always in the forms we might expect. Still, with the growth of mass media and consumerism, one has to wonder: What impact does commercialization have on subcultural resistance?

COMMODIFICATION—CAN THE REVOLUTION BE BOUGHT?

If you've ever walked into a Hot Topic store at your local mall you probably noticed a hodgepodge of styles representing a variety of scenes all mixed together in a kind of alternative stew. Whether you identify as punk, goth, emo, metal, as a gamer, or you just want a spiked belt, there is a tattooed, spiky-haired, black-clad employee ready to help you find what you're after. Subcultural fashion is easily commodified, and packaging subcultural style is nothing new—fashionable London boutiques marketed punk, mod, and new wave chic in the 1970s. The difference now is that scene marketing occurs on a massive scale. As much as Hot Topic tries to present itself as cool and underground, it is a large corporation with hundreds of stores in shopping malls everywhere. The Internet has also made marketing counterculture into big business. Sites like Interpunk.com, Gothshop.com, and dozens of online hip hop stores make purchasing subcultural style easier than ever.

Subculturists, as we've repeatedly observed, like to think of themselves as opposed to, separate from, and superior to mainstream capitalist society, often including the business world. Yet subcultural life depends upon production and consumption, so where is the line between underground economics and mainstream co-optation? A pessimistic (or realistic?) view is that simply engaging in market economics corrupts any real political potential of countercultures (Heath and Potter 2004). In fact, youth "rebellion" is a great marketing tool and fuels the ongoing innovation that capitalists need to sell us the "hot new thing." For example, companies use skateboarding to sell soda, video games, and clothing. Nike used The Beatles song "Revolution" to sell shoes (Frank 1998). *Rebellion sells.* Kids walking around with freedom fighter Ché Guevara's image on their t-shirts are likely not joining an armed revolution. Middle-class kids text-messaging each other about Fall Out Boy's performance on the Honda Civic Tour doesn't seem very subversive. Blogging about their alienating high school experience on Facebook or Livejournal hardly seems radical. The longer a subculture exists the more the mainstream becomes "acclimatized" and groups such as punk lose their capacity to "shock and dismay" (Clark 2003, 223–224). Subversive style diffuses through society, subsequently defusing its subversive potential (see Hall and Jefferson 1976).

Scenes are eventually co-opted by the mainstream, not to stifle their subver-siveness but because they help sell products (R. Moore 2005). Rather than resisting commercial mainstream society, marketers incorporate youth culture into their product lines and sales pitches. In fact, just as some segments of society (such as police and politicians) persecute marginal youth, business tries to figure out how to make money, as Ryan Moore (2005, 231) suggests:

> The authoritarian institutions of society try to censor and discipline young peo-ple, but at the same time the entertainment industry of fashion, music, and mov-ies knows that there is profit to be made from the extremely valuable and coveted demographic of young consumers. Corporations and advertisers know that this youth market is notoriously fickle and cannot be easily manipulated through simple marketing hype, and so they try to align themselves with music, fashion, images, and celebrities that appear to young people as authentic, cutting-edge, or cool.

Corporations even employ "cool hunters"—that is, young marketing professionals who scour underground youth scenes in search of hip fashions, slang, and activities that can be co-opted into the next big money-making trend. Commercialization might be more harmful to a subculture than authoritarian repression or disgust—the social stigma associated with subcultures may actually boost their adherents, but once an underground innovation becomes a marketable commodity, dollar signs often stifle subversion.

All this makes resisting the corporate machine sound pretty tough, if not impossible. However, from the idealistic subculturists' viewpoint there is still room for hope. Rather than stifling resistance completely, the commodification of youth subcultures creates new opportunities for subcultural resistance (Clark 2003). While still operating in a capitalist system, many subcultural businesses find small ways to resist commodification and remain independent of big busi-ness. Washington D.C.'s Dischord Records and bands such as Fugazi have long been held up as the epitome of independent rock. They sell music for reasonable prices, refuse to print t-shirts and other band merchandise, and insist on playing all-ages shows. Other labels, like Alternative Tentacles, Bridge 9, and SST, record and promote music that many mainstream labels would never touch. Hip hopper Sage Francis works largely independent of the mainstream hip hop world, often with an explicitly political message. Outside of music, hackers and other com-puter geeks write shareware and freeware programs, seeing their efforts as creative expression and subverting the Microsoft monopoly. Perhaps most importantly, older subculturists often shed the fashionable trappings of their youth and focus instead on living the values of their scene more fully (see Bennett and Hodkinson 2012). Imagine an "ex-hippy" who no longer smokes dope, engages in "free love," or wears tie-dye, beads, and flower power buttons but instead buys organic food, drives a hybrid car, gets involved in progressive politics, and works for a nonprofit agency promoting immigrants' rights. Once subculturists transcend the confor-mity within their own scene, they embrace the individuality their scene professed to offer all along. Substance supplants style, and "The threatening pose has been replaced by the actual threat" (Clark 2003, 234).

Indie-Nike?

Converse, maker of the Chuck Taylor All-Stars (which are, along with Doc Martens, the iconic subcultural shoe) is actually owned by Nike.[46]

DO DISTINCT SUBCULTURES EXIST?

One of the main problems with trying to define subcultures these days is that the term implies artificial boundaries between groups when in fact there is a great deal of overlap between them. Perhaps distinct subcultures don't really exist? Take heavy metal and rap, for instance. These music genres have converged for over two decades, beginning with Run D.M.C. and Aerosmith, then Ice T and Bodycount, and leading to bands such as Rage Against the Machine and even nu-metal act Korn and experimental hardcore band Candiria. Metal has also blended with goth (such as Marilyn Manson), and goth has returned to punk (for example, AFI). But beyond blends in music, many subcultures share common values and histories. The hippies emerged from the beats, skinheads from the mods. Fashions have certainly begun to overlap significantly. If you see a kid with a black shirt, dyed black hair, a spiked belt, eyeliner, and a lip ring, is he part of the punk, emo, goth, indie, or new metal scene? Many subcultures also share beliefs—most question government and religious authority and profess resistance to conformity. These common beliefs, practices, and histories have led to new ways of thinking about youth groups such as the *scenes* and *neo-tribes* I described in previous chapters.

The Cultic Milieu

Given the advances in media technology and the intense commodification of youth culture, it's easier than ever for youth to be exposed to a variety of different scenes within the cultic milieu. The **cultic milieu** encompasses the collective underground of seekers, followers of alternative religions, subculturists, and radicals, all considered deviant in one way or another (Campbell 1972; Kaplan and Lööw 2002). Within this milieu, subcultures tend toward both fragmentation into more specialized subgroups and "**syncretization**," or the convergence of ideas, values, and styles. Straight edge shares values with virginity pledgers, environmentalists, punks, metal kids, hippies, and skinheads, even while being distinct in many important ways (Haenfler 2006). Even seemingly disparate groups are often linked in the cultic milieu. Evangelical youth have appropriated the punk rock aesthetic (and vice versa), showing off their purple hair, torn pants, and tattoos as they rock out to Christian hardcore and nu-metal bands (Beaujon 2006; Sandler 2006). Both punks and Christians share dissatisfaction with the world and a search for collective meaning. Both emphasize resisting societal pressures and cultivating authenticity. In fact, there is likely a Christian-oriented faction to most youth cultures, including hip hop and heavy metal. As scenes splinter into more and more factions, spreading out over the subcultural terrain, it's almost inevitable that these different subgroups come into contact and gradually share and borrow ideas.

Genres of Metal

A Wikipedia search of "heavy metal" reveals the many subgenres within one overarching subculture and also the overlap between metal and other subcultures[47]:
Avant-garde metal—Black metal—Christian metal—Classic metal—Death metal—Doom metal—Folk metal—Glam metal—Gothic metal—Grindcore—Groove metal—Industrial metal—Metalcore—Nu metal—NWOBHM—Post-metal—Power metal—Progressive metal—Speed metal—Symphonic metal—Thrash metal—Viking metal.

The Internet has accelerated both syncretism and fragmentation and is perhaps one of the most striking developments in subcultural history. As we saw in Chapter 8, subcultures are less and less bound to specific places as online communities grow. Given so much overlap and fluidity in the cultic milieu and online, we have to ask whether the whole notion of subculture is outdated. After all, the Internet connects people on a global scale and makes access to the cultic milieu easier for more and more people.

American Juggalo

This short film documents the annual Gathering of the Juggalos where fans of rap duo Insane Clown Posse come together for a week of partying with their deviant "family." Juggalos draw upon a variety of youth cultures—hip hop, punk, stoners, metal—illustrating syncretism and bricolage as they combine a variety of styles into new forms.

SOURCE: http://www.americanjuggalo.com

WHAT HAPPENS WHEN YOUTH GROW UP?

Have you ever wondered what happened to the original hippies, skinheads, and punks? Did they sell out, get corporate jobs, have 2.1 kids, and move to suburbia? Some of them probably did. Yet not everyone "grows up," sheds their subculture identity, dons business attire, and moves on (A. Bennett 2006). Plenty of adults still identify as punks, hip hoppers, goths, and so on, reconciling their youthful identities and interests with careers, domestic life, and their ageing bodies (Hodkinson 2011). Others discover new scenes that accommodate their adult lives, and some start or work for businesses connected with subcultures, making a living while maintaining a connection to youth. Similar to someone pursuing an occupational career, subculturists have *deviant* careers with different stages.

Deviant Careers

A **deviant career** includes all the stages of a person's participation in deviance, especially how people enter and exit their deviant lifestyles. In accordance with labeling theory, Becker (1963) identifies several stages in a deviant career, focusing especially on adopting a deviant identity and engaging in an ongoing pattern of deviance. First, an individual commits a deviant act, sometimes on purpose but often by ignorance or accident. People who generally abide by conventional norms and laws then have to justify or neutralize their deviance. They may claim (to others and to themselves) that the deviant act was a one-time thing. An occasional shoplifter might justify his actions by claiming that the store makes so much money they won't miss a few small items. People for whom deviance becomes a way of life must somehow learn to enjoy deviance, often in the company of others. Becker, for example, noted that marijuana users had to learn to use and enjoy marijuana. Eventually, the individual may be caught and publicly labeled deviant, leading to a marred reputation and possible exclusion from more conventional social circles. In a conservative small town, an unmarried teenage girl known to have sex or an openly gay young man could be ostracized from their church youth group. The person's public identity has changed; in effect, her or his identity is "spoiled." Finally, as a result of being cut off from legitimate social groups, the person increasingly associates with other deviants, where she or he finds greater acceptance. Clearly, however, this only reinforces the deviant label.

Becker's Stages of Entering a Deviant Career

Commission of a nonconforming act

Justification and neutralization of deviance

Being caught and publicly labeled deviant

Being cut off from more legitimate groups

Increasing involvement with others who have been labeled deviant

---

While Becker focused primarily on entering a deviant career, later scholars investigated the other stages of deviant life, especially how people exit. Many kinds of deviance (particularly *illegal* behavior) are much more widespread among youth

(Best 2004). Remember from the introduction that control theory suggests that people who have strong social bonds and responsibilities are less likely to engage in deviant behavior. As people age, the hassles of maintaining a deviant identity often eventually outweigh the benefits. It's easier to dress strangely, go to clubs, and hang out when one is less worried about holding a job or supporting a family. For most, the costs of deviance become too high and the benefits of "legitimate life" become too appealing (ibid.).

While the notion of a deviant career is useful, comparing deviant and legitimate careers has its limitations, as they have significant differences (Best and Luckenbill 1982). In conventional careers, people generally expect to consistently gain status and compensation, progressing along a more or less linear promotion path. Deviant careers, however, are much less linear. People enter and exit, gain and lose status, and generally follow a less predictable and stable career path. Sometimes people have trouble leaving a deviant lifestyle for good. They move on only to return for a while before leaving once again. Drug dealers, for example, generally see dealing as a temporary occupation and often eventually tire of dodging law enforcement, managing their business, and taking too many drugs (Adler and Adler 1983). The risks begin to outweigh the excitement and benefits of dealing. However, several things make leaving the drug trade difficult. Dealers become accustomed to the easy money, high-spending, and free-wheeling lifestyle, they are reluctant to leave their dealer status and friends, and they have trouble finding other work (ibid.). They exit and reenter, sometimes a number of times, before finally (if ever) leaving their deviant careers behind. Still others walk the fine line between the deviant and legitimate worlds, continuing deals here and there while running legal businesses or working legitimate jobs.

Several studies of punks give us some idea of how subculturists age in their scenes. Davis (2006) argues that punks may take several paths as they age, each one interpreted differently by punks. "Scene rejecters" shift their energies from the scene toward other pursuits, often leaving remaining punks feeling betrayed. However, refusing to "grow up" entirely is also problematic. "Stagnant punks" remain heavily involved as they age and fail to "move on" in any significant way. Their "age inappropriate" involvement sometimes draws ridicule—punks may deem a thirty-five-year-old trying to look like a nineteen-year-old undignified. Yet punks do not view all of their aging counterparts with disdain. "Career punks" manage to assume adult responsibilities such as parenthood while maintaining their commitment to the scene, for example, making a modest living by running a record label. Scene "legends" are those who maintain involvement in the scene and forge a career out of the music, such as playing in a commercially successful band while staying true to punk's DIY ideals. Finally, "corporate incorporators" pursue careers outside punk but still make the scene a priority in their lives by hanging out with punks and going to shows when possible. All of the punk "career paths" demonstrate that aging in the scene is an ongoing, negotiated process lacking in clear-cut boundaries and age markers—graduating from college, having a child, or turning thirty does not automatically expel one from the punk identity. Many subculturists integrate scene skills and values into their work lives, often crafting DIY careers or using scene skills or reputations (e.g. networking and organization) in conventional careers (Driver 2011; Haenfler 2011).

Many punks negotiate ways of maintaining a punk identity while engaging in more adult/mainstream activities, often trading some of the punk style for a focus on the substance. They feel less need to outwardly demonstrate their commitment (A. Bennett 2006). Andes (1998) calls this **transcendence**, when subculturists focus less on fashion and the scene community and more on the ideals and philosophy underlying the identity. Subculturists have their own subjective interpretations of growing older in the scene and their interpretation of their deviant identity changes over time. Straight edge kids, for example, find new expressions for their subcultural values as their involvement wanes, creating new meanings and incorporating new understandings that are compatible with life outside of the subculture (Haenfler 2006). They keep their straight edge identity relevant to their lives by redefining their commitment to the identity. For example, being drug-free might become part of being a good parent or mentor to younger kids. For some, wearing Xs, band shirts, and showing tattoos continues to be a form of resistance in their adult lives, even as they enter into conventional workplaces; for others, showing their "edge" identity feels unnecessary or awkward, like being "stuck" in their youth (Haenfler 2012). Commitment is less about going to every show and more about maintaining and demonstrating a personally meaningful set of values. Even those who no longer claim the straight edge identity or practice its core values report that the scene has significant and lasting residual impacts on their lives (Torkelson 2010).

"Adult" Subcultures

Although the focus of this book has been youth-oriented subcultures, it's not as if adults don't participate in subcultural groups. Some adult groups seem relatively tame compared to scenes we have studied; wine, ballroom dancing, and book clubs hardly seem deviant and would even be considered mainstream. Yet many of these groups often have their own vocabulary, status hierarchy, and history, potentially making them worthy of consideration as subcultures. Some adult groups rival skinheads and goths in their deviance—sexual swingers, outlaw biker gangs, and transvestite troupes, to name but a few. Other adults become involved in religious or spiritual subcultures, sometimes called "new religious movements." Wiccans, Scientologists, and "New Agers" fall into this category. Still others, motivated by a passion for social justice or the environment, join activist groups that comprise a subculture even while being part of social movements. Feminist and queer groups often combine political activism with alternative culture. While not all of these groupings are subcultures in the strictest sense, they all have subcultural elements.

"Adult" Subcultures?

Bikers

Feminist and queer groups

Sexual swingers

Activists

Mountain climbers

Religious groups and new religious movements

Gamers

Science fiction

Bar/club cultures

Slow food and simple living

Many (if not most) subcultures are neither distinctly youth nor adult oriented. In fact, perhaps "youth" or "youth culture" has less to do with age than with identity, lifestyle, and consumption. Many people extend their "youth" well into their thirties, postponing careers, families, and other markers of adulthood, and some subcultures span many generations. The tattoo and body modification subcultures, for instance, transcend age boundaries to some degree. Computer gaming culture and fan fiction are not confined to youth but instead stretch into adulthood. The rodeo circuit involves both youth and adults. Still, people of different ages participate in different ways; sixteen-year-old and forty-year-old metal fans generally have different perceptions of slam-dancing. As I've repeatedly shown, the old idea of subcultures as distinct, stable, oppositional, youth-oriented groups hasgiven way to a more fluid understanding of subculture, scene, neo-tribe, and so on. It's up to you to decide if the theories I've presented throughout this book help you make sense of whatever groups you might encounter.

FINAL THOUGHTS

Subcultures may seem like a silly topic to have garnered so much attention from academics; perhaps our focus would be better spent on the economy, war, poverty, or other seemingly "bigger" issues. While I might argue that any part of human experience is worthy of investigation, I believe there are a number of more "practical" reasons for the importance of youth culture studies. First, as I mentioned in the introduction, youth subcultures often shine a light on the "invisible," or taken-for-granted (and often arbitrary) rules, inequalities, and hypocrisies embedded in our relationships and social institutions—why are neck tattoos deviant but breast implants are not? Why is spending hundreds of dollars on a designer handbag considered rational while spending hundreds of hours in virtual worlds is weird?

Subcultures challenge conventional ways of thinking, even while reflecting the world in which they exist. They also give many youth a voice, via music, art, or the expression of alternative identities and ideas. Subcultural expression offers youth a meaningful way to counter their marginalization. Young people, especially those associated with subcultures, face significant challenges, and the media, politicians, and other authorities too often cast kids and their activities as a social problem without understanding youths' daily lives. Finally, youth involved in subcultures *do* get older, and as I've shown in this chapter subcultural experiences often translate into adulthood in one way or another. To begin to understand our social institutions it is probably a good idea to consider people's formative experiences and identities.

As this book comes to an end, I think it's great if you're wondering, "Why didn't he have a chapter on electronic dance music? Or graffiti writers? Or lowrider culture? Or skateboarders? Or…?" You get the idea. Any book of this kind necessarily leaves out more than it includes—I've only scratched the surface of youth subcultures and deviance. While I may not have been able to discuss every subculture out there, I hope to have accomplished something more important—helping you cultivate the theoretical tools and the intellectual curiosity to examine and ask meaningful questions about *any* subculture or deviant group. Just because we discussed race and gender in relation to hip hop doesn't mean you can't consider white privilege, sexism, and racism in other contexts. We may have used computer gaming to illustrate virtual communities, but you can use what you learned to think about other online groups. You might never read about goths again, but if you understand the concept of stigma and can apply it to other subcultures, we've achieved some measure of success. Even if you couldn't relate to heavy metal, I hope you can think critically in the future when the next set of moral entrepreneurs stokes the fire of moral panic. The power to ask your own meaningful questions is one of the gifts of social theory.

I hope you understand the constructed nature of deviance, in particular that powerful people and industries define what is "normal" and what is deviant. Recognizing that social forces outside of us influence our beliefs and choices is a humbling, but empowering, insight. The next time you see someone covered in tattoos, a guy wearing makeup, or a kid with pants fifteen sizes too big, perhaps you'll stop and consider what you've learned before rushing to judgment. Acknowledging that "right" and "wrong," "weird" and "normal" are not always black and white can be disorienting and disconcerting, but ultimately it leads to greater compassion and understanding. There are no impenetrable walls between subcultures and popular culture, and most of us have more in common than we might think. Finally, I hope you see that life can be fun at the margins, people find meaning in difference, and that diversity keeps life interesting.

KEY IDEAS

Cultic Milieu: The collective underground of seekers, followers of alternative religions, subculturists, and radicals who share alternative beliefs and are connected by virtue of their deviance.

Deviant career: The stages of a person's participation in deviance.

Syncretization: The convergence of ideas, values, and styles in the cultic milieu.

Transcendence: Stage of a subcultural career when individuals focus less on fashion, music, and the scene and more on personal values and philosophies.

RESOURCES

Exit Through the Gift Shop (film, Banksy 2010) Thierry Guetta follows world-renowned street artists such as Banksy, Invader, and Shepard Fairey as they practice their craft, eventually manufacturing his own fame as artist "Mr.Brainwash." This award-winning film wrestles with issues of commercialization, incorporation, and resistance, as well as the question of what "counts" as art.

Merchants of Cool: A Report on the Creators and Marketers of Popular Culture for Teenagers (film, Rachel Dretzin and Barak Goodman 2001)

A PBS *Frontline* documentary about how corporations and the media use youth culture to make millions and, in the process, influence youth attitudes and values. You can watch it online at www.pbs.org/wgbh/pages/frontline/shows/cool.

The Other F Word (film, Andrea Blaugrund Nevins 2011)

A documentary about being a punk rock father, featuring members of Rancid, Rise Against, Pennywise, Bad Religion, and other bands, as well as pro skater Tony Hawk.

Ageing and Youth Cultures: Music, Style and Identity

Edited by Andy Bennet and Paul Hodkinson, 2012. Oxford: Berg.

A collection of scholarly essays about "older" participants in a variety of youth scenes, including sections on style, the body, and community.

References

Aapola, Sinikka, Marnina Gonick, and Anita Harris. 2005. *Young Femininity: Girlhood, Power and Social Change.* New York: Palgrave Macmillan.

Adler, Patricia, and Peter Adler. 1983. "Shifts and Oscillations in Deviant Careers: The Case of Upper-Level Drug Dealers and Smugglers." *Social Problems* 31 (2): 195–207.

Agger, Ben. 2004. *The Virtual Self: A Contemporary Sociology.* Oxford: Blackwell Publishing.

Andersen, Mark, and Mark Jenkins. 2001. *Dance of Days: Two Decades of Punk in the Nation's Capital.* New York: Soft Skull Press.

Anderson, Elijah. 1991. *Street Wise: Race, Class, and Change in an Urban Community.* Chicago: University of Chicago Press.

Andes, Linda. 1998. "Growing Up Punk: Meaning and Commitment Careers in a Contemporary Youth Subculture." In *Youth Culture: Identity in a Postmodern World*, ed. Jonathan Epstein, 213–231. Malden, MA: Blackwell.

Aranza, Jacob. 1983. *Backward Masking Unmasked: Backward Satanic Messages of Rock and Roll Exposed.* Shreveport, LA: Huntington House.

Archer, Debbie. 1998. "Riot Grrrl and Raisin Girl: Femininity Within the Female Gang." In *The British Criminology Conferences: Selected Proceedings. Volume 1: Emerging Themes in Criminology*, ed. Jon Vagg and Tim Newburn. Papers from the 1998 British Criminology Conference, Londonborough University. https://docs.google.com/viewer?a=v&q= cache:3c9dRuTpNrkJ:www.britsoccrim.org/volume1/002.pdf+%E2%80%9CRiot- +Grrrl+and+Raisin+Girl:+Femininity+Within+the+Female+Gang.%E2%80%9D &hl=en&gl=us&pid=bl&srcid=ADGEESg9f9Mx3ZBbAnhqyh8TNRgBL65HnL4- UEOIYaw8Ip3f9muIpZv-do46qe2AxxcZji8KuCWKnmZeu1DjKYImDxAMpfpdEA zNG8psVFBSeUzpawl8DFJfdWEGH975-rCo0pKYF5zwk&sig=AHIEtbRkquGWF_ agyIAY70cJ1nPIGIYOSw (accessed December 10, 2011).

Arnett, Jeffrey. 1991. "Adolescents and Heavy Metal Music: From the Mouths of Metalheads." *Youth and Society* 23: 76–98.

Arnett, Jeffrey Jensen. 1996. *Metalheads: Heavy Metal Music and Adolescent Alienation.* Boulder, CO: Westview Press.

Atkinson, Michael. 2003. "The Civilizing of Resistance: Straightedge Tattooing." *Deviant Behavior* 24: 197–220.

Attwood, Feona. 2007. "Sluts and Riot Grrrls: Female Identity and Sexual Agency." *Journal of Gender Studies* 16 (3): 233–247.

Bailey, Brian. 2005. "Emo Music and Youth Culture." In *Contemporary Youth Culture: An International Encyclopedia*, eds. Shirley R. Steinberg, Priya Parmar and Bergit Richard, 338–343. Westport, CT: Greenwood Press.

Baron, Stephen W. 1989. "Resistance and Its Consequences: The Street Culture of Punks." *Youth and Society* 21 (2): 207–237.

Bearman, Peter S., and Hannah Brückner. 2001. "Promising the Future: Virginity Pledges and First Intercourse." *American Journal of Sociology* 106 (4): 859–912.

Beaujon, Andrew. 2006. *Body Piercing Saved My Life: Inside the Phenomenon of Christian Rock*. New York: Da Capo Press.

Becker, Howard. 1963. *Outsiders: Studies in the Sociology of Deviance*. New York: Free Press.

Bennett, Andy. 1999. "Subcultures or Neo-Tribes? Rethinking the Relationship Between Youth, Style and Musical Taste." *Sociology* 33 (3): 599–617.

———. 2000. *Popular Music and Youth Culture: Music, Identity and Place*. New York: Palgrave Macmillan.

———. 2001. *Cultures of Popular Music*. Maidenhead, UK: Open University Press.

———. 2006. "Punk's Not Dead: The Significance of Punk Rock for an Older Generation of Fans." *Sociology* 40 (1): 219–235.

Bennett, Andy, and Keith Kahn-Harris. 2004. *After Subculture: Critical Studies in Contemporary Youth Culture*. New York: Palgrave Macmillan.

Bennett, Andy, and Paul Hodkinson. 2012. *Ageing and Youth Cultures: Music, Style, and Identity*. Oxford: Berg.

Bennett, Andy, and Richard A. Peterson, eds. 2004. *Music Scenes: Local, Translocal, and Virtual*. Nashville: Vanderbilt University Press.

Bennett, William. 1994. *De-Valuing of America: The Fight for Our Culture and Our Children*. New York: Simon & Schuster.

Berger, Peter L., and Thomas Luckman. 1966. *The Social Construction of Reality: A Treatise in the Sociology of Knowledge*. New York: Doubleday and Co.

Bersamin, Melina M., Samantha Walker, Elizabeth D. Waiters, Deborah A. Fisher, and Joel W. Grube. "Promising To Wait: Virginity Pledges and Adolescent Sexual Behavior." *Journal of Adolescent Health* 36 (5): 428–436.

Best, Joel. 2004. *Deviance: Career of a Concept*. New York: Wadsworth.

Best, Joel, and David F. Luckenbill. 1982. *Organizing Deviance*. Englewood Cliffs, NJ: Prentice-Hall.

Bianco, David P., ed. 1998. *Parents Aren't Supposed to Like It: Rock and Other Pop Musicians of the 1990s*. Detroit: UXL.

Bigg, Matthew. 2006. Fewer US High School Students Having Sex: Report. *Reuters*, August 10, 2006. http://www.redorbit.com/news/health/611216/fewer_us_high_school_students_having_sex_report/index.html (accessed April 14, 2008).

Blumer, Herbert. 1969. *Symbolic Interactionism: Perspective and Method*. Englewood Cliffs, NJ: Prentice-Hall.

Blush, Steven. 2001. *American Hardcore: A Tribal History*. Los Angeles: Feral House.

Bonilla-Silva, Eduardo. 2009. *Racism Without Racists: Colorblind Racism and the Persistence of Racial Inequality in America* (3rd edition). Lanham, MD: Rowan and Littlefield.

Brake, Mike. 1980. *The Sociology of Youth Culture and Youth Subcultures: Sex and Drugs and Rock 'n' Roll*. London: Routledge and Kegan Paul.

Brake, Mike. 1985. *Comparative Youth Culture: The Sociology of Youth Culture and Youth Subcultures in America, Britain, and Canada.* London: Routledge and Kegan Paul.

Brill, Dunja. 2008. *Goth Culture: Gender, Sexuality and Style.* Oxford: Berg.

Brückner, Hannah, and Peter Bearman. 2005. "After the Promise: The STD Consequences of Adolescent Virginity Pledges." *Journal of Adolescent Health* 36: 271–278.

Brumberg, Joan Jacobs. 1997. *The Body Project: An Intimate History of American Girls.* New York: Random House.

Buford, William. 1992. *Among the Thugs: The Experience, and the Seduction, of Crowd Violence.* New York: W. W. Norton & Company.

Burghart, Devin (ed.). 1999. *Soundtracks to the White Revolution: White Supremacist Assaults on Youth Music Subcultures.* Chicago: Center for New Community.

Bury, Rhiannon. 2005. *Cyberspaces of Their Own: An Ethnographic Investigation of Fandoms and Femininities.* New York: Peter Lang Publishers.

Butler, Judith. 1997. *Excitable Speech: A Politics of the Performative.* New York and London: Routledge.

Campbell, Colin. 1972. "The Cult, the Cultic Milieu and Secularization." In *A Sociological Yearbook of Religion in Britain* 5, 119–136. London: SCM Press.

Castronova, Edward. 2005. *Synthetic Worlds: The Business and Culture of Online Games.* Chicago: University of Chicago Press.

———. 2008. *Exodus to the Virtual World: How Online Fun is Changing Reality.* New York: Palgrave Macmillan.

Chee, Florence, Marcelo Vieta, and Richard Smith. 2006. "Online Gaming and the Interactional Self: Identity Interplay in Situated Practice." In *Gaming as Culture: Essays on Reality, Identity, and Experience in Fantasy Games*, ed. J. P. Williams, S. Q. Hendricks, and W. K. Winkler, 154–174. Jefferson, NC: McFarland Publishing.

Chesney-Lind, Meda, and Katherine Irwin. 2008. *Beyond Bad Girls: Gender, Violence, and Hype.* New York: Routledge.

Clark, Dylan. 2003. "The Death and Life of Punk, the Last Subculture." In *The Post-Subcultures Reader*, ed. David Muggleton and Rupert Weinzierl, 223–236. Oxford: Berg.

Cohen, Albert. 1955. *Delinquent Boys.* New York: The Free Press.

Cohen, Stanley. 1993. *Folk Devils and Moral Panics: The Creation of the Mods and the Rockers.* Cambridge, MA: Blackwell. (Orig. pub. 1972.)

Coleman, Gabriella. 2010. "The Anthropology of Hackers." *The Atlantic* September 21, 2010. http://www.theatlantic.com/technology/archive/2010/09/the-anthropology-of-hackers/63308 (accessed November 7, 2011).

———. 2011. "Anonymous: From the Lulz to Collective Action." In the "Politics in the Age of Secrecy and Transparency" cluster. The New Everyday. http://mediacommons. futureofthebook.org/tne/pieces/anonymous-lulz-collective-action (accessed November 8, 2011).

Collins, Randall. 1975. *Conflict Sociology: Toward an Explanatory Science.* New York: Academic Press.

Comstock, Michelle. 2001. "Grrrl Zine Networks: ReComposing Spaces of Authority, Gender, and Culture." *Journal of Advanced Composition* 21 (2): 383–409.

Condry, Ian. 2006. *Hip-Hop Japan: Rap and the Paths of Cultural Globalization.* Durham, NC: Duke University Press.

Constantine, Norman A., and Braverman, Marc T. 2004. "Appraising Evidence on Program Effectiveness." In *Foundations and Evaluation: Contexts and Practices for Effective*

Philanthropy, ed. Marc T. Braverman, Norman A. Constantine, and Jana K. Slater, 236–258. San Francisco: Jossey-Bass.

Correll, Shelley. 1995. "The Ethnography of an Electronic Bar: The Lesbian Café." *Journal of Contemporary Ethnography* 24 (3): 270–298.

Cressey, Paul G. 1932. *The Taxi Dance Hall: A Sociological Study of Commercialized Recreation and City Life*. New York: Greenwood Press.

Crowe, Nic, and Simon Bradford. 2007. "Identity and Structure in Online Gaming: Young People's Symbolic and Virtual Extensions of Self." In *Youth Cultures: Scenes, Subcultures, and Tribes*, ed. Paul Hodkinson and Wolfgang Deicke, 215–228. London: Routledge.

Davis, Joanna R. 2006. "Growing Up Punk: Negotiating Aging Identity in a Local Music Scene." *Symbolic Interaction* 29 (1): 63–69.

Decker, J. L. 1994. "The State of Rap: Time and Place in Hip Hop Nationalism." In *Microphone Fiends: Youth Music and Youth Culture*, ed. Andrew Ross and Tricia Rose, 99–121. New York: Routledge.

Deicke, Wolfgang. 2007. "Resistance and Commercialisation in 'Distasteful Movements': Right-Wing Politics and Youth Culture in East Germany." In *Youth Cultures Scenes, Subcultures and Tribes*, ed. Paul Hodkinson and Wolfgang Deicke, 93–110. London: Routledge.

Denski, Stan, and David Sholle. 1992. "Metal Men and Glamour Boys: Gender Performance in Heavy Metal." In *Men, Masculinity, and the Media*, ed. Steve Craig, 41–60. Thousand Oaks: Sage Publications.

Doll, Lynda, Lyle Peterson, Carol White, Eric Johnson, John Ward, and the Blood Donor Study Group. 1992. "Homosexually and Non-homosexually Identified Men Who Have Sex With Men: A Behavioral Comparison." *The Journal of Sex Research* 29: 1–14.

Driver, Christopher. 2011. "Hardcore Bodies in The Labour Market: On Subcultural Capital and Careers." Paper presented at the annual meetings of The Australian Sociological Association. November 2011. Newcastle, Australia.

Dunning, Eric, Patrick Murphy, and John Williams. 1986. "Spectator Violence at Football Matches: Towards a Sociological Explanation." *The British Journal of Sociology* 37 (2): 221–244.

Dyson, Michael Eric. 2001. *Holler If You Hear Me: Searching for Tupac Shakur*. New York: Basic Civitas Books.

Edelman, Murray. 1977. *Political Action: Words that Succeed and Policies that Fail*. New York: Academic.

———. 1988. *Constructing the Political Spectacle*. Chicago, IL: University of Chicago Press.

Esping-Andersen, Gøsta. 2007. "Equal Opportunities and the Welfare State." *Contexts* 6 (3): 23–27.

Feldman, Christine Jacqueline. 2009. *We Are the Mods: A Transnational History of a Youth Subculture*. New York: Peter Lang Publishing.

Fine, Gary Alan. 2002. *Shared Fantasy: Role Playing Games as Social Worlds*. Chicago: University of Chicago Press. (Orig. pub. 1983.)

Fox, Kathryn Joan. 1987. "Real Punks and Pretenders: The Social Organization of a Counterculture." *Journal of Contemporary Ethnography* 16 (3): 344–370.

Frank, Thomas. 1998. *The Conquest of Cool: Business Culture, Counterculture, and the Rise of Hip Consumerism*. Chicago: University of Chicago Press.

Gagnon, John, and William Simon. 1973. *Sexual Conduct: The Social Sources of Human Sexuality*. Chicago: Aldine Publishing Co.

Gaines, Donna. 1991. *Teenage Wasteland*. New York: Pantheon.

———. 1994. "The Local Economy of Suburban Scenes." In *Adolescents and Their Music: If It's Too Loud, You're Too Old*, ed. J. Epstein, 47–65. New York and London: Garland Publishing.

Gelder, Ken, and Sarah Thornton. 1997. *The Subcultures Reader*. London: Routledge.

Gergen, Kenneth. 1991. *The Saturated Self: Dilemmas of Identity in Contemporary Life*. New York: Basic Books.

Gilligan, Carol. 1982. *In a Different Voice: Psychological Theory and Women's Development*. Cambridge: Harvard University Press.

Glassner, Barry. 1999. *The Culture of Fear: Why Americans Are Afraid of the Wrong Things*. New York: Basic Books.

Goffman, Erving. 1963. *Stigma: Notes on the Management of Spoiled Identity*. New York: Simon & Schuster.

Goode, Erich. 1991. "Positive Deviance: A Viable Concept?" *Deviant Behavior* 12: 289–309.

———. 1994. *Deviant Behavior*. 4th edition. Englewood Cliffs, NJ: Prentice-Hall.

Goode, Erich, and Nachman Ben-Yehuda.1994. *Moral Panics: The Social Construction of Deviance*. Oxford: Blackwell.

Goodlad, Lauren M. E., and Michael Bibby, eds. 2007. *Goth: Undead Subculture*. Durham, NC: Duke University Press.

Gosling, Tim. 2004. " 'Not for Sale': The Underground Network of Anarcho-Punk." In *Music Scenes: Local, Translocal, and Virtual*, ed. Andy Bennett and Richard A. Peterson, 168–183. Nashville, TN: Vanderbilt University Press.

Gottfredson, Michael R., and Travis Hirschi. 1990. *A General Theory of Crime*. Los Alamos, CA: Stanford University Press.

Gottlieb, Joanne, and Gayle Wald. 1994. "Smells Like Teen Spirit: Riot Grrrls, Revolution and Women in Independent Rock." In *Microphone Fiends: Youth Music and Youth Culture*, ed. Andrew Ross and Tricia Rose, 250–274. New York: Routledge.

Gramsci, Antonio. 1971. *Selections from the Prison Notebooks*. New York: International Publishers.

Gray, Jonathan, Cornel Sandvoss, and C. Lee Harrington. 2007. *Fandom: Identities and Communities in a Mediated World*. New York: New York University Press.

Green, Shoshanna, Cynthia Jenkins, and Henry Jenkins. 1998. "Normal Female Interest in Bonking: Selections from *The Terra Nostra Underground* and *Strange Bedfellows*. In *Theorizing Fandom: Fans, Subculture, and Identity*, ed. Cheryl Harris, 8–38. Cresskill, NJ: Hampton Press.

Greenwald, Andy. 2003. *Nothing Feels Good: Punk Rock, Teenagers, and Emo*. New York: St. Martins.

Griffiths, Mark D., Mark N. O. Davies, and Darren Chappell. 2004. "Demographic Factors and Playing Variables in Online Computer Gaming." *CyberPsychology & Behavior* 7 (4): 479–487.

Gunn, Joshua. 2007. "Dark Admissions: Gothic Subculture and the Ambivalence of Misogyny and Resistance." In *Goth: Undead Subculture*, ed. Lauren M. E. Goodlad and Michael Bibby, 41–64. Durham, NC: Duke University Press.

Haenfler, Ross. 2004a. "Collective Identity in the Straight Edge Movement: How Diffuse Movements Foster Commitment, Encourage Individualized Participation, and Promote Cultural Change." *The Sociological Quarterly*, 45 (4): 785–805.

———. 2004b. "Manhood in Contradiction: The Two Faces of Straight Edge." *Men and Masculinities* July (7): 77–99.

———. 2004c. "Rethinking Subcultural Resistance: Core Values of the Straight Edge Movement." *Journal of Contemporary Ethnography* 33 (1): 406–436.

———. 2006. *Straight Edge: Clean-Living Youth, Hardcore Punk, and Social Change*. New Brunswick, NJ: Rutgers University Press.

———. 2011. "Making a Living While Living Clean: Older Straight Edgers' Pathways Into Work and Careers." Paper presented at the annual meetings of The Australian Sociological Association. November 2011. Newcastle, Australia.

———. 2012. " 'More than the X's on My Hands'—Older Straight Edgers and the Meaning of Style." In *Ageing and Youth Cultures: Music, Style and Identity*, Andy Bennett and Paul Hodkinson, eds. Oxford: Berg.

Hains, Rebecca. 2004. "Power(puff) Feminism: The Powerpuff Girls as a Site of Strength and Collective Action in the Third Wave." Paper presented at the annual meeting of the International Communication Association, New Orleans, LA.

Hall, Stuart, and Tony Jefferson, eds. 1976. *Resistance Through Rituals: Youth Subcultures in Post-War Britain*. London: Unwin Hyman.

Hamm, Mark S. 1993. *American Skinheads: The Criminology and Control of Hate Crime*. Westport, CT: Praeger.

Harris, Anita. 2004. *Future Girl: Young Women in the Twenty-First Century*. New York: Routledge.

Harris, Cheryl. 1998. *Theorizing Fandom: Fans, Subculture, and Identity*. Cresskill, NJ: Hampton Press.

Healey, Joseph R. 2005. *Race, Ethnicity, Gender, and Class: The Sociology of Group Conflict and Change*. 4th edition. Thousand Oaks, CA: Pine Forge Press.

Heath, Joseph, and Andrew Potter. 2004. *Nation of Rebels: Why Counterculture Became Consumer Culture*. New York: HarperCollins.

Hebdige, Dick. 1979. *Subculture: The Meaning of Style*. London: Routledge.

Heckert, Alex, and Druann Maria Heckert. 2002. "A New Typology of Deviance: Integrating Normative and Reactivist Definitions of Deviance." *Deviant Behavior* 23: 449–479.

Heckert, Druann Maria, and Amy Best. 1997. "Ugly Duckling to Swan: Labeling Theory and the Stigmatization of Red Hair." *Symbolic Interaction* 20 (4): 365–384.

Henry, Tricia. 1989. *Break All Rules!: Punk Rock and the Making of a Style*. Ann Arbor, MI: UMI Research Press.

Hewitt, John. 2000. *Self and Society*, 8th edition. New York: Allyn and Bacon.

Heylin, Clinton. 1993. *From the Velvets to the Voivods: A Pre-Punk History for a Post-Punk World*. Harmondsworth: Penguin.

Hirschi, Travis. 1969. *Causes of Delinquency*. Berkeley: University of California Press.

Hodkinson, Paul. 2002. *Goth: Identity, Style and Subculture*. Oxford: Berg.

———. 2003. " 'Net.Goth': Internet Communication and (Sub)Cultural Boundaries." In *The Post-Subcultures* Reader, ed. David Muggleton and Rupert Weinzierl, 285–298. Oxford: Berg.

———. 2004. "Translocal Connections in the Goth Scene." In *Music Scenes: Local, Translocal, and Virtual*, ed. Andy Bennett and Richard A. Peterson, 131–148. Nashville, TN: Vanderbilt University Press.

———. 2011. "Ageing in a Spectacular 'Youth Culture': Continuity, Change and Community Amongst Older Goths." *British Journal of Sociology* 62 (2): 262–282.

Hollander, D. 2006. "Many Teenagers Who Say They Have Taken a Virginity Pledge Retract That Statement After Having Intercourse." *Perspectives on Sexual and Reproductive Health*, 38 (3): 168.

hooks, bell. 1994. *Outlaw Culture: Resisting Representations*. New York: Routledge.

Hornsby, Anne M. 2005. "Surfing the Net for Community: A Durkheimian Analysis of Electronic Gatherings." In *Illuminating Social Life: Classical and Contemporary Theory Revisited*, ed. Peter Kivisto, 59–91. Thousand Oaks, CA: Pine Forge Press.

Hutcherson, Ben and Ross Haenfler. 2010. "Musical Genre as a Gendered Process: Authenticity in Extreme Metal." *Studies in Symbolic Interaction* 35: 99–120.

Introvigne, Massimo. 2002. "The Gothic Milieu: Black Metal, Satanism and Vampires." In *The Cultic Milieu: Oppositional Subcultures in an Age of Globalization*, ed. Jeffrey Kaplan and Heléne Lööw, 138–151. Walnut Creek, CA: Alta Mira Press.

Irwin, Darrell. 1999. "The Straight Edge Subculture: Examining the Youths' Drug-Free Way." *Journal of Drug Issues* 29 (2): 365–380.

Irwin, John. 1977. *Scenes*. Beverly Hills, CA: Sage.

Irwin, Katherine. 2001. "Legitimating the First Tattoo: Moral Passage through Informal Interaction." *Symbolic Interaction* 24: 49–73.

Jacques, Alison. 2001. "You Can Run but You Can't Hide: The Incorporation of Riot Grrrl Into Mainstream Culture." *Canadian Women's Studies* 20/21 (4/1): 46–50.

Jenkins, Henry. 1992. *Textual Poachers: Television Fans and Participatory Culture*. New York: Routledge.

———. 2006. *Fans, Bloggers, and Gamers: Exploring Participatory Cutlure*. New York: New York University Press.

Jenks, Chris. 2005. *Subculture: The Fragmentation of the Social*. London: Sage Publications.

Jensen, Joli. 1992. "Fandom and Pathology." In *The Adoring Audience*, ed Lisa A. Lewis, 9–29. New York: Routledge.

Kahn-Harris, Keith. 2004. "Unspectacular Subculture? Transgression and Mundanity in the Global Extreme Metal Scene." In *After Subculture: Critical Studies in Contemporary Youth Culture*, ed. Andy Bennett and Keith Kahn-Harris, 107–118. New York: Palgrave Macmillan.

——— 2007. *Extreme Metal: Music and Culture on the Edge*. Oxford: Berg.

Kaplan, Jeffrey, and Helene Lööw, eds. 2002. *The Cultic Milieu: Oppositional Subcultures in an Age of Globalization*. Walnut Creek, CA: AltaMira Press.

Kearney, Mary Celeste. 1998. "Producing Girls: Rethinking the Study of Female Youth Culture. In *Delinquents & Debutantes: Twentieth Century American Girls' Cultures*, ed. Sherrie Inness, 285–310. New York: New York University Press.

———. 2006. *Girls Make Media*. New York: Routledge.

Keller, Wendy. 1999. *The Cult of the Born-Again Virgin: The New Sexual Revolution*. Deerfield Beach, FL: Health Communications.

Kelly, R. V. 2004. *Massively Multiplayer Online Role-Playing Games: The People, the Addiction, and the Playing Experience*. Jefferson, NC: McFarland & Company.

Kendall, Lori. 2002. *Hanging Out in the Virtual Pub: Masculinities and Relationships Online*. Berkeley: University of California Press.

Kennedy, Helen W. 2011. "Female *Quake* Players and the Politics of Identity." In *The New Media and Technocultures Reader*, ed. Seth Giddings with Martin Lister, 201–214. London and New York: Routledge.

Keyes, Cheryl L. 2002. *Rap Music and Street Consciousness*. Urbana and Chicago: University of Illinois Press.

Kilpatrick, Nancy. 2004. *The Goth Bible: A Compendium for the Darkly Inclined*. New York: St. Martin's Griffin.

Kitwana, Bakari. 2002. *The Hip Hop Generation: Young Blacks and the Crisis in African American Culture*. New York: Basic*Civitas* Books.

———. 2005. *Why White Kids Love Hip Hop: Wangstas, Wiggers, Wannabes, and the New Reality of Race in America*. New York: Basic*Civitas* Books.

Krenske, Leigh, and Jim McKay. 2000. " 'Hard and Heavy': Gender and Power in a Heavy Metal Music Subculture." *Gender, Place and Culture* 7 (3): 287–304.

Kruse, Holly. 1993. "Subcultural Identity in Alternative Music Cultures." *Popular Music* 12 (1): 31–43.

Lamont, Michèle. 2003. "Who Counts as 'Them?' Racism and Virtue in the United States and France." *Contexts* 2 (4): 36–41.

Lancaster, Kurt. 2001. *Interacting with Babylon 5: Fan Performances in a Media Universe*. Austin: University of Texas Press.

Laumann, Edward O., John H. Gagnon, Robert T. Michael, and Stuart Michaels. 1994. *The Social Organization of Sexuality: Sexual Practices in the United States*. Chicago, IL: University of Chicago Press.

Leblanc, Lauraine. 1999. *Pretty in Punk: Girl's Gender Resistance in a Boy's Subculture*. New Brunswick: Rutgers University Press.

Lee, Kylie. 2007. "My Life as an Enterprise Slash Writer." In *Youth Subcultures: Exploring Underground America*, ed. Arielle Greenberg. New York: Longman Pearson.

Leonard, Marion. 1997. "Paper Planes: Travelling the New Grrrl Geographies." In *Cool Places: Geographies of Youth Cultures*, ed. Tracey Skelton and Gill Valentine, 101–118. New York: Routledge.

———. 1998. "Rebel Girl, You Are the Queen of My World: Feminism, 'Subculture' and Grrrl Power." In *Sexing the Groove: Popular Music and Gender*, ed. Sheila Whiteley, 230–255. London and New York: Routledge.

Levy, Ariel. 2005. *Female Chauvanist Pigs: Women and the Rise of Raunch Culture*. New York: Free Press.

Levy, Steven. 2001. *Hackers: Heroes of the Computer Revolution* (updated version). Harmondsworth: Penguin.

Lorber, Judith. 1994. *Paradoxes of Gender*. New Haven, CT: Yale University Press.

Macdonald, Nancy. 2001. *The Graffiti Subculture: Youth, Masculinity and Identity in London and New York*. New York: Palgrave Macmillan.

Maffesoli, Michael. 1996. *The Time of the Tribes: The Decline of Individualism in Mass Society*. London: Sage.

Majors, Richard, and Janet Mancini Billson. 1992. *Cool Pose: The Dilemmas of Black Manhood in America*. New York: Lexington Press.

Margolis, Eric. 2005. "White Ethnics." Photo essay in *Race, Ethnicity, Gender, and Class: The Sociology of Group Conflict and Change*. 4th edition., Joseph F. Healey. Thousand Oaks, CA: Pine Forge Press.

Marshall, George. 1994. *Spirit of '69: A Skinhead Bible*. 2nd edition. Lockerbie, Scotland: S. T. Publishing.

McIntosh, Peggy. 1988. "White Privilege: Unpacking the Invisible Knapsack." Excerpted from Working Paper 189. "White Privilege and Male Privilege: A Personal Account of Coming to See Correspondences through Work in Women's Studies."

McLeod, Kembrew. 1999. "Authenticity Within Hip-Hop and Other Cultures Threatened with Assimilation." *Journal of Communication* 49 (4): 134–150.

McRobbie, Angela. 2000. *Feminism and Youth Culture*. 2nd edition. New York: Routledge.

McRobbie, Angela, and Jenny Garber. 1976. "Girls and Subcultures." In *Feminism and Youth Culture*. 2ⁿᵈ edition, ed. Angela McRobbie. New York: Routledge.

Mercer, Mick. 2002. *21ˢᵗ Century Goth*. London: Reynolds & Hearn.

Merskin, Debra. 2006. "Jammer Girls and the World Wide Web: Making an About-Face." *Global Media Journal* 5 (9). http://lass.calumet.purdue.edu/cca/gmj/fa06/gmj_fa06_merskin.htm (accessed February 20, 2012).

Merton, Robert K. 1938. "Social Structure and Anomie." *American Sociological Review* 3: 672–682.

———. 1957. *Social Theory and Social Structure*. Glencoe, IL: Free Press.

Miller, Daniel, and Don Slater. 2000. *The Internet: An Ethnographic Approach*. New York: Berg.

Miller, Timothy. 1991. *The Hippies and American Values*. Knoxville: The University of Tennessee Press.

———. 1999. *The 60s Communes: Hippies and Beyond*. Syracuse, NY: Syracuse University Press.

Moore, Jack B. 1993. *Skinheads Shaved for Battle: A Cultural History of American Skinheads*. Bowling Green, OH: Bowling Green State University Popular Press.

Moore, Ryan. 2005. "Alternative to What? Subcultural Capital and the Commercialization of a Music Scene." *Deviant Behavior* 26 (3): 229–252.

Moore, Ryan, and Michael Roberts. 2009. "Do-It-Yourself Mobilization: Punk and Social Movements." *Mobilization: An International Journal* 14 (3): 273–291.

Morgan, Joan. 1999. *When Chickenheads Come Home to Roost: My Life as a Hip Hop Feminist*. New York: Simon and Schuster.

Moynihan, Michael, and Didrik Søderland. 1998. *Lords of Chaos: The Bloody Rise of the Satanic Metal Underground*. Venice, CA: Feral House.

Mudrian, Albert. 2004. *Choosing Death: The Improbable History of Death Metal and Grindcore*. Los Angeles: Feral House.

Muggleton, David. 2000. *Inside Subculture: The Postmodern Meaning of Style*. Oxford; New York: Berg.

Muggleton, David, and Rupert Weinzierl. 2003. *The Post-Subcultures Reader*. Oxford; New York: Berg.

Mullaney, Jamie L. 2006. *Everyone Is NOT Doing It: Abstinence and Personal Identity*. Chicago: University of Chicago Press.

Mungham, Geoff, and Geoff Pearson. 1976. *Working Class Youth Culture*. London: Routledge and Keagan Paul.

Murray, Scott, and Angela Aguayo. 2008. "Reconstructing the Discursive Hymen: Virginity Pledges and the Performance of Agitation." Paper presented at the 94ᵗʰ annual meeting of the National Communication Association, San Diego, CA.

Nack, Adina. 2000. "Damaged Goods: Women Managing the Stigma of STDs." *Deviant Behavior* 21 (2): 95–121.

Nie, Norman H., and Lutz Erbring. 2000. "Our Shrinking Social Universe." *Public Perspective* 11 (3): 44–45.

Niesel, Jeff. 1997. "Hip-Hop Matters: Rewriting the Sexual Politics of Rap Music." In *Third Wave Agenda: Being Feminist, Doing Feminism*, ed. Leslie Heywood and Jennifer Drake, 239–253. Minneapolis: University of Minnesota Press.

Norton, Quinn. "Anonymous 101: Introduction to the Lulz." *Wired* November 8, 2011. http://www.wired.com/threatlevel/2011/11/anonymous-101 (accessed November 8, 2011).

Ntarangwi, Mwenda. 2009. *West African Hip Hop: Youth Culture and Globalization*. Chicago: University of Illinois Press.

Oliver, William. 1989. "Sexual Conquest and Patterns of Black-on-Black Violence: A Structural-Cultural Perspective." *Violence and Victims* 4: 379–390.

Park, Robert E. 1925. "The City: Suggestions for the Investigation of Human Behavior in the Urban Environment." In *The City*, ed. Robert E. Park, Ernest W. Burgess, and Roderick D. McKenzie, 1–46. Chicago, IL: University of Chicago Press.

Pilkington, Hilary. 2010. "No Longer 'On Parade': Style and the Performance of Skinhead in the Russian Far North." *The Russian Review* 69 (2): 187–209.

Pilkington, Hilary, Al'bina Garifzianova, and Elena Omel'chenko. 2010. *Russia's Skinheads: Exploring and Rethinking Subcultural Lives*. London: Routledge.

Pipher, Mary. 1995. *Reviving Ophelia: Saving the Selves of Adolescent Girls*. New York: Ballantine.

Plante, Rebecca F. 2006. *Sexualities in Context: A Social Perspective*. Boulder, CO: Westview Press.

Platt, Anthony M. 1969. *The Child Savers: The Invention of Delinquency*. Chicago: University of Chicago.

Polhemus, Ted. 1998. "In the Supermarket of Style." In *The Clubcultures Reader*, ed. Steve Redhead, Derek Wynne, and Justin O'Connor, 148–151. Oxford: Blackwell.

Pough, Gwendolyn. 1999. *Check It While I Wreck It: Black Womanhood, Hip-Hop Culture, and the Public Sphere*. Lebanon, NH: Northeastern University Press.

Pray, Doug (director). 2005. *Infamy*. Documentary film. Chatsworth, CA: Image Entertainment.

Pugh, Sheenah. 2004. "The Democratic Genre: Fan Fiction in a Literary Context." *Refractory: A Journal of Entertainment Media* 5: 1–9.

Purcell, Natalie J. 2003. *Death Metal Music: The Passion and Politics of a Subculture*. Jefferson, NC: McFarland and Co.

Rafalovich, Adam, and Andreas Schneider. 2003. "Metal Music Motifs as the Politics of Youth Culture." Paper presented at the annual meeting of the American Sociological Association, Atlanta, GA.

Rathus, Spencer A., Jeffrey S. Nevid, and Lois Fichner-Rathus. 2000. *Human Sexuality in a World of Diversity*. 4th edition. Boston: Allyn and Bacon.

Rector, Robert E., Kirk A. Johnson, and Jennifer A. Marshall. 2004. Teens Who Make Virginity Pledges Have Substantially Improved Life Outcomes (Center for Data Analysis Report #04–07). *The Heritage Foundation*, September 21, 2004. www.heritage.org/Research/Family/cda04-07.cfm (accessed August 24, 2006).

Redhead, Steve. 1993. *Rave Off: Politics and Deviance in Contemporary Youth Culture*. Aldershot: Avebury.

Redhead, Steve, Derek Wynne, and Justin O'Connor. 1998. *The Clubcultures Reader: Readings in Popular Cultural Studies*. Oxford: Blackwell.

Regnerus, Mark, and Jeremy Uecker. 2011. *Premarital Sex in America: How Young Americans Meet, Mate, and Think About Marrying*. New York: Oxford University Press.

Rheingold, Howard. 2000. *The Virtual Community: Homesteading on the Virtual Frontier*, rev. edition. Cambridge, MA: MIT Press.

Ridenhour, Carlton, and Yusuf Jah. 1997. *Fight the Power: Rap, Race, and Reality*. New York: Delta.

Roberts, Mike, and Ryan Moore. 2009. "Peace Punks and Punks Against Racism: Resource Mobilization and Frame Construction in the Punk Movement." *Music and Arts in Action* 2, 1: 21–36.

Roediger, David. 1998. "What to Make of Wiggers: A Work in Progress." In *Generations of Youth: Youth Cultures and History in Twentieth-Century America*, ed. Joe Austin and Michael Nevin Willard, 358–366. New York: New York University Press.

Rose, Tricia. 1994a. *Black Noise: Rap Music and Black Culture in Contemporary America.* Hanover, NH: Wesleyan University Press.

———. 1994b. "A Style Nobody Can Deal With: Politics, Style and the Postindustrial City in Hip Hop." In *Microphone Fiends: Youth Music and Youth Culture*, ed. Andrew Ross and Tricia Rose, 71–88. New York: Routledge.

———. 2008. *The Hip Hop Wars: What We Talk About When We Talk About Hip Hop—And Why It Matters.* New York: Basic Books.

Rosenbaum, Janet. 2006. "Reborn a Virgin: Adolescents' Retracting of Virginity Pledges and Sexual Histories." *American Journal of Public Health* 96 (6): 1098–1103.

Rothenberg, Paula S. 2005. *White Privilege: Essential Readings on the Other Side of Racism.* 2nd edition. New York: Worth Publishers.

Rubington, Earl, and Martin S. Weinberg. 2005. *Deviance: The Interactionist Perspective.* 9th edition. Boston: Allyn and Bacon.

Sabin, Roger. 1999. " 'I Won't Let That Dago By': Rethinking Punk and Racism." In *Punk Rock: So What?: The Cultural Legacy of Punk*, ed. Roger Sabin, 199–218. London: Routledge.

Sandler, Lauren. 2006. *Righteous: Dispatches from the Evangelical Youth Movement.* New York: Viking.

Sandstrom, Kent L. 1990. "Confronting Deadly Disease: The Drama of Identity Construction Among Gay Men with AIDS." *Journal of Contemporary Ethnography* 19 (3): 271–294.

Sandstrom, Kent L., Daniel D. Martin, and Gary Alan Fine. 2006. *Symbols, Selves, and Social Reality: A Symbolic Interactionist Approach to Social Psychology and Sociology.* Los Angeles: Roxbury Publishing Company.

Schilt, Kristen. 2003a. " 'I'll Resist with Every Inch and Every Breath': Girls and Zine Making as a Form of Resistance." *Youth and Society* 35 (1): 71–97.

———. 2003b. "A Little Too Ironic": The Appropriation and Packaging of Riot Grrrl Politics by Mainstream Female Musicians." *Popular Music and Society* 26 (1): 5–16.

———. 2004. "Riot Grrrl Is: Contestations over Meaning in a Music Scene." In *Music Scenes: Local, Translocal and Virtual*, ed. Andy Bennett and Richard Peterson, 115–130. Nashville, TN: Vanderbilt Press.

Seale, Bobby. 1991. *Seize the Time: The Story of The Black Panther Party and Huey P. Newton.* Baltimore, MD: Black Classics Press. (Orig. pub. 1970.)

Seymour, Elaine, and Nancy M. Hewitt. 1999. *Talking About Leaving: Why Undergraduates Leave the Sciences.* Boulder, CO: Westview Press.

Shaw, Clifford R., and Henry D. McKay. 1942. *Juvenile Delinquency in Urban Areas.* Chicago: University of Chicago Press.

Sheel, Karen R., and John S. Westefeld. 1999. "Heavy Metal Music and Adolescent Suicidality: An Empirical Investigation." *Adolescence* 34 (134): 253–273.

Shrover, Neal, and John Paul Wright. 2000. *Crimes of Privilege: Readings in White-Collar Crime.* Oxford: Oxford University Press.

Shuker, Roy. 1994. *Understanding Popular Music.* London: Routledge.

Straw, Will. 1991. Systems of Articulation, Logics of Change: Scenes and Communities in Popular Music. *Cultural Studies* 5 (3): 361–375.

Sutherland, Edwin H. 1939. *Principles of Criminology*. Chicago, IL: University of Chicago Press.

Sutherland, Edwin H., and Donald R. Cressey. 1978. *Principles of Criminology*. 10th edition. Philadelphia, PA: Lippencott.

Sykes, Gresham, and David Matza. 1957. "Techniques of Neutralization: A Theory of Delinquency." *American Sociological Review* 22: 664–670.

Taylor, Jodie. 2009. "Spewing Out of the Closet: Musicology on Queer Punk." In *Musical Islands: Exploring the Connections Between Music, Place, and Research*, ed. Elizabeth Mackinlay, Brydie-Leigh Bartleet, and Katelyn Barney, 221–241. Newcastle upon Tyne, U.K.: Cambridge Scholars Publishing.

Taylor, T. L. 2006. *Play Between Worlds: Exploring Online Game Culture*. Cambridge: The MIT Press.

Tewksbury, Richard. 1996. "Cruising for Sex in Public Places: The Structure and Language of Men's Hidden, Erotic Worlds." *Deviant Behavior* 17 (1): 1–19.

Thomas, Douglas. 2002. *Hacker Culture*. Minneapolis: University of Minnesota Press.

Thomas, William I. 1923. *The Unadjusted Girl*. Boston: Little, Brown, and Co.

Thomas, William I., and Florian Znaniecki. 1918. *The Polish Peasant in Europe and America*. Boston: Richard G. Badger, The Gorham Press.

Thornton, Sarah. 1995. *Club Cultures: Music, Media and Subcultural Capital*. Hanover, NH: University Press of New England.

Tittle, Charles R., and Raymond Paternoster. 2000. *Social Deviance and Crime*. Los Angeles, CA: Roxbury.

Torkelson, Jason. 2010. "Life After (Straightedge) Subculture." *Qualitative Sociology* 33: 257–274.

Turkle, Sherry. 1997. *Life on the Screen: Identity in the Age of the Internet*. New York: Simon & Schuster.

Turner, Cherie. 2001. *Everything You Need to Know About the Riot Grrrl Movement: The Feminism of a New Generation*. New York: The Rosen Publishing Group.

Victor, Jeffrey S. 1993. *Satanic Panic: The Creation of a Contemporary Legend*. Chicago, IL: Open Court Publishing.

Voltaire. 2004. *What Is Goth?* Newburyport, MA: Weiser Books.

Wald, Gayle. 1998. "Just a Girl? Rock Music, Feminism, and the Cultural Construction of Female Youth." *Signs* 23 (3): 585–610.

Walser, Robert. 1993. *Running with the Devil: Power, Gender, and Madness in Heavy Metal Music*. Hanover, NH: Wesleyan University Press.

Weinstein, Deena. 2000. *Heavy Metal: The Music and Its Culture*. Rev. ed. Cambridge, MA: Da Capo Press.

Weitzer, Ronald, and Steven A. Tuch. 2004. "Race and Perceptions of Police Misconduct." *Social Problems* 51 (3): 305–325.

West, Candace, and Don H. Zimmerman. 1987. "Doing Gender." *Gender & Society* 1 (2): 125–151.

West, Cornell. 2001. *Race Matters*. Rev. edition. Boston, MA: Beacon Press.

Whyte, William Foote. 1943. *Street Corner Society: The Social Structure of an Italian Slum*. Chicago, IL: University of Chicago Press.

Widdicombe, Sue, and Robin Wooffitt. 1995. *The Language of Youth Subcultures: Social Identity in Action*. London and New York: Harvester Wheatsheaf.

Wilkins, Amy C. 2004. " 'So Full of Myself as a Chick': Goth Women, Sexual Independence, and Gender Egalitarianism." *Gender and Society* 18 (3): 328–349.

———. 2005. " 'It's an Aesthetic': Goth Freakiness and the Reproduction of White Middle Classness." Paper presented at the annual meeting of the American Sociological Association, Philadelphia, PA.

———. 2008. *Wannabes, Goths, and Christians: The Boundaries of Sex, Style, and Status.* Chicago, IL: University of Chicago Press.

Williams, J. Patrick. 2003. "The Straightedge Subculture on the Internet: A Case Study of Style-display Online." Media International Australia Incorporating Culture and Policy 107: 61–74.

———. 2006. "Authentic Identities: Straightedge Subculture, Music, and the Internet." *Journal of Contemporary Ethnography* 35 (2): 173–200.

———. 2007. "Youth-Subcultural Studies: Sociological Traditions and Core Concepts." *Sociology Compass* 1 (2): 572–593.

Williams, J. Patrick, and Heath Copes. 2005. " 'How Edge Are You?' Constructing Authentic Identities and Subcultural Boundaries in a Straightedge Internet Forum." *Symbolic Interaction* 28 (1): 67–89.

Willis, Paul. 1977. *Learning to Labor: How Working Class Kids Get Working Class Jobs.* New York: Columbia University Press.

———. 1978. *Profane Culture.* London: Routledge and Kegan Paul.

Wood, Robert T. 1999. "The Indigenous Nonracist Origins of the American Skinhead Subculture." *Youth and Society* 31 (2): 131–151.

———. 2006. *Straightedge: Complexity and Contradictions of a Subculture.* Syracuse, NY: Syracuse University Press.

Wooden, Wayne S., and Randy Blazak. 2001. *Renegade Kids, Suburban Outlaws: From Youth Culture to Delinquency.* 2nd edition. Belmont, CA: Wadsworth.

Wright, R. 1996. "The Occupational Masculinity of Computing." In *Masculinities in Organizations*, ed. C. Cheng, 77–96. Thousand Oaks, CA: Sage.

Yee, Nick. 2006. "Demographics, Motivations and Derived Experiences of Uses of Massively Multi-User Online Graphical Environments." *Presence: Teleoperators and Virtual Environments* 15, 309–329.

Young, Kevin, and Laura Craig. 1997. "Beyond White Pride: Identity, Meaning and Contradiction in the Canadian Skinhead Subculture." *Canadian Review of Sociology and Anthropology* 34 (2): 175–206.

Zellner, William W. 1994. *Countercultures: A Sociological Analysis.* New York: Worth Publishers.

Zurcher, Louis. 1977. *The Mutable Self.* Beverly Hills, CA: Sage.

Notes

1. www.tedpolhemus.com/main_concept5.html (accessed June 28, 2007).
2. "Federal Crack Cocaine Sentencing." Report by The Sentencing Project, May 2009, www.sentencingproject.org/PublicationDetails.aspx?PublicationID=573 (accessed June 12, 2009).
3. See Robert M. Regoli and John D. Hewitt, *Delinquency in Society* (New York: McGraw-Hill, 1997).
4. Noah Wildman, "So You Want to Be a Rude Boy?", *rootsworld.com*, www.rootsworld.com/rw/feature/rudeboy.html (accessed January 15, 2007).
5. For a fictional depiction of mods and rockers, check out the film *Quadrophenia*.
6. Other popular acts that commanded large skinhead followings included Judge Dread, Slade, Madness, Sham 69, and Blitz. Oi! music, a punk-influenced sound characterized by rowdy singalongs and shouts of "Oi! Oi! Oi!" (Hey! Hey! Hey!), became increasingly popular with bands such as The Cockney Rejects, Sham 69, Agnostic Front, Cro-Mags, Rancid, Dropkick Murphys, and Mighty Mighty Bosstones, attracting both skinheads and punks.
7. The "no future" self-destructive lifestyle ended in early deaths for the Sex Pistols' Sid Vicious and the Germs' Darby Crash, both of whom died of heroin overdoses.
8. "One Life Drug Free," "It's OK Not to Drink," and "Straight Edge for Life," in addition to simply "Straight Edge" and "XXX," are among the most common slogans appearing on t-shirts, jackets, and tattoos.
9. Especially the music of Rites of Spring.
10. Jam Master Jay was shot and killed in 2002 at a recording studio in Queens, New York.
11. "Bush Doesn't Care About Black People" http://www.youtube.com/watch?v=zIUzLpO1kxI (accessed March 6, 2012).
12. "Reaction to Katrina Split on Racial Lines," *CNN.com*, September 13, 2005, www.cnn.com/2005/US/09/12/katrina.race.poll/index.html (accessed January 9, 2007).
13. See http://poplicks.com/2005/06/race-and-rap-revisited-again.html for a summary of a panel about hip hop that addresses these very questions.
14. American Rhetoric Top 100 Speeches www.americanrhetoric.com/speeches/mlkihaveadream.htm (accessed March 6, 2012).

15. "Skate-thrash" bands like Suicidal Tendencies and Dirty Rotten Imbeciles (DRI) bridged the skateboarder–metalhead gap.
16. This form of metal gained prominence in the mid-1990s with Korn and continues in popularity with Linkin Park, Limp Biskit, and Slipknot, minus much of RATM's radical political message.
17. Nearly absent of guitar solos, special effects, and costumes, metalcore carries the ongoing themes of alienation and politics of thrash while extolling the virtues of friendship and family. Such bands attract both hardcore and metal kids who occasionally come into conflict at concerts due to their different dancing styles and expectations.
18. Alienation in this context is not the same as Karl Marx's concept of alienated labor.
19. As unlikely as it may seem, there are Christian metal bands (e.g., Stryper in the 1980s and later P.O.D.), a Christian death metal niche, and, believe it or not, even Christian *black* metal scenes (e.g., Extol, Lengsel). Alienation leads Christian metal fans to *embrace* rather than reject dominant pro-social goals.
20. Centers for Disease Control and Prevention: http://www.cdc.gov/teenpregnancy/LongDescriptors.htm (accessed 11/4/2011).
21. Rebecca Leung, "Taking the Pledge," *cbsnew.com*, Sept. 18, 2005, www.cbsnews.com/stories/2005/05/20/60minutes/main696975_page2.shtml (accessed August 24, 2006).
22. http://archives.cnn.com/2001/HEALTH/children/01/04/virginity.study/ (accessed August 24, 2006).
23. Lifeway Student Ministry, "True Love Waits" home page. www.lifeway.com/tlw/ (accessed August 24, 2006).
24. National Mental Health Association. "Factsheet: Bullying and Gay Youth." www.nmha.org/go/information/get-info/children-s-mental-health/bullying-and-gay-youth (accessed June 13, 2009).
25. http://archives.cnn.com/2001/HEALTH/children/01/04/virginity.study/ (accessed November 23, 2005).
26. http://archives.cnn.com/2001/HEALTH/children/01/04/virginity.study/ (accessed November 23, 2005). Also 0/60minutes/main696975_page2.shtml (accessed August 24, 2006).
27. Christopher Trenholm, Barbara Devaney, Ken Fortson, Lisa Quay, Justin Wheeler, and Melissa Clark, "Impacts of Four Title V, Section 510 Abstinence Education Programs," Mathematica Policy Research, Inc., April 2007, www.mathematica-mpr.com/publications/PDFs/impactabstinence.pdf (accessed July 19, 2007).
28. http://www.revolutionabstinence.org/about.htm (accessed November 1, 2011).
29. About half of the grant money was eventually returned when officials could not really identify a "goth problem." See Casey Logan, "Oh My Goth," *The Pitch*, May 30, 2002, www.pitch.com/2002–05–30/news/oh-my-goth/ (accessed June 12, 2007).
30. Bela Lugosi (1882–1956) was an actor who played Dracula and other horror icons in early black-and-white horror films.
31. See www.goth.net/goth.html (accessed September 29, 2006).
32. See www.vamp.org/Gothic/clublist.html (accessed June 14, 2007).
33. Blizzard Entertainment, Press release, December 23, 2008, http://eu.blizzard.com/en/press/081223.html (accessed March 1, 2009).
34. While the classic pen-and-paper game *Dungeons and Dragons* launches an online version, some MMORPGs, such as *Everquest* and *World of Warcraft* have already been translated into pen-and-paper games. Thus there is no fixed trajectory for the life of a game franchise.

35. Roles include the "healer," whose primary purpose is to keep the group members alive as they take damage from monsters and NPCs; the "damage dealer," characters whose abilities inflict most damage against foes (often called "dps" for damage per second); and the "tank," or hardy characters in heavy armor who try to hold monsters' attention and protect groupmates from harm.

36. Nick Yee, WoW Basic Demographics, *The Daedalus Project*, March 19, 2009, www. nickyee.com/daedalus/archives/001365.php (accessed March 19, 2009).

37. James Hursthouse, "MMOG Demographics: Perspectives from Industry Insiders," *IGDA Online Games Quarterly*, Spring 2005, www.igda.org/online/quarterly/1_2/mmogdemographics.php (accessed May 20, 2008).

38. Source: "An Analysis of MMOG Subscription Growth Version 23.0" (last updated on April 9th, 2008) www.mmogchart.com (accessed March 19, 2009).

39. Some gamers even run power-leveling services where, for a fee, they will rapidly advance your character. Again, more casual gamers see this as less authentic; it's almost cheating to have a powerful character without having to work for it yourself.

40. Computer Addiction Services, www.computeraddiction.com (accessed 10/21/06). These addictions are not officially listed as disorders in the Diagnostic and Statistical Manual of Mental Disorders, the diagnostic guide for mental health professionals published by the American Psychiatric Association.

41. William Gibson, *Neuromancer* (New York: Ace Books, 1983).

42. "Gamer Buys $26,500 Virtual Land," *BBC News*, December 17, 2004, http://news.bbc.co.uk/1/hi/technology/4104731.stm (accessed May 29, 2006).

43. Evan Shamoon, "3BR w/VU of Asteroid Belt: One Man's Plan to Turn Virtual Real Estate into Cold Hard Cash," *Wired*, April (2006): 130.

44. Early hackers substituted numbers for letters to avoid having their Web sites picked up in simple term searches. In the mid-1990s, online gaming necessitated a fast, shorthand language that players could quickly type as they battled other players. "I am elite" and similar trash-talking phrases emerged and were eventually shortened to "leet," "133t," and "1337." See www.urbandictionary.com for more history.

45. "[I]f the CCCS over-politicized youth formations, then post-modernist and other post-subcultural positions have been equally guilty of under-politicizing them" (Muggleton and Weinzierl 2003, p. 14).

46. Associated Press, "Nike Hopes to Cash in on 'Retro' Converse," *ESPN.com*, July 9, 2003, http://espn.go.com/sportsbusiness/news/2003/0709/1578731.html (accessed June 24, 2007).

47. *Wikipedia.org*, s.v. "Heavy metal." http://en.wikipedia.org/wiki/Heavy_metal (accessed June 27, 2007).

Index